GROWTH AND INEQUALITY
IN PAKISTAN

Growth and Inequality in Pakistan

Edited by

Keith Griffin
Fellow of Magdalen College, Oxford

and

Azizur Rahman Khan
Research Fellow of Nuffield College, Oxford

Macmillan
St. Martin's Press

First published 1972 by
THE MACMILLAN PRESS LTD

London and Basingstoke
Associated companies in New York Toronto
Dublin Melbourne Johannesburg and Madras
Library of Congress catalog card no. 70–190776

SBN 333 12921 0

Printed in Great Britain by
A. WHEATON & CO
Exeter

To
Nurul Islam
Anisur Rahman
Rahman Sobhan
and
Swadesh Bose

whose dream was growth and equality

*In human society extremes of wealth
and poverty are the main sources of
evil... Where a population is divided
into the two classes of the very
rich and the very poor, there can
be no real state; for there can
be no real friendship between the
classes; and friendship is the
essential principle of all association.*

Aristotle

Contents

viii   *Contents*

PART FOUR: WAGES, INCOME DISTRIBUTION
AND SAVINGS

Preface

THE experience of the underdeveloped countries in the last
two decades has shown that faster growth does not inevitably
lead to greater prosperity. It has often led instead to greater
inequality, and in some countries, e.g. Pakistan and India, it
has actually led to an absolute decline in the standard of living
of the urban and rural poor. Contrary to what was expected,
the beneficial effects of growth have not trickled down to the
impoverished masses. The initial reaction of many economists
to these facts was to claim they were not true, that the data
were too few and insufficiently reliable. Later, when this objec-
tion became untenable, it was claimed that the distribution of
income did not matter, that a concern with equity was a luxury
poor countries could not afford. Growth remained supreme as
an objective of economic policy.

More recently, however, there has been a change of emphasis. Economists have begun to reconsider the bundle of policies
which constitute a development strategy. The objective no
longer is merely to accelerate the rate of growth of national
product per head; the objective is to reduce poverty and
inequality. This does not imply that growth is unimportant, but
it does imply that the rate of growth will become little more
than a reflection at the aggregate level of the consequences of
policies which were designed to tackle problems at a much
more disaggregated level. This change of emphasis from
national product to individual welfare will force economists to
place the well-being of specific groups and classes in the fore-
front of their analysis rather than obscure social conditions
behind aggregate index numbers. Growth targets as such will
become meaningless.

   Pakistan was one of the largest countries in the world and in
August 1972 it would have been independent for twenty-five
years. The purpose of this book is to examine the policies pursued
by the government in the last quarter-century and to assess the
consequences for group and regional welfare. Until recently
Pakistan was widely acclaimed for its rapid growth of output
per head. It was less widely recognised abroad, however, that
this growth was accompanied by an increase in the number of
poor people and a decline in their standard of living. But
within the country the issue of equality, and the fact of growing
inequality, have led to intense political controversy, to attempts
by East Pakistan to achieve regional autonomy and, finally, to
the declaration of an independent Bangla Desh. This book
explains the economic origins of the Free Bengal movement and
the policies which have culminated in civil war. It is a sobering
story, and one which should be of interest not only to students
of Asia, but to everyone engaged in the struggle against poverty
and inequality, wherever it is found.

   All of the contributors to this volume have been associated
with the Pakistan Institute of Development Economics, and
most of the chapters appeared in their original version as articles
in the Institute's journal, the *Pakistan Development Review*. When
we first decided to prepare a volume on growth and inequality
in Pakistan it was not our intention to select contributors solely
from the ranks of the staff and foreign advisors of the Institute.
That the volume is so exclusive is largely an accident, although
a happy one. It was not altogether surprising, however, since
the Institute has for many years been the only organisation
wholly concerned with applied economic research on the
problems of Pakistan. Most scholars with a serious interest in
South Asia have worked at the Institute or visited it on at least
one occasion, and this volume is but a modest tribute to the
high quality and social relevance of the investigations spon-
sored there.

Oxford   K. B. Griffin
June 1971   A. R. Khan

Introduction

On 14 August 1972 Pakistan was to celebrate twenty-five years of independence. What was to be the occasion for quarter-centennial celebrations is in danger of being transformed into a funeral. In view of the ongoing struggle for the freedom of the more populous eastern region of the country, it is not impossible that Pakistan will soon be a name like Austria-Hungary. In this context a quarter-century, although not a long period of history under usual circumstances, is surely a milestone in the life of this young nation. Whether the quarter-centenary is viewed as the beginning of another lease of life or as the end of an ill-fated experiment, it indicates a turning point of history. It is a time for sober assessment of the past events and policies which have led the country to this turning point.

The creation of Pakistan was, of course, a remarkable event. The nation is as much the embodiment of an idea as a geographical area. It was meant to be a spiritual as well as a physical home for Muslims of the subcontinent, a place where the followers of Islam were to constitute the majority and where they could develop in accordance with their own preferences, unencumbered by the fear of Hindu discrimination, communal violence or the rigidities of the caste system.

The territory of Pakistan was carved out of the eastern and western extremities of northern India, and the two wings of the country are divided by a thousand miles. A quick glance at a map might suggest that Pakistan consists of little more than two backwaters, a pair of fragments split off from the British Raj. Such a judgement would be only partially correct, however. East Pakistan – a low-lying, rain-drenched, disaster-prone deltaic plain – is highly fertile and is the world's largest producer of jute. At the time of independence East Pakistan was cut off from the rest of Bengal, and in particular, the jute-processing centre of Calcutta. West Pakistan is an arid region, but large parts of it – notably the Punjab and the Sind – are traversed by the Indus, and cotton and wheat are cultivated under irrigation. Thus both wings of the nation were primarily agricultural areas.

At the time of partition approximately 77·5 million people lived in the country, 42·2 million in East Pakistan and 35·3 million in West Pakistan. Population growth has been rapid and may still be accelerating. During the 1950s it is estimated that the population rose 2·4 per cent a year; in the following decade the rate increased to 2·7 per cent and the current rate probably is even faster. It is widely feared, for instance, that in East Pakistan the demographic increase may be over 3 per cent per annum. The population of the country as a whole is now about 130 million.

It is widely believed that rapid population growth has been a major obstacle to development. In general, we share this opinion. It must be recognised, however, that the interactions between demographic and economic phenomena are still not well understood and it is impossible to demonstrate conclusively that a lower rate of population growth would have caused a faster rate of growth of per capita income. Indeed, a superficial examination of the data would suggest the opposite: it is precisely during the period when population growth is reported to have accelerated that per capita income began to expand rapidly.

Nonetheless, it has been government policy, particularly while Ayub Khan was President, to restrict the rate of demographic expansion. The family planning programme received considerable support during the Third Plan and slightly more than one per cent of government development expenditure occurred in this sector. This percentage is expected to increase somewhat during the Fourth Plan. Although the results so far have been rather modest, the planners expect that by 1975 the birth rate will have fallen from 45 to 40 per thousand.

The structure of the economy has changed considerably since independence. In 1949 agriculture accounted for nearly

60 per cent of G.D.P.; today it accounts for slightly more than 45 per cent. Industrial output has doubled its share and now accounts for about a quarter of G.D.P. We have less satisfactory data on the composition of employment, but it is clear from a comparison of the 1951 and 1961 censuses that the change in the structure of employment has not been as dramatic as the change in the pattern of production. Between the two census years the percentage of the labour force employed in agriculture declined only fractionally, viz., from 76·5 to 74·3. Sample survey estimates reveal a more rapid decline in agriculture's share of employment in more recent years – to 67·1 per cent in 1966–7 – but the differences between the census and survey methods and definitions have to be allowed for before drawing any firm conclusions.

These national averages obscure important regional differences. The rate of industrialisation, measured as the increase in the share of industrial output in G.D.P., has been much lower for East Pakistan than for West. If the share of industrial employment in total labour force is used as an index, then East Pakistan failed to industrialise during the decade between the two census years, while West Pakistan achieved a significant rate of industrialisation during the same period. Between the census years the percentage of the labour force employed in agriculture increased from 84·7 to 85·3 in the East and decreased from 65·3 to 59·3 in the West. Correspondingly, the proportion of the labour force employed in industry declined by 0·6 points in East Pakistan (to 6 per cent) and rose by 8·6 points in West Pakistan (to 20·2 per cent).

The differential rates of industrialisation were accompanied by differential rates of growth of the two regions, leading to a widening disparity between the average standard of living of the two regions. In 1949–50 per capita income in West Pakistan was 17 per cent higher than that in the East. This difference increased to 32 per cent by 1959–60 and to 60 per cent by 1969–70. Given, first, the considerably lower purchasing power of a unit of income in the East as compared to that in the West and, second, evidence of a relative overstatement of various components of the East's G.D.P. in the national income estimates, even these rates of disparity would appear to understate the real differential between regional standards of living.

TABLE Intro. 1

COMPOSITION OF OUTPUT IN PAKISTAN AND ITS TWO REGIONS

	1949–50	*1959–60*	*1969–70*
Pakistan			
Agriculture	59·9	53·2	45·3
Industry	12·0	17·5	24·0
Services	28·1	29·3	30·7
East Pakistan			
Agriculture	65·2	63·5	55·7
Industry	9·4	13·7	20·2
Services	25·4	22·8	24·1
West Pakistan			
Agriculture	54·5	49·1	41·6
Industry	14·7	20·7	28·3
Services	30·8	30·2	30·1

Note: 1. Industry consists of manufacturing, mining, construction and transport. 2. Estimates of regional products which form the basis of these shares do not add up to national product because some small transport and services items of national product are not distributed between the regions.
Source: For 1949–50, Khan and Bergan, 'Measurement of Structural Change in the Pakistan Economy', *The Pakistan Development Review*, summer 1966. For 1959–60, C.S.O., *Final Report of the National Income Commission*, Karachi, 1966. For 1969–70, C.S.O., *Draft Minutes of the Fifth Meeting of the National Accounts Committee*, mimeographed, Karachi, 1970.

TABLE Intro. 2

COMPOSITION OF EMPLOYMENT IN PAKISTAN AND ITS TWO REGIONS

	1951	*1961*	*1966–7*
Pakistan			
Agriculture	76·5	74·3	67·1
Industry	8·7	12·0	16·5
Services	14·8	13·7	16·4
East Pakistan			
Agriculture	84·7	85·3	77·8
Industry	6·6	6·0	9·6
Services	8·7	8·7	12·6
West Pakistan			
Agriculture	65·3	59·3	53·4
Industry	11·6	20·2	25·4
Services	23·1	20·5	21·2

Source: 1951 and 1961 estimates are based on Population Censuses of the respective years. 1966–7 estimates from C.S.O., *Summary Report of Population and Labour Force in Pakistan* (Labour Force Sample Survey).

The main reasons for the differential rates of growth have been the differential shares of investment and foreign exchange – East Pakistan, the home of about 55 per cent of the nation's population, had about 30 per cent of each over the period as a whole.

The structural change that we have noted was a product of growth, especially in the non-agricultural sectors. Rapid growth, however, is a fairly recent phenomenon in Pakistan. Indeed even as late as the *Mid-Plan Review of the Second Five Year Plan*, 1960–5, the authorities were worried about the poor performance of the economy, particularly in the agricultural sector. The best estimates available indicate that in the period 1949/50 to 1959/60 gross national product in constant prices increased at a trend rate of 2·4 per cent a year. Population is officially reported to have increased at the same rate, so that for the country as a whole there was no increase in real income per head. Since the official estimates probably understate the true increase in population, it is possible that per capita income actually fell.

There is no doubt that it fell in East Pakistan. Total output grew only 1·4 per cent a year, so that output per head declined by at least one per cent per annum. In West Pakistan, on the other hand, total output increased 3·5 per cent a year and per capita output increased 1·1 per cent a year.[1]

Despite the acceleration in the rate of growth of population, the rate of growth of G.N.P. rose to 5·5 per cent during the Second Five Year Plan and increased further to 5·7 per cent during the Third Plan. The corresponding rates of growth of per capita income were 2·8 and 3·0 per cent.

Although all sectors grew faster in the Second Plan than previously, much of the success achieved in the 1960s must be attributed to the breakthrough in agriculture. This breakthrough was immensely important for four reasons. First, since agricultural output accounted for over half the nation's total production, stagnation in this sector was bound to retard the overall rate of advance. Second, many of Pakistan's industries, particularly textiles, were dependent upon agricultural raw

[1] See Taufiq M. Khan and Asbjorn Bergan, 'Measurement of Structural Change in the Pakistan Economy: A Review of the National Income Estimates 1949/50 to 1963/64', *Pakistan Development Review*, summer 1966.

materials. Hence slow growth of, say, jute and cotton would adversely effect the possibilities for rapid expansion in the industrial sector. Third, agricultural exports were the largest source of foreign exchange earnings. Jute and cotton alone accounted for over 75 per cent of exports in the 1950s. Thus the nation's capacity to import, and invest, were largely determined by the export performance of the agricultural sector. Finally, the breakthrough in agriculture was important on grounds of welfare. As we have seen, the great majority of the people lived and worked in rural areas, and the most direct way – in fact possibly the only feasible way – of improving their standard of living was by raising output in the sector on which they depended for their livelihood.

TABLE Intro. 3

AVERAGE ANNUAL PERCENTAGE RATES OF
GROWTH

	Pre-Plan (1949/50 to 1954/5)	First Plan (1955–60)	Second Plan (1960–5)	Third Plan (1965–70)
Agriculture	1·3	1·4	3·4	4·5
Manufacturing	9·1	5·7	10·0	6·8
Public Administration and Defence	3·2	1·4	6·2	13·7
G.N.P.	2·6	2·4	5·5	5·7
G.N.P. per capita	0·2	0·15	2·8	3·0

Sources: Three plan periods—*Pakistan Economic Survey, 1969–70*, pp. 2, 5; pre-plan period—T. M. Khan and A. Bergan, 'Measurement of Structural Change in the Pakistan Economy: A Review of the National Income Estimates 1949/50 to 1963/64', *Pakistan Development Review*, summer 1966.

West Pakistan continued to grow about two percentage points faster than East Pakistan. During the Second Plan the West grew about 6·4 per cent a year and the East 4·3 per cent. In the Third Plan the growth rate in both West and East declined (to 6·1 and 4·1 per cent, respectively), but because of the change in weights in favour of the West, the average for the entire country rose. As regards per capita income, it seems that it is rising a bit over one per cent a year in the East wing and over 3 per cent in the West wing.

These differences in regional performance are due in large part to the fact that agriculture is far more important in the East than in the West and is growing much more slowly. Because of pronounced fluctuations in output due to changes in weather, trends in agricultural output over short planning periods are frequently misleading. The best evidence we have, however, indicates that in the 1960s – 1960/1 to 1967/8 to be precise – agricultural production increased 2·1 per cent a year in the East and 4·6 per cent in the West.[1] That is, agricultural production per head is declining by 0·6 – 0·9 per cent a year in East Bengal and rising by about 1·9 per cent a year in West Pakistan, particularly in the Punjab and parts of Sind. Presumably changes in real income in rural areas have been moving in a similar direction.

In the G.D.P. estimates, the manufacturing sector is subdivided into large-scale and small-scale manufacturing. All manufacturing establishments employing 20 or more workers and using power in the process of production are considered to be large-scale. The rest are small-scale. As can be seen in the previous table, the manufacturing sector in Pakistan has grown quite rapidly, especially since the beginning of the Second Plan. The figures must be interpreted with caution, however, because the quality of the data in the two subsectors is not uniform. Statistics on large-scale manufacturing are reasonably reliable, but the data on small-scale manufacturing are not. Surveys of small-scale industries have been in existence for both the regions of Pakistan for some years. But for reasons which have not been explained, the information from these surveys has not been incorporated into the national income estimates prepared by the Central Statistical Office (C.S.O.). The C.S.O. continues to base its estimates of output in small-scale manufacturing on the crude assumption that value-added per employee is the same in all urban areas, be they located in the East or West wing; similarly, it is assumed that value-added per employee is identical in all rural areas. Estimates for the benchmark year were obtained from a very limited and antiquated survey of rural East Pakistan and urban West Pakistan. Output is obtained by applying the estimated population growth rate to these benchmark data.

[1] See Chapter 2 below.

Table Intro. 4

THE PERCENTAGE SHARE OF MANUFACTURING OUTPUT IN GROSS NATIONAL PRODUCT AND GROSS REGIONAL PRODUCT

	1949/50	1959/60	1969/70
Pakistan			
Manufacturing/G.D.P.	5·8	9·4	12·0
Large-scale manufacturing/G.D.P.	1·0	5·0	8·8
Small-scale manufacturing/G.D.P.	4·8	4·4	3·2
East Pakistan			
Manufacturing/G.R.P.	3·8	6·1	8·4
Large-scale manufacturing/G.R.P.	0·5	2·7	5·4
Small-scale manufacturing/G.R.P.	3·3	3·4	3·0
West Pakistan			
Manufacturing/G.R.P.	7·9	12·3	15·8
Large-scale manufacturing/G.R.P.	2·2	7·0	12·0
Small-scale manufacturing/G.R.P.	5·7	5·3	3·8

This statistical convention would not matter very much if the small-scale manufacturing sector was in fact very small. Unfortunately, this is not the case. In 1949/50 large-scale manufacturing accounted for only 24 per cent of estimated production in the manufacturing sector and one per cent of G.N.P. These ratios rose rapidly, but it was not until 1956 that the two subsectors are reported to have become equally large and not until 1960 did large-scale manufacturing account for as much as 5 per cent of G.N.P.

The importance of manufacturing in the two regions varies enormously. At the time of independence there was virtually no large-scale manufacturing activity in East Pakistan. In 1949/50 over 85 per cent of all output in the sector is believed to have originated in small-scale establishments. Large-scale manufacturing remained less important than small-scale production until 1961 and it was not until the end of the Second Plan that the former contributed 5 per cent to East Pakistan's gross regional product. In West Pakistan, in contrast, large-scale manufacturing became the more important of the two subsectors around 1957 and a decade later accounted for about 9 per cent of West Pakistan's G.R.P.

Quite apart from the regional location of industry is the question of the welfare implications of industrialisation. The expansion of the large-scale manufacturing sector in Pakistan was a response to profit incentives created by the government rather than a response to price signals originating in the world market. That is, it became profitable for entrepreneurs to engage in industrial activity despite the fact that the country's comparative advantage lay elsewhere. Tariffs, quantitative

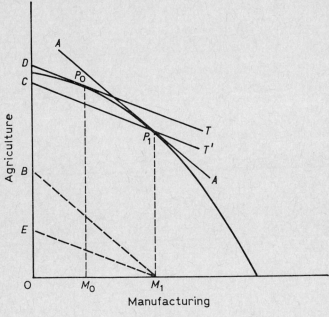

Fig. Intro. 1

trade restrictions, tax policy, foreign exchange policy and licensing were all used to alter relative prices in favour of the manufacturing sector and against agriculture.

This development strategy had several consequences, two of which are important in the present context. First, by altering relative commodity prices, resources became misallocated and the level of national income fell below what it otherwise would have been. This is illustrated in Fig. Intro. 1. Assume that under free trade conditions Pakistan would have produced at *Po* in response to relative world prices as indicated by the terms of trade line *DT*. Under these conditions *Mo* manufactured goods would have been produced. If instead relative domestic prices were changed to AA, the economy would adopt a pattern of production P_1 and output of manufactured goods would rise to M_1. The level of income at P_1, however, is lower than at Po. In fact, if output at P_1 is valued at relative world prices ($CT' = DT$) it can be seen that national income is lower by an amount CD.[1] This lower income is likely to be associated with lower savings, a lower rate of accumulation of capital and slower growth.

Second, if manufacturing output M_1 is valued at local prices AA ($=BM_1$), its contribution to national income will be overstated. This is because the opportunity cost of manufactured goods in terms of agricultural goods is not properly reflected in domestic prices – because these are 'distorted' by tariffs and quotas; the real rate at which agricultural goods can be exchanged for manufactures is indicated by relative world prices DT ($=EM_1$). If local prices are used, M_1 manufactures have an apparent value of OB, but if world prices are used the value of output in the manufacturing sector is only OE. In other words, national accounting conventions which use local prices as weights overstate the value of manufacturing output by EB. In extreme cases, the real value added in manufacturing may be negative, whereas the apparent value added (using local prices) may be positive.[2] Moreover, if the output of the manufacturing sector is overvalued, the rate of growth of national product will be overstated. In welfare terms, or in opportunity cost terms, Pakistan has not been growing as rapidly as the G.D.P. figures at domestic prices indicate, and because of the loss in income which results from resource misallocation, the country probably has not been growing as rapidly as it could.

Industrialisation has occurred under conditions of quasi-autarky, largely through a process of import substitution of consumer goods. This would appear to affect the measurement of the distribution of income. The measurement of the absolute level of living for the low income groups, i.e. their real wage

---

[1] This conclusion does not depend on whether world prices or domestic prices are used, although the precise measure of the income loss does depend upon which set of price weights is used.

[2] See Chapter 4 below.

rate, would overstate the level of consumption in so far as manufactured consumption goods are overpriced in the domestic market. The effect on the measurement of the distribution of income *between groups* is more difficult to ascertain. It appears, however, that the degree of overstatement of consumption would be greater for wage-earners than for very high income groups. The consumption surveys show that the weight of manufactured goods in total consumption, though an increasing function of income between one group of wage-earners and another, is considerably lower for very high income groups of non-wage earners as compared to the average wage-earner. The consumption of high income groups tends to be concentrated in services such as housing, transport, travel and personal services for which the gap between domestic and world prices is unlikely to be as large as for manufactured goods.

Between the Second and Third Plans the rate of expansion of manufacturing output declined by over 30 per cent. The growth of services, particularly public administration and defence, accelerated dramatically, however, and this prevented the rate of growth of G.N.P. from falling. In fact, as we have seen, national income grew slightly faster in the second half of the 1960s than in the first half. According to the official data, non-commodity producing sectors grew 50 per cent faster than the commodity producing sectors during the Third Plan period: agriculture and industry combined increased 26·5 per cent in the five years, whereas the other sectors, i.e. services, grew 39·2 per cent. Half of the increase in total output during this period is attributed to services.

It is possible, but not very probable, that even in a country as poor as Pakistan the demand for services grows considerably faster than the demand for goods. A better explanation is that the rapid growth of services is due to a combination of a very high income elasticity of demand among the richer classes and increasing inequality in the distribution of income. Even so, it seems intuitively implausible that services could have grown so much faster than the production of commodities. Our suspicion is that the growth rate of services is exaggerated somewhat. It is most unlikely that they could have grown 6·9 per cent a year when commodity production was increasing only 4·8 per cent a year.

This suspicion is strengthened when one disaggregates the data. One finds that, in general, services which are closely linked to the production of commodities grew less rapidly during the Third Plan than during the Second. For example, wholesale and retail trade increased 29·7 per cent between 1960/1 and 1964/5, but increased only a further 25·8 per cent by 1969/70. Similarly, services rendered by the ownership of dwellings grew 11·1 per cent in the first period and 10·0 per cent in the second. Construction increased 141·3 per cent in the first period and only 53·6 per cent in the second. These are the trends one would expect if the aggregate growth rate were declining, but the official figures indicate a slight acceleration.

The two subsectors which account for the rapid growth of services (and, hence, of G.N.P. as a whole) are (i) banking and insurance and (ii) public administration and defence. Between 1960/1 and 1964/5 the former increased 44·5 per cent; from then until 1969/70 it increased further by a fantastic 131 per cent. Public administration and defence could not match this record, but it did manage to grow nearly 14 per cent a year during the Third Plan. Few would claim, however, that this represented a growing contribution to the welfare of the community. Indeed many would argue that the welfare contribution of this subsector is zero or negative. Defence expenditure alone now accounts for nearly 3·5 per cent of the national income, and its share in G.D.P. has gone up by a full percentage point in the last five years. The civil service and the army are perhaps extreme cases of economic activity in Pakistan which does not increase the welfare of the majority (or at least not very much), but a cautious analyst should cast a sceptical eye on the services figures before making any judgements about increased welfare. It certainly would be rash to assume that the contribution of services to the nation's welfare was increasing at anything like 6·9 per cent per annum.

The public sector has assumed a large and increasing responsibility for investment. In 1949/50 state investment accounted for less than 35 per cent of total capital formation. The share rose to nearly 63 per cent in 1959/60 and a decade later the state still accounted for over 55 per cent of total investment. As we can see in the table below, government development expenditure, i.e. state investment plus current expenditure which affects development, has been concentrated on infra-structure, i.e. water, power, transport and communications. There has been a tendency for expenditure on the social services to rise (education, health, housing, family planning, etc.) and for investment in directly productive activities to fall.

TABLE Intro. 5

PERCENTAGE ALLOCATION OF PUBLIC
SECTOR OUTLAYS

	First Plan (actual)	Second Plan (actual)	Third Plan (est. actual)	Fourth Plan (allocation)
Infrastructure	53·5	59·0	56·0	47·9
Social services	17·7	11·1	20·4	29·4
Directly productive activities	28·8	29·9	23·6	22·7

Source: Government of Pakistan, *The Fourth Five-Year Plan* (*1970–75*), Feb. 1970, p. 28.

Responsibility for investment in directly productive activities lies mainly with the private sector, but this does not mean that the government has pursued a policy of non-intervention in economic affairs. On the contrary, the government has been very active indeed in providing incentives to private entre-preneurs to invest initially in industry and more recently in the agricultural sector as well. Government assistance has taken a variety of forms and has had two major consequences. First, domestic producers have been sheltered from foreign competi-tion and this has enabled them to raise the prices of their products above competitive levels. The protected industries have tended to become oligopolistically organised and in many cases entry into an industry has been restricted as a result of administrative controls, e.g. licenses. The government has created a small class of privileged industrial monopolists who reap enormous profits on a small turnover. The justification for this policy is that a redistribution of income toward profits will raise the rate of private savings and accelerate the growth of the economy.

Second, public policy and private monopoly have combined to ensure that privileged producers receive scarce factors of production, notably foreign exchange and capital, at less than their opportunity cost. The exchange rate has been overvalued, excess demand for foreign exchange has been created, and the limited supply has been allocated by the bureaucracy.[1] Similarly, the price of capital has been far below an equilibrium price and as a result capital has had to be rationed. In some instances this has occurred through state-owned financial institutions and in other cases capital has been rationed by private banking oligopolies which provide credit at a low rate of interest to favoured clients, usually members of the family which own the bank. As a result, most people are unable to obtain foreign exchange or capital except at an exorbitant price, while a minority of wealthy and privileged producers can obtain these inputs at highly subsidized prices.

Presumably the justification for providing cheap inputs is that it lowers the cost of production, raises profits and hence stimulates investment and growth. It sounds obvious, but the argument is almost entirely fallacious. Let us consider the price of capital in some detail in order to see why.

The price of capital, i.e. the rate of interest, is not an ordinary price; it plays a strategic role in determining the distribution of income, the level of employment, the composition of output and the rate of growth. First, the rate of interest influences household decisions to save. Particularly when deposit rates in financial intermediaries are low, or even negative in real terms, personal savings are likely to be adversely affected.[2] A low savings rate, everything else being equal, is likely to imply a slow rate of growth. Next, even if the volume of savings is not reduced by low rates of interest, the form in which assets are held is almost certain to be affected. Savers will be discouraged from accumulating financial assets and encouraged to accumulate real assets, e.g. gold, jewelery and consumer durables.[3] This will retard the development of a capital market, increase the difficulty of channelling investment resources to the most

---

[1] For an examination of the problems this creates see Chapter 6 below.

[2] For evidence of negative interest rates in Pakistan see A. H. M. Nuruddin Chowdhury, 'Some Reflections On Income Redistributive Intermediation in Pakistan', *Pakistan Development Review*, summer 1969.

[3] There is some evidence, for example, that time deposits in commercial banks are highly sensitive to changes in the real rate of interest.

productive sectors, raise the capital-output ratio and reduce the rate of growth.

Third, the rate of interest will help determine the commodity composition of output and the techniques of production. A low rate of interest will induce entrepreneurs who have access to credit to enter sectors which are relatively capital-intensive and to adopt methods of production with high capital-labour ratios. This will tend to generate unemployment in the economy or, more likely, to force those who cannot find employment in the capital-intensive sectors to enter low wage, labour intensive sectors such as services. That is, excessively low interest rates tend to fragment the economy into high and low productivity sectors. This leads to a misallocation of resources and lowers the level of national income;[1] it also produces either unemployment or underemployment.[2]

Finally, if profit rates are high and borrowing rates are low entrepreneurs are able, if they wish, to consume a substantial part of borrowed credit. This point seems not to have been recognised.

Assume a businessman in year o borrows Rs. B from a bank at a rate of interest of i repayable in equal annual instalments over n years without any initial grace period. His payment to the bank in the first year will be

$$B \ (i + 1/n).$$

It will be possible for the businessman to consume some fraction c of the borrowed capital immediately and yet meet all his obligations to the lender if the rate of profit r is high relative to interest and repayment obligations. The maximum value of c will be given by the inequality

$$B \ (1 - c) \ r \geqslant (i + 1/n) \ B$$

or

$$c \leqslant \frac{r - (i + 1/n)}{r}$$

---

[1] It might also reduce the rate of growth if either the marginal propensity to save is higher than the average or if (as neo-classical theory would predict) sectors with high capital-labour ratios also have high capital-output ratios.

[2] The Planning Commission claims that 7·5 million man-years, equivalent to 17·7 per cent of the labour force, are unemployed (*Outline of the Fourth Five-Year Plan* (*1970–75*) p. 30.).

Note that it varies directly with the rate of profit and the length of the repayment period and inversely with the rate of interest. Interest and repayment in any subsequent year t will together be

$$B\left(\frac{n-(t-1)}{n}\, i + \frac{1}{n}\right)$$

This repayment is less than in the first year, so that the consumption of cB in the initial year will not create a problem of financing the loan in later years as long as the rate of profit remains as high as r. One can also allow for the possibility that total profit in later years will decline as capital depreciates and the rate of profit remains unchanged. The above upper limit on c would still hold as long as depreciation is not greater than B/n, i.e., given straight-line depreciation, the life of capital is at least n years.

The rate of interest on borrowed capital in Pakistan has been no higher than 6 per cent and the repayment period to a favoured client has typically been 5 or more years. Under these assumptions, entrepreneurs could consume a positive amount out of their borrowing if the rate of profit is higher than 26 per cent. It is widely believed that the rate of profit in many activities has been much higher, viz., between 50 and 100 per cent. Assuming the lower limit of this range, an entrepreneur could consume as much as 48 per cent of his borrowed capital.

How much of the loan business men would in fact consume cannot be determined without specifying the preference function of the borrowers. Studies have suggested, however, that a very large proportion of the resources transferred from agriculture to industry are used to supplement consumption rather than investment. One estimate put the figure between 63 and 85 per cent.[1] In view of the results of the above exercise, these

---

[1] See Chapter 1 below. It has been claimed by K. Haq and M. Baqai, on the basis of a study of 104 companies, that corporations save a high proportion of their profits in the form of depreciation allowances and retained earnings. (See 'Savings and Financial Flows in the Corporate Sector, 1959–63', *Pakistan Development Review*, autumn 1967.) At least two objections can be made to this study. First, corporations are known to grossly understate their true profits and, hence, to overstate their true rate of savings. Second, even the reported net savings of corporations, i.e. gross profits minus taxation, depreciation and dividend payments, are only slightly higher than dividend payments.

figures still remain plausible. Until we find evidence to the contrary it would seem safe to assume that a significant fraction of all bank credit is used to increase current consumption rather than accelerate capital accumulation.

The very policies designed to encourage investment are responsible for making higher consumption possible. It is government policy which allowed the financial system to become highly concentrated and which tolerates its continuation. It is government policy to keep interest rates low and provide credit to private industrialists on favourable terms. Similarly, it is government policy which shields industrialists from competition and allows them to make fantastic profits. It is the huge gap between profit rates and interest rates which makes it possible to consume credit, and this gap is a consequence of government policy. Moreover, the harder the government tries to redistribute income to the industrial sector by raising commodity prices and lowering the prices of inputs, the larger the fraction of the resource transfer that can be consumed. As long as present institutional arrangements exist, a redistribution of income toward profits is likely to have a negligible effect on raising private savings.

Furthermore, given the strategy pursued, it was inevitable that the level of taxation and public savings would be low. The whole thrust of government policy was to encourage industrial entrepreneurship and to minimise the burden of taxation on the business community. As a consequence the total tax burden, i.e., the ratio of central government tax revenue to G.N.P., is low and rising only very slowly. In the period 1950–4 the tax burden was 6·8 per cent, and it actually declined to 6·1 per cent in the following five years. In the early 1960s, however, it rose to about 7·5 per cent, and by the end of the decade the tax burden was about 8·5 per cent. In the twenty years 1950–70 the ratio of taxes to G.N.P. rose two percentage points. At this rate of increase it will be another 70 years before the tax burden is 16 per cent.

Not only is the tax burden low, it is also regressive.[1] This

---

[1] This conclusion has been reached by other observers as well. Angus Maddison, for example, writes as follows: 'The net impact of the tax system is probably to increase inequality rather than reduce it. . . . In the past, the regressive tax system has been justified on the grounds that it

should be expected, given the intention of the government to redistribute income to corporate profits and high income groups. There has been no tendency for increased reliance to be placed on direct taxation. On the contrary, direct taxes are declining in relative importance and their share of total taxes at the end of the 1960s was lower than at the beginning. In the period 1948 to 1950 direct taxes[2] accounted for 10·8 per cent of total central government tax receipts. The proportion rose to 22·8 per cent in 1957–9 and declined thereafter. Today, direct taxes account for less than 17 per cent of total tax revenues.[3]

Government current, non-development expenditure is concentrated on defence and items which largely benefit middle and upper income groups. Defence expenditure alone absorbs between 60 and 75 per cent of tax revenues (or 40–50 per cent of total tax plus non-tax revenue); at its peak in 1965/6 it absorbed 112 per cent of tax revenue. What is left over after the armed forces are paid and equipped is devoted in large part to high-cost public housing (two-thirds of which is for civil servants[4],) higher education[5] (mostly of a non-technical nature), and urban health facilities.[6] As a result, the poor pay most of

---

Footnote 1 (contd.)

promoted growth . . . the industrial sector seems to have saved only half its profits. . . . There is no evidence that rural capitalists have a particularly high savings rate. By international standards the savings rate in Pakistan is not high. The tax system does not contribute much to welfare, efficiency or capital accumulation.' ('Social Development in Pakistan 1947–1970', paper presented to the June 1970 meeting at Dubrovnik of the Harvard Development Advisory Service, p.26.)

[2] That is, personal plus corporation income tax.

[3] As a result, the elasticity of the tax system is only 0·89, and the elasticity of corporate taxation is only 0·46.

[4] During the Third Plan Rs. 821 million was spent on public servants' housing, government offices and buildings and the new capital at Islamabad.

[5] The per cent allocated to primary education was 18 per cent in the First Plan, 14·7 per cent in the Second Plan and 13·6 per cent in the Third Plan. This trend is expected to be reversed during the Fourth Plan. Over the period 1949–69 enrolments increased 5·8 per cent a year in primary schools. 7·0 per cent in secondary schools and 12·7 per cent in colleges and universities.

[6] 'Most of the hospitals and doctors are in urban areas, where the major beneficiaries are the relatively richer part of the population.' (*Outline of the Fourth Five-Year Plan*, p. 302.)

the taxes and the prosperous receive most of the benefits of the current expenditure programme.

The incentive and tax system that has evolved has not been very successful in generating a high and rising savings rate. Over the 20-year period 1949/50 to 1969/70 the ratio of gross domestic savings to G.N.P. increased annually by 0·005.[1] This simple linear trend implies, of course, a diminishing percentage rate of increase. In fact, however, the situation is even worse than this. Between 1949 and 1958 the rate of savings remained roughly constant at 3–4 per cent. It then rose swiftly to a peak of 12·2 per cent in 1963–4. Thereafter it declined, and by 1969/70 the savings rate was about 9·8 per cent. In other words, throughout most of the two decades the savings rate either remained constant or declined; it was only during the early years of the Second Plan period that the rate rose sharply. This improved performance caught everyone by surprise and it was promptly called an "economic miracle", but the miracle was short lived.

The behaviour of private savings was almost identical to that of total savings. The private savings ratio was constant at 3–4 per cent until 1958 and then rose sharply to a peak of 12·1 per cent in 1965/6. In the following years the ratio declined very quickly. In 1969/70 private savings were only 7·9 per cent of G.N.P., the lowest proportion since 1960/1. Over the period as a whole the private savings rate increased only 0·004 a year.[2]

Given the high level of defence expenditures and the low tax burden one would not expect the public sector to make a significant contribution to domestic savings. Indeed between 1949 and 1958 public savings were persistently negative. During the next nine years, i.e. through 1967, public savings were at least positive, although they accounted for less than one per cent of G.N.P. In the next two years, however, the public savings rate rose substantially, and in 1969/70 it represented almost 1·9 per cent of G.N.P.

In the absence of reliable data on the rate of capital replace-

---

[1] $S/\text{GNP} = 0\cdot0127 + 0\cdot0049\ T;\ \bar{R}^2 = 0\cdot68.$
   $(0\cdot0007)$

[2] $\dfrac{\text{Gross private savings}}{\text{GNP}} = 0\cdot021 + 0\cdot0040\ T;\ \bar{R}^2 = 0\cdot61$
   $(0\cdot0007)$

ment it is impossible to know precisely how large are net savings as a proportion of national income. It is unlikely, however, that depreciation of the capital stock would be less than, say, four per cent of G.N.P., and hence the current rate of net savings must be about six per cent. This is a remarkably poor performance, particularly for a country which has consciously pursued a policy of redistributing income to the "saving sectors". In retrospect it has become painfully obvious that the savings strategy followed in Pakistan has failed. If the government is serious about wanting to attain a high rate of savings, much greater reliance must be placed in future on fiscal policy.

Once the emphasis shifts from private savings to public savings it will become possible to combine greater equality with a higher rate of domestically financed investment. The conflict that was assumed to exist between growth and equality was a consequence of the savings behaviour that was postulated. Such a conflict need not arise under a different strategy. In principle there is no reason why government policies cannot be designed both to achieve a high rate of savings and to ensure that consumption is distributed equitably.

At present gross personal income is distributed very un-equally. According to Bergan's data, households in the eighth decile receive 12·5 per cent of the total income, those in the ninth decile receive 15 per cent and those in the highest decile receive 30 per cent.[1] Virtually complete equality could be achieved (*a*) by taxing households in such a way that the shares of the top three deciles declined to 11·3, 13·7 and 15·0 per cent, respectively; and (*b*) by redistributing the proceeds to the bottom 40 per cent of households. This would require heavy taxation only of the richest 10 per cent of households, yet it would raise the income of the poorest households in the community by exactly 100 per cent. Even if only half the in-come taxed away from the rich were used to supplement directly the consumption of the poor, their standard of living would rise by a substantial amount; the other 50 per cent could then be channelled directly into investment and thereby help to raise the gross domestic savings rate.

One cannot predict the amount by which domestic savings would increase, since we do not know how the rich would

[1] See Chapter 8 below.

respond to increased taxation or the poor to increased income. It is evident, however, that under no circumstances need the domestic savings rate decline. Even if (i) all private savings were done by the upper 30 per cent of households, (ii) their savings fell to zero as a result of higher taxation, and (iii) the beneficiaries of redistribution consumed all their additional income, the domestic savings rate could be prevented from falling simply by ensuring that of the 17·5 per cent of income that was taxed away, roughly 7·9 percentage points (the amount currently saved in the private sector) were devoted to public savings. The worst that could occur under this programme is that domestic savings remained constant at the current level and the income of the poor rose by nearly 55 per cent. There is no question, therefore, but that a radical programme of taxation, income redistribution and public savings could simultaneously raise the standard of living of those most in need and accelerate the growth rate.

PART ONE

Post-Independence
Development Strategy

Post-Independence Development Strategy

Commentary

Economic policy in Pakistan has been concerned primarily with accelerating the rate of growth of gross national product. This objective has been pursued with extraordinary determination and other possible social goals have been neglected. Indeed, as we shall see, the single-minded pursuit of growth has resulted not only in a frequent failure to increase welfare, but in some respects policies have led to an actual deterioration of the well-being of the majority of the population. Production has expanded rapidly but little development has occurred.

The situation in which Pakistan finds itself today is a direct consequence of the government's growth strategy. This strategy contained, until recently, essentially two elements. First, expansion was to occur largely through industrialisation. Second, expansion was to be financed in part by redistributing income to the capitalist class, who were assumed to have a high propensity to save, and in part with foreign aid. Taxation and public savings were intentionally kept low so as to provide strong incentives to private entrepreneurs.

In Part three we discuss in great detail how the quasi-autarkic industralisation strategy imposed a loss of welfare on the society. Here we briefly indicate the main reasons for this loss. First, the extreme protection of industry implied a relative misallocation of resources in favour of industry and against agriculture beyond the limits of comparative advantage. Second, the arbitrary trade controls distorted the relative price structure to such an extent as to make intra-industrial priorities unrecognisable; within the industrial sector resources were allocated in favour of the wrong sectors and in favour of the

wrong techniques of production. Third, many of the new industries were technically inefficient and the period required for
these infant industries to mature seems to have been quite
long. In other words, Pakistan has been neglecting agriculture
relative to industry and has been producing the wrong industrial goods in the wrong way and, moreover, has been doing so
inefficiently.

The method used to finance industrialisation also had
unfortunate effects. The process of redistributing resources
from agriculture to industry was accompanied by, and in fact
was an integral part of, a redistribution of income from the
poor to the rich and from East to West Pakistan. It is possible to
show with the aid of a simple arithmetic example that a misallocation of resources may have only a marginal effect on
national income and at the same time have a very large adverse
effect on the income received by one sector.[1]

Imagine that a country has two sectors. Agriculture initially
produces 2000 bushels of wheat, 800 of which are sold abroad
and 200 to urban areas. The manufacturing sector produces
400 bolts of cloth, half of which is sold in the agricultural
sector at the international exchange rate of 1 bushel = 1 bolt.
The original position is as follows:

	Production	Sales		Purchases		Consumption
		Domestic	Foreign	Domestic	Foreign	
Agri-culture	2000W	200W	800W	200C	800C	1000W + 1000C = 2000
Industry	400C	200C	—	200W	—	200W + 200C = 400
G.N.P.	2400					

National income is 2400; income in agriculture is 2000 and
income in industry is 400.

Now assume that the government decides to encourage
domestic industry by imposing a tariff which alters the domestic
exchange ratio to 2 bushels = 1 bolt, i.e. the price of cloth has
doubled in terms of wheat. This change in relative commodity

---

[1] We are grateful to Stanislaw Wellisz for help in preparing this example.
Note that in this example only the first type of waste mentioned above has
been accounted for, while wastes of the other two types have been neglected
completely.

prices (a) will reduce imports of cloth, let us say to zero, (b) will reduce the domestic demand for cloth both because its price has risen and because national income has declined, and (c) will lead to a transfer of resources from the agricultural to the industrial sector. Let us assume that domestic production of cloth rises by 400 bolts, i.e. to 800. In the initial position one bushel of wheat could be converted, on the margin, into one bolt of cloth. In order to increase production of cloth by 400 bolts, however, more than 400 bushels of wheat must be sacrificed, since we are no longer dealing with marginal changes. Let us assume that the decline in wheat output is 500 bushels. The new position is as follows:

	Production	Sales	Purchases	Consumption
Agriculture	1500W	700W	350C	800W + 350C = 1150
Industry	800C	350C	700W	700W + 450C = 1150

GNP at world prices = 2300 and at domestic market prices = 3100.
Welfare loss (decline in GNP at world prices) = 100 (2400−2300)
Agricultural loss (at world prices) = 850 (2000−1150)
Industrial gain (at world prices) = 750 (1150−400)

Foreign trade has ceased. Instead of trading at international prices agriculture sells 700 bushels of wheat in exchange for 350 bolts of cloth. Measured at the initial price ratio, agriculture's welfare has declined by 850, i.e. to 1150. Industry, on the other hand, has increased its welfare by 750, i.e. to 1150. Because of the misallocation of resources, national income has declined from 2400 to 2300, i.e. by 100. In other words, a massive transfer of resources from agriculture to industry has reduced the national income by little more than four per cent, but in the process the income of the agricultural sector declined by 43 per cent.

In Pakistan, of course, a transfer of resources from agriculture to industry also implies a transfer from the East to the West wing, since during most of the period under review more than 60 per cent of East Pakistan's gross output originated in agriculture and about 40 per cent in West Pakistan. Attempts have been made to estimate the extent of the transfer by constructing East Pakistan's balance of payments. The data used in preparing the estimates are rather poor and hence the results must not be taken too literally, but at least we now have a rough idea of the order of magnitude of the income transfer.

To understand the measurement of resource transfer from East to West Pakistan, it is useful to divide the transfer into three components: (i) the value of goods and services exported abroad by East Pakistan less the value of goods imported from abroad $(X - M)$; (ii) the volume of goods and services traded between the regions and their prices (ideally

$$\sum_i p_i x_i{}^r - \sum_i p_i m_i{}^r,$$

where p_i is the ratio of the world price to the internal price for the ith good, but more conveniently $P(X^r - M^r)$, assuming some constant degree of overvaluation of the rate of exchange for all domestically traded goods); and (iii) East Pakistan's share of the total foreign aid inflow into Pakistan (αA). Thus the total resource outflow from the East would amount to

$$(X - M) + P(X^r - M^r) + \alpha A.$$

Note that this measurement is in terms of foreign exchange, so that in order to measure the resource outflow in rupees or as a percentage of domestic income it will have to be inflated by the inverse of P.

In order to measure resource transfer quantitatively, values of the parameters P and α have to be established. There is considerable dispute about the level of P, but all available studies suggest that 0·6 is something like an upper limit. Limits on α would be even more difficult to specify. But a lower limit seems to be the value of the aid projects actually approved for location in East Pakistan. This would put the value of α somewhere between 0·2 and 0·3. Another possibility, more like a reasonable value than an upper limit, would be the East's share of Pakistan's population, N_e/N, or about 0·55. In estimating resource transfer this may be treated as an upper limit on the grounds that it might be thought to be unreasonable for the East to claim more than 55 per cent of foreign aid.

It is important to note that for about a decade and a half since independence, i.e. until 1961 – 2, the following relation held for East Pakistan

$$(X - M) + (X^r - M^r) \geqslant 0$$

so that irrespective of the values of α and P East Pakistan suffered an unambiguous resource transfer. Since 1962 – 3 $(X - M)$ has continued to be positive (except in two years when there were small deficits) but the surpuls has in general been less than $(X^r - M^r)$ in absolute value. Thus, an estimate of resource transfer for these years has to be based on plausible estimates of P and α. Using the upper limit of 0·6 as the value of P, East Pakistan can be said to have been making a substantial resource transfer even if the value of α is as low as 0·2. For example, during the three years 1966 – 67 to 1968 – 69 $(X - M + 0·6 \ (X^r - M^r)$ has been less than 0·2A in absolute value.

It has been estimated by a group of highly competent economists from East Pakistan that on the assumption of $\alpha = N_e/N = 0·55$, the total transfer of resources over the two decades up to 1968 – 69 would amount to Rs. 31,120 million, or over \$100 per head of East Pakistan's population.[1]

Further evidence of the neglect of East Pakistan is provided by the division of development expenditure between the two wings. In the first half of the 1950s East Pakistan received only 20 per cent of public and private development expenditure. The proportion rose steadily throughout the years, but by the last half of the 1960s the province still was receiving only 36 per cent of total development resources. If one corrects for differences in population size between the two wings the comparison is even worse. In the period 1950/1 – 1954/5 development expenditure per head was nearly 4·9 times larger in West Pakistan than in East. By 1965/6 – 1969/70 the West wing was still receiving 2·17 times as much as the East wing.

These differences in per capita development expenditure are largely responsible for the differences in the rates of growth of G.D.P. in the two wings. Between 1959/60 and 1969/70 per capita G.D.P. at 1959/60 constant prices rose from Rs. 269 to Rs. 314 in East Pakistan, or by 1·5 per cent per annum. In West Pakistan the rise was from Rs. 355 to Rs. 504, or by 3·6 per cent per annum.

After a quarter-century of independence and the completion of three five year plans Pakistan's government has failed to

[1] Government of Pakistan, Planning Commission, *Report of the Panel of Economists on the Fourth Five-Year Plan (1970–75)*, May 1970, p. 75.

reduce the disparity between the two wings of the country.
Indeed, the disparity is growing, although the rate of increase of
disparity may be slowing down a bit. It is obvious, however,
that regional income inequality will not be eliminated by
1985, as the 1962 constitution provides, unless many more
resources are directed to the East wing.

The essay which follows contains an estimate of the extent of
resource transfer out of agriculture during the Second Five
Year Plan. It is shown that roughly 15 per cent of the value of
agricultural output, when measured in local prices, was
transferred to urban areas. Moreover, a very large proportion
of this resource transfer – say, about 75 per cent – was used to
increase urban consumption rather than investment. In a
subsequent study, first published three and a half years later,
Dr A. H. M. Nuruddin Chowdhury showed that if all transactions are valued at world prices, the reduction in income of
the agricultural sector is much greater than our estimate of
resource transfer would imply. In fact, under reasonable
assumptions about the terms of trade, the 'real' income loss
may be two or three times larger than the 'nominal' transfer.[1]

[1] A. H. M. N. Chowdhury, 'Some Reflections On Income Redistributive
Intermediation in Pakistan', *Pakistan Development Review*, summer 1969.

1 Financing Development Plans in Pakistan

KEITH GRIFFIN*

PAKISTAN is beginning her Third Five Year Plan[1] in a mood of great optimism. After the disappointment of the First Plan, the country was able to make undoubted progress during the Second. All the major objectives of the Second Five Year Plan were exceeded and there were few important short falls of the specific sub sector targets. Perhaps the most important of these were (a) the failure to use all the resources allocated to family planning, and (b) the relatively slow rate of growth of exports of cotton manufactures; of second-order importance was (c) the growing shortage of cement.[2]

Industrial output continued to grow rapidly. Although consumer goods still account for over 50 per cent of gross value added in industry, investment and intermediate goods have shown rapid rates of growth during the last ten years [17, p. 108]. One must be careful, however, not to extrapolate these growth rates too far into the future as the base upon which these calculations were made is extremely small. 'Large-scale manufacturing' in Pakistan still means, in essence, textiles and a handful of food-processing industries.

Exports grew at the extraordinary rate of 7 per cent per annum during the Second Plan, as compared with the 3 per cent rate anticipated. Almost all of the above-target achievements can be attributed to three items – raw cotton,

* This chapter originally appeared in the Winter 1965 issue of the *Pakistan Development Review*. The author is indebted to Bruce Glassburner and Mark Leiserson for helpful criticisms on the earlier draft.

[1] The third-plan period officially began on 1 July 1965.

[2] Only half the budget allocated to family planning was spent; exports of cotton manufactures were 250 million rupees less than planned; output of cement in 1964/5 was 2·4 million tons less than the 4·0 million ton target.

TABLE 1.1

PLANNING OBJECTIVES AND
ACHIEVEMENTS, 1955–65

Per cent increase over plan period	First 5-year plan		Second 5-year plan	
	Target	Achievement	Target	Achievement
G.N.P.	15	11	24	29
Agricultural output	15[a]	7	14	19
Industrial output	68[b]	32	47	51
Exports	33	13	15	40
Per capita income	7	3	10	13

[a]Food grain and fibre output only.
[b]Gross value added in large-scale industry only.
Sources: [29; 30; 31; 32]

miscellaneous exports and invisibles, with the last-named being
nearly as important as the other two combined.

A summary of the country's export performance over the last
ten years is included in Table 1.2 below.

TABLE 1.2

GROWTH RATE OF MAJOR EXPORTS,
1954/5–1964/5

	1954/5	1964/5	Annual compound percentage rate of growth
	(million rupees)		
All exports	1918	3050	4·7
Raw jute	857	820	−0·46
Manufactured jute	16	350	36·1
Raw cotton	496	400	−2·0
Cotton manufactures	32	170	18·0
Hides and skins	45	70	4·5
Wool	80	90	1·2
Miscellaneous	258	480	6·4
Invisibles	166	530	12·2

The behaviour of raw-cotton exports appears quite different
when viewed over the two plan periods as a whole. In spite of
the dramatic increase in exports beginning in 1962/3, by the end
of the second-plan period the value of exports was still slightly
lower than that prevailing ten years before. The explanation of

this is that throughout most of the period there were two conflicting trends at work: until 1960/1 cotton production in West Pakistan was stagnant; at the same time domestic consumption of cotton by the new textile industry grew rapidly. As a result, the volume of cotton available for export diminished. More recently, cotton output has increased and the rate of growth of domestic consumption has been reduced. This has led to a sharp rise in exports of raw cotton [19].

In some respects the most surprising accomplishment during the Second Plan was the rapid growth of agricultural output. The sector had been badly neglected during the previous ten years and it was largely responsible for the failure of the First Plan. During the last five years, however, the production of both food and fibre crops – and, as we have seen, particularly of cotton – is reported to have greatly increased. Jute production was the only serious disappointment. The average increase in output over the four years ending in 1963/4 was 8·4 per cent for wheat, 27·5 per cent for rice, 20 per cent for cotton, 26·5 per cent for surgarcane and minus 1·7 per cent for jute.

Cotton, wheat and sugarcane are produced principally in West Pakistan. We know there has been a substantial increase in private investment in tubewells and the use of fertilizers in this province [18]. Thus, the increase in output can easily be understood. Jute and rice are grown in East Pakistan; jute output declined; rice output increased enormously. Yet we know that neither the area cultivated nor the use of unconventional inputs rose very much, so – at least on the surface – it is very difficult to explain the reported increase in rice yields.[1]

Still, after all the qualifications are made, it is clear that physical output and G.N.P. per capita increased rather than decreased during the last ten years, and it is quite likely – at least in the latter half of the period – that they did so at a fairly substantial rate.

[1] Rice yields are reported to have risen 36 per cent between 1957 and 1964. Cf. *Pakistan Economic Survey, 1964/65* [27]. Yet as the National Income Commission stated, '. . . estimates of yield per acre in both parts of Pakistan are subjective estimates' [26, p. 18]. The decline in prices in 1964 is used as evidence of increased yield, but the large harvest in that year was probably due to favourable weather conditions.

THE ADOPTED STRATEGY

The strategy for development in Pakistan has been to channel resources to those groups in the community whose average and marginal savings rates are thought to be relatively high. In practice, this has meant that income should be redistributed away from the massive agricultural population and in favour of the small class of wealthy urban industrial entrepreneurs.[1] The surplus thus accumulated and available for investment would be guided into high priority projects through the use of indirect (monetary and fiscal) controls. After the unhappy experience of the early 1950s there has been a general tendency to avoid direct controls, state ownership of industries, and government intervention.

These domestic resources would then be supplemented with large imports of foreign capital, i.e. grants, loans and private foreign investment. Capital imports would be concentrated in the early periods of the development effort so that by the end of the Perspective Plan in 1985 we would witness the "elimination of dependence on foreign assistance" [31, p. 17].

Such, in outline, has been the strategy for development. Let us consider its consequences and implications.

(a) Decontrol and Free Enterprise

Large-scale textile manufacturing and some food-processing industries began to appear a few years after Pakistan achieved her independence. The major impetus to industrialize, however, came during the Korean War boom of 1950/1. Export prices rose over 26 per cent in two years, and foreign exchange was readily available to finance imports of machinery. When the boom ended export prices collapsed: cotton prices fell nearly 50 per cent and jute prices by 68 per cent. Imports of consumer goods were sharply curtailed, 'thereby giving the newly established industries a monopoly of the domestic market' [38, p. 54]. Profits were high and their reinvestment contributed to further growth.

[1] The 'trickle-down' effects in the urban areas are very slight. There is evidence that people in the bottom 50 per cent of the income scale in Karachi have a lower standard of living than those in the bottom half of the rural income scale. In fact, they are even poorer than the equivalent East Pakistani peasant! [31, p. 29].

The government provided additional assistance to private capitalists in 1952 when it established the Pakistan Industrial Development Corporation (P.I.D.C.). This is a semi-autonomous agency controlled and financed by the state which is responsible both for participating in private ventures and in starting projects of its own. P.I.D.C. has been instrumental in promoting such industries as sugar refineries, jute textiles, fertilizers and cement plants. More recently, it has begun to concentrate less on consumer-goods industries and more on basic industries, such as machine tools, heavy electrical equipment and petro-chemicals.

It has been the policy of the P.I.D.C. to divest itself of its projects once they have become well established. Of the 43 large industry projects completed by the West Pakistan Industrial Development Corporation (W.P.I.D.C.),[1] 24 have been converted into public limited companies and 19 of them are now under private management [27, p. 34]. Thus, considerable effort has been made to encourage private enterprise: private industrialists have been shielded from foreign competition; they have been given credit if they were short of capital, tax concessions to ensure that profits were high, and export bonuses to encourage them to sell abroad; and when these were not sufficient the government has established the industry and turned it over to private enterprise once it was under way.

The alternative policy of maintaining state ownership could have been advantageous for at least two reasons: first, since private capitalists consume some of their profits, state ownership and the assumed 100 per cent reinvestment of profits from the nationalized industries could in principle have led to a higher savings rate and rate of growth.[2] Second, state ownership

[1] The former P.I.D.C. was divided into two organisations, one for each wing, in July 1962.

[2] It is frequently asserted that 'the experience gained in these countries (that is, "in countries that are following a socialistic pattern") indicates that public enterprise has not been as efficient as private enterprise . . .' [21, pp. 5–6]. Such a statement cannot be supported with empirical evidence, and there are many reasons to believe that it is utterly false. There are numerous examples of efficient public enterprises not only in socialistic economies but in capitalist and mixed economies as well. The cases of Volkswagen in Germany (now private), the electricity company in France, the Suez Canal in Egypt, or the National Petroleum Co. in Chile come readily to mind.

would have eliminated the justification for the growing concentration of incomes and wealth which are such prominent features of the country today. The authorities, however, chose to move in the opposite direction.

The tone of the First Five Year Plan has been described as 'moralistic and libertarian' [38, p. 63]. By the time the Second Plan was published in June 1960 the general strategy of development was seldom questioned. The document contained only a few assertions and short statements of policy. A sample might include the following: 'The creative energies of the people can be best harnessed to the needs of development if policies of economic liberalism are pursued'; 'Private investment in industry is to be given maximum encouragement'; '. . . the Plan places greater reliance on the market mechanism and fiscal and monetary policies . . .' [30, pp. xiv, 5, 8]. The apparent success of the Second Plan has further reduced the need to justify the policies pursued. As far as the planners are concerned 'it is clear that the distribution of national product in the Third Plan should be such as to favour the saving sectors' [31, p. 33].

(b) The Distribution of Income

In order to enjoy a higher level of consumption in the future, present consumption must be restrained and the surplus thus mobilized must be used for productive investment. Evidently, a growing proportion of the national income must be saved and invested if growth is to be accelerated, and it is this refraining from consuming which constitutes the real sacrifice or cost of economic development. What is of crucial importance is *whose* consumption is restrained, i.e. the way in which these sacrifices are distributed among the population, because the control of the surplus and the way in which it is mobilized determine not only the distribution of income throughout the development period but also the form and composition of development itself.

To the extent that domestic resources have been mobilized in Pakistan it has been achieved by restraining the growth of the living standards of the poorest members of society – the rural masses. The Third Plan states: "There was a considerable transfer of savings from the agricultural to the industrial sector . . . as terms of trade were deliberately turned against agriculture through such policies as licensing of scarce foreign exchange earned primarily by agriculture to the industrial sector, compulsory government procurement of foodgrains at low prices to subsidize the cost of living of the urban, industrial workers, generous tax concessions to industry and lack of similar incentives for commercial agricultural investment" [31, p. 7]. These measures were particularly strong in the 1950s; they have been modified since then but have not been abandoned completely.

The evidence is quite strong that agricultural prices were squeezed in the early years of the 1950s through such policies as compulsory delivery of foodgrains and export taxes on cotton and jute. At the same time tariff protection, import licensing and other exchange controls allowed industrial prices to soar. But, as a result of a modification of policy, by the end of the decade agriculture's terms of trade appear to have greatly improved, although in recent years they may have declined again slightly.

The government's measures had the effect of reducing per capita income and consumption in rural areas relative to the rate of growth of G.N.P. per capita and, perhaps, also in absolute terms. It was mostly in the agricultural sector that consumption was restrained and a surplus generated.

Table 1.3 presents the existing data on real G.N.P. per capita, rural income per capita, and the per capita availability of foodgrains. It shows clearly that throughout most of the past 15 years average agricultural incomes were declining. During the last five years they rose fairly rapidly, but at the end of the period they were still no higher than at the beginning. G.N.P. per capita, on the other hand, rose by about 50 rupees.

Column (3) indicates that in spite of the massive imports of PL 480 commodities the per capita availability of foodgrains is no higher today than at the time of Partition. Moreover, these official estimates quite likely are overestimated. Total availability of foodgrains is obtained by subtracting a 10-per-cent allowance for seed, animal feed and wastage from domestic production, adding all imports and subtracting exports. This figure is then divided by the official estimate of population size. Most competent observers, however, believe that (a) the population size is underestimated and (b) its rate of growth is accelerating. (See, for example, [9, 14, 39].) If these demographers are correct then the per capita availability of foodgrains, particularly in the later periods, is overestimated. The level of food consumption in rural areas must be even lower as income has been sharply redistributed to the urban sector. The conclusion of all this is that the vast majority of the Pakistani population probably has a lower standard of living today than when the country achieved its independence in 1947.

TABLE 1.3

PER CAPITA INCOME AND
CONSUMPTION

	G.N.P. per capita (1) (Rupees)	Rural income per capita (2) (Rupees)	Foodgrains per capita* (3) (ounces per day)
1948/9			16
1949/50	311	207	15 (15)
1950/1	312	205	14 (14)
1951/2	313	204	13 (13·3)
1952/3	314	202	13 (13·6)
1953/4	315	202	15 (13·6)
1954/5	316	201	13 (13·3)
1955/6	316	199	12 (13·3)
1956/7	316	198	15 (13·6)
1957/8	317	195	14 (14)
1958/9	317	195	13 (13·6)
1959/60	318	194	14 (14)
1960/1	326	197	15 (14·3)
1961/2	334	199	14 (14)
1962/3	342	202	13 (14)
1963/4	351	205	15
1964/5	360	207	

*Numbers in parentheses are three-year moving averages.
Sources: Cols (1) and (2), Appendix Table 1; Col. (3) (27, Table 13).

Looking at the evidence in Table 1.4, which refers to the two plan periods, it would appear that average urban incomes are six times higher than rural (1278 *v.* 207 rupees) and that they grew four times faster (12·8 per cent over ten years *v.* 3 per cent). Even though the number of urban residents increased 60 per cent over the 10 years (it is not unusual to have high percentage rates of growth when the base is small), the absolute number of rural people increased by 18 million. Hence, it is clear that income distribution is becoming more unequal. The fruits of development are being reaped by the minority of urban rich while the majority of the nation remains the rural poor. Moreover, the growing inequality in income distribution is also reflected in the economic relations between the two wings. In terms of its contribution to the Gross Regional Product

TABLE 1.4

RURAL–URBAN INCOME DISTRIBUTION

			Increase	
	1954/55	*1964/65*	*Absolute*	*Percentage*
Population (million)	88	112	27	27·3
Urban	10	16	6	60·0
Agricultural	78	96	18	23·1
Income per capita (rupees)	316	360	44	13·9
Urban	1133	1278	145	12·8
Agricultural	201	207	6	3·0

Source: Calculated from data in Appendix Table 1.

agriculture is 11 times larger than "large-scale" manufacturing[1] in East Pakistan, whereas in West Pakistan it is only 4·7 times larger.

It is, of course, a gross simplification to assume that all who live in rural areas are poor and all urban dwellers are rich.

The distribution of land in West Pakistan is very unequal and a commission was appointed in 1958 to recommend reforms. The commission proposed (i) that the government expropriate all holdings of irrigated land above 500 acres and those of other lands (with exceptions) in excess of 1000 acres. Compensation would be paid at something less than the market value and the land would be sold to small cultivators. The commission also recommended (ii) that the methods of collecting rents be modified and that tenants be given greater security, and (iii) that the fragmentation of holdings be stopped and that already fragmented holdings be consolidated.

[1] Large-scale manufacturing is defined by the National Income Commission to include any establishment which employs at least 20 persons and uses mechanical power.

The commission's report was accepted and the programme was begun in January 1959. By the end of the Second Plan 2·2 million acres, or about 2 per cent of the land in the province, had been expropriated and resold. Compensation was assessed at 76 million rupees and bonds were issued for the entire amount. By July 1965 half the bonds had been redeemed for cash payment. The expropriated land was largely marginal and uncultivated while many large holdings have been left untouched; tenant relations were largely unchanged and 'about 6·7 million acres (50 per cent of the target) were consolidated' [32, p. 41].

There is very little information about the distribution of income in urban areas. M. Shoaib, the Finance Minister, has, however, recognized that: 'There is a growing discontent in the country about increasing concentration of income and wealth and economic power in the hands of a relatively few' [37, para 40]. It is common knowledge that 'the rich have certainly become very rich indeed, and persons and families which were worth millions a decade ago are now worth hundreds of millions ... The same family groups own industrial undertakings, banks, insurance companies, consultancy offices, construction firms, distribution trade, etc., etc., so that not only is there a horizontal but also a vertical concentration of wealth, and a tremendous concentration of economic power' [11, p. 9]. Only one-tenth of 1 per cent of the population pays income tax, yet the plan informs us that the top 5 per cent in Karachi have incomes 27 times higher than the bottom 5 per cent (who are even poorer than the equivalent rural group) [31, p. 29]. The exemption limit for personal income tax is 6000 rupees or nearly 17 times the per capita income. There is little to warrant this policy as it has even been shown that the nominal level of non-corporate private savings has not risen substantially since 1949 [16]. Furthermore, a sample survey in Dacca also reveals that as much as 42·5 per cent of personal 'savings' in the urban sector is in the form of gold and ornaments, consumer durables and housing [7, p. 26].

(c) Private Savings

We have shown so far (i) that the development strategy has placed considerable reliance on private enterprise and that it has been government policy to protect and strengthen private capitalists; (ii) that the rural areas have been squeezed to such an extent that the level of rural consumption per capita possibly is lower and certainly no higher than it was fifteen years ago; and (iii) that the strategy adopted has led to the creation of a privileged class and an unequal distribution of income. We must now consider more closely to what extent the strategy has been successful in achieving a high rate of domestic savings.

TABLE 1.5

GROSS DOMESTIC SAVINGS AND INVESTMENT
AS PERCENTAGE OF G.N.P.

	1949/50	*1954/55*	*1959/60*	*1964/65*
Domestic savings as a percentage of G.N.P.	4·6	6·8	5·9	9·5
Investment as a percentage of G.N.P.	4·6	7·9	10·9	15·8

Source: [31].

The Planning Commission has repeatedly called attention to what it considers the 'remarkable acceleration in gross investment' and the 'considerable increase in domestic savings' [31, pp. 4 and 6]. The data it presents would appear to substantiate this claim. Yet if one accepts the estimate that 'depreciation accounts for 4 per cent of G.N.P.' [18, p. 5], then the net domestic savings ratio on the most optimistic assumption is only slightly higher than 5 per cent. This can hardly be considered a respectable savings effort. If the government is serious about outrunning the population increase (which is currently estimated at 3 per cent per annum and still accelerating) and eliminating its dependence on foreign aid by 1985, it will have to raise the net savings ratio to roughly 12–15 per cent. The perspective plan is somewhat more ambitious: it envisages a 25 per cent marginal rate of savings leading to a 21·8 per cent gross savings ratio by the end of the period [31, p. 19].

Since a great deal depends upon the behaviour of private savings it is worth while to examine what occurred during the Second Plan more closely. It is estimated that about 11,474 million rupees were invested in the private sector over the last five years. Of this amount, 451 million rupees were financed by private foreign investment and 1,600 million rupees by foreign loans and grants. A further 221 million rupees represent investment by the two P.I.D.C.s. Roughly 2,525 million rupees were spent on private housing, apparently mostly for the wealthy. The Planning Commission candidly states that: 'In the private sector, the construction activity has been impressive, especially in the upper income groups' [32, p. 76].

These four items account for 4,797 million rupees of investment in the private sector. This means that private initiative and savings were responsible for only 6,677 million rupees of investment in directly productive activities.[1] This effort of private savers represents only slightly more than 3 per cent of the Gross National Product.

TABLE 1.6

PRIVATE DOMESTIC SAVINGS IN DIRECTLY PRODUCTIVE ACTIVITIES DURING THE SECOND PLAN

		(Rs. million)
1. Total investment in private sector		11,474
2. Foreign private investment	451	
3. Foreign loans and grants	1600	
4. Investment in P.I.D.C.s	221	
5. Investment in housing	2525	
6. Sub-total: rows 2 through 5		4,797
7. Private savings in directly productive activities (row 1–row 6)		6,677
8. Private savings in directly productive activities as percentage of G.N.P.		3·3

Source: [32, pp. 26, 28, 54, 116].

This, however, is only part of the story. We have shown earlier that the strategy of development was to restrain the growth of agricultural incomes and facilitate investment in industry by private entrepreneurs. Up to now we have implied that all private saving was in fact done by this class and invested

[1] All that is meant by 'directly productive activities' in this context is investment in anything other than housing. This definition, of course, begs the important question of whether private investment in such things as cigarettes, perfumes and cosmetics is in any sense 'directly productive'.

in manufacturing. Yet we know that during the Second Plan there was a substantial amount of private investment in rural areas; just how much is still uncertain. The best estimate we have was prepared by W. Falcon and C. Gotsch. They reached the conclusion that in 1962/3 private investment in agriculture was of the order of 781 million rupees [4, p. 6].

Now if we take the annual average of item 7 in Table 1.6 we get 1335 million rupees as an estimate of private investment in directly productive activities. As we have seen, 781 million rupees were invested in agriculture, so the approximate amount of private savings invested in directly productive activities *outside agriculture* was only 554 million rupees. This was only slightly more than 1 per cent of the G.N.P. or 3 per cent of total urban income in 1962/3. The Falcon-Gotsch estimate of private investment in agriculture, however, was made independently of the estimates included in Table 16. Thus there is no assurance that this estimate is included in the figure we are using for private savings in directly productive activities; we can only be confident that non-agricultural productive investment is somewhere between 3·3 per cent and 1 per cent of G.N.P.

As long ago as 1959 the Credit Enquiry Commission revealed that nearly 60 per cent of the bank credit was secured by 222 families. From the viewpoint of equity it is highly doubtful that the 'sizable transfer of saving . . . taking place through the rural branches of the commercial banks to the urban centres' can be considered a 'great help' [31, p. 33]. Further provision of credit is only likely to perpetuate this socio-economic system.

The desirability of well-meaning proposals to raise savings through a 'reduction of the corporation tax rate to either a nominal payment or to zero' is highly doubtful [15, p. 268]. Corporate tax rates already are quite moderate and income from this source accounts for only about 5 per cent of all tax revenues. Preliminary findings of a study under way at the Pakistan Institute of Development Economics by Abdur Rab indicate that the effective corporate tax rate (on net taxable income, i.e. net of exemptions) is only about 25 per cent. In fact, the total tax burden is unusually low [20]: only 7 – 9 per cent of G.N.P. is currently paid in taxes and the government hopes to raise this to 10 per cent during the third Plan.

The government has become increasingly unable to finance its expenditures with tax receipts. In 1960/1 government receipts (taxes plus other revenues) covered over 68 per cent of total expenditures (both non-development and development expenditures); by 1964/5 they covered barely 66 per cent. This was a continuation of a long trend. As Chowdhury states 'though there has been some growth of tax revenues, this has been slower than the growth of total budgeted expenditure. There has been, however, much greater availability of foreign aid' [3, p. 108].

(d) *The Savings Transfer from Agriculture*

Assuming additional unemployed resources cannot be readily mobilised, if the domestic savings rate is to increase, consumption must be restrained, i.e. resources must be transferred from consumption-use to investment-use. Consumption, in turn, may be restrained more severely in some sectors than in others – just as investment may increase more in some sectors than in others. If we find, for example, that the relative reduction in consumption in sector A during some period exceeds the increase in investment in that sector, we say there has been a transfer of resources to the other sector N. If we should also find that the transfer of resources from A to N is greater than investment in sector N, then we say there has been a transfer of savings from sector A to consumption in sector N.

We have tried to obtain a rough measure of the transfer of savings from the agricultural to the non-agricultural sector by constructing the 'balance of payments' of agriculture for the fiscal year July 1964 – June 1965. Relevant data are scarce and of poor quality and our estimate has been pieced together from a variety of sources. Hence, the estimate in Table 17 must be viewed only as an indication of the order of magnitude.

It appears that agriculture annually transfers about 3600 million rupees of resources to the urban sector. This represents over 15 per cent of the value of its gross output. Total development expenditure during the five years of the Second Plan was 26,330 million rupees, of which 10,100 million rupees were financed by capital imports. Domestic resources accounted for only 16,230 million rupees of plan expenditure, or an annual average of 3246 million rupees. On pages [42–3] we argued that private non-agricultural investment probably was somewhere between 554 to 1335 million rupees on the average. If this estimate is correct it implies that at least 63 to 85 per cent of the savings transferred from agriculture are dissipated in higher consumption in urban areas.

TABLE 1.7

SALES AND PURCHASES OF THE AGRICULTURAL SECTOR, 1964/65

	(Rs. million)
1. Sales by agriculture to urban sector and foreign countries	14,425
2. Purchases of intermediate goods	1,518
3. Purchases of capital goods from foreign countries	69
4. Purchases of capital goods from urban sector	262
5. Purchases of consumer goods	8,914
6. Total purchases	10,763
7. Sales minus purchases (=resource transfer)	3,662

Sources: Rows (1) and (2): [10]. Row (3): [15]. Row (4): [7]. The 1959/60 estimates of the output of agricultural machinery and appliances, cement, strainers, engines and turbines, pumps and compressors were brought up to 1964/5 by assuming a 13 per cent annual compound rate of growth— which was the rate experienced by large-scale manufacturing as a whole. Row (5): [11]. The estimates were brought up to 1964/5 by using income elasticities of demand suggested by the survey data and assuming per capita rural income increased by 5 per cent as suggested by the data in Appendix Table 1. The estimate is known to be overstated by a considerable amount because village-produced textiles and footwear are treated as purchases from the urban sector.

We cannot conclude from this, however, that the agriculturists are rapidly becoming industrial capitalists. Without a flow-of-funds statement it is impossible to trace the financial flows and determine the form in which assets are accumulated. Some of the savings, of course, are transferred through taxation, but at the same time fertilizers, pesticides and water are heavily subsidized. Some of the savings are deposited in rural branches of national banks and then transferred to the urban sector. Probably, a larger proportion is deposited directly in urban banks by large landowners who reside in, say, Lahore or Karachi. Some of the funds may be invested directly in manufacturing activities, but the volume may prove to be small. Further research on this topic is obviously necessary, but it does seem clear that if the agricultural surplus were mobilized and combined with high urban savings the need for foreign aid would soon disappear.

FOREIGN AID AND INVESTMENT

Private savings and the government's surplus on current expenditure account were totally inadequate to finance the development effort during the first two plans. The relative success of the plans and the consequent performance of the economy depended to a great extent on the availability of foreign assistance and its efficient utilization.

During 1955/60 Pakistan's capital imports were over 5 billion rupees. 56 per cent of this was in the form of grants; the remainder composed of loans and a small flow of private foreign investment (see Table 1·8). These external resources financed half the plan expenditure and a third of the total imports; they supplemented Pakistan's earnings from exports by over 50 per cent. In the next plan period the volume of aid doubled and the proportion of loans rose to 80 per cent. Aid now supplemented export earnings by over 76 per cent and financed nearly 40 per cent of all imports, although the proportion of development expenditure financed by aid declined to 38 per cent.

Thus, between the two plans, there was an abrupt change in the composition of capital imports. Grants declined by 762 million rupees while the volume of loans increased by almost 444 per cent. It is perhaps unfair as well as indelicate to suggest that grants decreased once Pakistan's alignment with the West, its acceptance of United States military aid, and its membership in SEATO and the Baghdad Pact (later CENTO) were assured – but the suspicion remains nevertheless. This de-emphasis of grants was associated with a dramatic increase in 'tied' loans. The immediate consequences are reflected in the fact that from 1960/1 to 1963/4 the share of dollar-area imports rose from 26 to 46 per cent.

The long-run consequences of tied aid can be quite serious. It is a common belief that products purchased under tied-loan agreements usually cost 15–25 per cent more than world prices. It is quite likely that this is an underestimate since (*a*) foreign suppliers frequently raise their prices when loans are tied and world competition is eliminated; and (*b*) there is evidence that German industrialists charge 40 per cent more than world prices under their tied-loan agreement.[1] In comparison with untied aid, these practices squeeze the developing countries in three ways: first, by definition, by raising the cost of imports, tied loans augment the deficit on current account of the

TABLE 1.8

CAPITAL IMPORTS AND FOREIGN DEBTS

	1955-60	*1960-5*	*1965-70*
		(Rs. million)	
1. Total capital imports	5,070	10,100[b]	16,500[b]
(a) grants	2,837	2,075	n.a.
(b) loans	1,808	8,025	n.a.
(c) private foreign investment	425	450	700
2. Capital imports as per cent of			
(a) export earnings	55·3	76·2	82·0
(b) total imports	35·0	39·3	46·5
(c) development expenditure	52·0	38·4	31·7
3. Servicing of foreign debt	161·1[a]	951	2810
(a) debt servicing as per cent of capital imports	3·2	9·4	17·0
(b) debt servicing as per cent of export earnings	1·8	7·2	14·0

Source: [27; 30; 31; 34, various years].
[a] Repayment of principal only.
[b] The Second and Third Plans exclude the 945·9 million dollar Indus Basin Project. All but 29 million dollars of this will be financed from external resources, according to the terms of the 1960 treaty signed with India.

balance of payments and lead to a deterioration of the terms of trade. The deterioration of the terms of trade will be a once-for-all change except in so far as the proportion of tied aid increases. This terms-of-trade effect can be partially offset by diversifying the sources of aid. In other words, by raising the cost of development expenditure, tied loans lead to a higher capital-output ratio and lower rate of growth. Secondly, this effect may be permanent as the industrial apparatus of the borrowing country

[1] See the statement by Mr A. Jawad, President of the Karachi Chamber of Commerce, as reported in *Dawn* (Karachi), 10 July 1965, p. 5.

may become permanently dependent upon a high-cost supplier for spare parts, replacements and ancillary equipment. Thirdly, tied loans lead to higher debt repayment obligations and a greater foreign debt burden. Assume, for example, that Pakistan obtains a tied loan of 1000 dollars at 5 per cent repayable over 10 years from the Eximbank to buy a piece of machinery which costs only 800 dollars on the world market. Total debt servicing on this loan will be 1,275 dollars, i.e. 1000 dollars for repayment of principal and 275 dollars for interest charges. In comparison, if Pakistan had been able to obtain an (hypothetical) untied loan for 800 dollars on the same terms, total debt servicing would have been only 1020 dollars, or 255 dollars less.

Aid in the form of surplus agricultural commodities under the P.L. 480 programme increased from 1618 million to 1970 million rupees over the two plan periods. 723 million rupees were spent in support of the public works programme which is attempting to provide employment and increase productivity by undertaking labour-intensive investment projects in rural areas. It could be argued that this is the most effective use to which P.L. 480 aid has been put, and certainly in principle such programmes deserve to be supported. Critics of the programme, however, frequently allege that in practice the public works programme has contributed much less than one would hope because (a) corruption is widespread, (b) the type and location of projects is determined by political rather than economic factors, and (c) the work (including maintenance) has been poorly done through lack of skills and technical knowledge. Evidently, more research is needed on this topic.

It has been suggested that in other respects P.L. 480 assistance has been harmful. Beringer and Ahmad believe 'that there is a danger that the relatively stable food-price situation which has been maintained with the help of P.L. 480 imports is beginning to blur the government's vision of the seriousness of the agricultural supply situation in Pakistan' [2, p. 59]. It is uncertain whether the government's vision is blurred, i.e. whether agriculture has been neglected in general, but it is a fact (a) that the index of wheat output was 100 in 1960 and only 106 by 1963/4 and (b) that the average acreage devoted to wheat increased from 10·4 million in 1950/5 to 11·7 million in

1955/60 to over 12 million in the early 1960s [25, p. 1]. Thus, there is a clear association between P.L. 480 imports and stagnating wheat production.

It could be argued that Pakistan should concentrate her efforts on increasing the output of jute and cotton – which earn foreign exchange – and continue to rely on P.L. 480 imports to meet her food requirements. This, however, would seem to be an unwise policy as it would give a foreign government extra-ordinary power to influence this country's internal and external affairs. Alternatively, one could argue that Pakistan should export jute and cotton in return for foodgrains purchased from commercial sources. The advisability of this policy would depend upon where the country's comparative advantage lies and what are the likely future changes in costs and prices in the cash crop and foodgrain industries. It certainly isn't obvious that Pakistan can best feed her growing population by selling cotton rather than by growing wheat.

(a) Foreign Aid in the Third Plan
The Planning Commission has tried to give the impression that the country's dependence on foreign assistance is diminishing. It is true that capital imports as a percentage of G.N.P. are expected to be lower in the Third Plan than in the Second (6·7 per cent *v.* 8·1 per cent), but they will still be higher than the 4·8 per cent which prevailed during the First Plan. It is also true that foreign assistance as a percentage of total development expenditure is expected to be somewhat lower in the Third Plan than in the last (see Table 1.8). More to the point, however, capital imports appear to be a growing proportion of total government expenditures, foreign-exchange receipts and total imports. Moreover, the amount of foreign aid requested to finance the Third Plan is 60 per cent greater than the amount received during the second-plan period.

Capital exports, in the form of repatriation of private capital, repayment of principal on foreign debts and interest charges have begun to rise at a substantial rate. In fact, private capital outflows appear to exceed the inflow, i.e. Pakistan is a net capital exporter on private account. As a government spokesman has stated: 'It is estimated that in 1963/4 the level of such out-flow was in the neighbourhood of 150 million rupees exceeding the direct inflow of private capital by 50 million rupees' [12, p. 11].

The rate of interest on Pakistan's foreign debt varies from 0·75 per cent for I.D.A. loans to 6 per cent for German 10-year credits. At present, the average rate is approximately 3 per cent[1] and seems to be rising – although it is difficult to document this precisely. An increasing volume of debt is being incurred simply to pay off previous debts: during the First Plan the proportion of debt servicing to capital imports was 3·2 per cent: it rose to 9·4 per cent in the Second Plan and is expected to be 17·0 per cent during the Third. This can be a costly policy especially if the average rate of interest on new debts is higher than on the old.

Debt servicing also is a growing percentage of export earnings. During the First Plan only 3·8 per cent of the country's earnings of foreign exchange were used to service the debt; the proportion rose to 10 per cent in the last year of the Second Plan and is expected to be 16 per cent in the last year of the Third Plan. At this rate of increase a quarter of Pakistan's export earnings will be needed by 1974/5 to service the debt and nearly a half by 1979/80. Even this projection is optimistic, however.

The notable feature of the Second Plan was the extent by which exports exceeded their target. Had exports grown at the planned rate of 3 per cent per annum, instead of the 7 per cent rate actually achieved, the foreign debt position would appear much worse today than it does. Had exports not grown at the rate they did, foreign-exchange earnings would have been lower and the need for capital imports consequently greater. It is probably safe to say that in the absence of an export boom debt servicing in the last year of the plan would have absorbed 12 to 15 per cent of export earnings. This speculation after the event is important because it is planned to accelerate the rate of growth of exports even further during the Third Plan to 9·5 per cent per annum. Failure to meet this target would be serious, for if exports grow only 20 per cent over the plan period,

---

[1] The estimate was obtained by weighting 9 interest rates reported in [27] by the debt outstanding at the end of 1964. The weighted average obtained was 3·01 per cent.

for example, the ratio of debt service to exports will be 20·5 per cent in 1969/70.

(b) The Foreign-Trade Targets

A detailed analysis of the balance-of-payments projections of the Third Plan is the subject for another essay [6]. All that can be done here is to indicate the broad lines of the foreign trade strategy and comment upon them. The basic information presented in Table 1.9 will help us to do this.

TABLE 1.9

EXPORT TARGETS OVER THIRD PLAN

	1964/5	1969/70	Compound percentage rate of growth
	(Rs. million)		
Raw jute	820	750	−1·8
Raw cotton	400	550	6·7
Hides and skins	70	80	2·8
Wool	90	90	0·0
Rice	140	300	16·4
Total primary commodities	1,705	2,120	4·5
Jute manufactures	350	800	18·0
Cotton manufactures	170	350	15·6
Total manufactures	815	2,000	19·7
Invisible earnings	530	680	5·2
Total exports	3,050	4,800	9·4

Source: [5].

The first thing to notice is that exports are expected to grow almost 50 per cent faster than G.N.P. Thus, to use Rostow's terminology, foreign trade is to become Pakistan's leading sector. This is to be achieved by a rapid expansion of five commodity groups: rice, raw cotton, cotton manufactures, jute manufactures and other manufactures.

The second thing to notice is that 'for most products, both agricultural and industrial, for which exports are planned, domestic consumption constitutes an alternative market' [31, p. 90]. This means that domestic consumption will have to be restrained and increased production channelled to export markets. This is likely to be quite difficult. First, the Planning

Commission has assumed the population will grow at 2·7 per cent per annum even though there is good reason to believe that the rate is at least 3 per cent (cf. p. 38 above). Thus, internal pressure for additional consumer goods is likely to be more intense than is anticipated. Secondly 'the shift from direct to indirect controls . . . will be intensified during the next five years' [31, p. 89]. If the planners are serious, this implies that precisely at the moment when efficient discriminatory controls on consumption would be most useful in accelerating exports, the existing measures will not be improved but rather discarded in favour of instruments whose impact is diffused and unpredictable. Insufficient consideration, for example, seems to have been given to the desirability of establishing a government trading corporation and an export quota system. Such direct controls could be powerful instruments in achieving the government's stated aim – although it must be recognised that direct controls can have undesirable distributive effects depending upon the way the controls are administered and the honesty of the civil service.

A consideration of the export targets by separate commodity groups does not lead to greater optimism. The planned 16·4 per cent annual rate of growth of high-quality rice exports appears to be too high. It is unlikely that world demand will be great enough to absorb this quantity without a substantial price decline [10].

Cotton production is expected to increase by 50 per cent during the Third Plan and exports of raw cotton are expected to grow 6·7 per cent per annum. Whether the export target can be met depends upon whether domestic supply increases by the required amount and whether purchases of cotton by the textile industry can be kept within bounds. The former problem may prove to be the more difficult.

Cotton output has substantially increased in the last few years, due primarily to private investment in tubewells. Further increases in output will depend upon a continuation of this investment as well as additional use of non-conventional inputs, particularly fertilizers. There is a danger, which seems to have been ignored, that private investment in tubewells during the next five years may not be as buoyant as is hoped. In the past, these investments have been undertaken by relatively large and wealthy farmers: 77 per cent of all tubewells are found on holdings of 25 acres or larger; 82 per cent of all tubewells were installed without recource to borrowing [18, pp. 20–21]. It is quite possible that within the next two or three years most large farmers will have installed their tubewells. Expansion of the programme will then rest upon the small farmers – who own over half of the cultivable land in West Pakistan. These small farmers may not invest either because their financial resources do not enable them to do so or because their fragmented holdings do not justify such a large capital expenditure. For these reasons the provision of more generous credit facilities coupled with an acceleration of the process of land consolidation may be essential. Without them the chances of meeting the export target for raw cotton are less certain.

Exports of manufactured products are expected to grow 19·7 per cent per annum, i.e. almost twice as fast as industrial output and three times faster than they grew over the Second Plan. If this target is achieved it would represent a complete reversal of past trends. The proportion of industrial output that is exported has declined steadily from 4 per cent at the beginning of the Second Plan to 3 per cent at the end. Now the Planning Commission has decided that the ratio should increase to 'at least 5 per cent' by 1970. How this is to be accomplished is not clearly stated. Until the commission specifies in detail the policy measures it intends to introduce to achieve such results the target for exports of manufactured goods should be viewed with scepticism.

The import targets are equally ambitious. Total imports and debt servicing are expected to grow by 7·3 per cent per annum during the Third Plan as compared with 15·8 per cent during the Second. Imports, exclusive of debt servicing, are expected to grow less rapidly than G.N.P. This is to be achieved by restricting the rate of growth of imports of capital goods to 4·5 per cent per annum, of raw materials to 11 per cent per annum, and of consumer goods to 3·3 per cent per annum. At the same time that this is to occur the government insists that the regulation of imports will shift to indirect methods and that gradually they will be decontrolled [31, p. 123].

The gap between imports and exports has been growing steadily throughout the last ten years, and the need for capital

imports has consequently been increasing. The Third Plan
proposes to reverse this trend. Yet it appears that both the
export and import targets are completely unrealistic, especially
in the context of the government's philosophy of economic
liberalism. It has already been shown above, contrary to what
the Planning Commission would like to imply, that by almost
any reasonable measure the Third Plan envisages an increase
in Pakistan's dependence on foreign assistance. The increased
dependence may have been understated, however. If the
foreign-trade targets are not achieved, either greater aid will
be requested or the Plan's objectives will be scaled down. In
either case dependence on capital imports will increase. The
only way to avoid this dilemma is to place greater stress on
mobilising the nation's resources.

SUMMARY AND CONCLUSIONS

Planning in Pakistan has been a curious exercise. It has been
the intention of the government to liberalise the economy as
much as possible and to redistribute income to the industrial
classes in the expectation that this would lead to a high rate of
domestic savings.

In the first half of the essay it is shown that the government
did introduce the social and economic changes it proposed:
the economy was liberalised and income was redistributed. In
fact, it is argued that the redistribution of income was so
pronounced that the standard of living of the average rural
inhabitant is no higher today than it was fifteen years ago and
it may be lower. The poor are little better off and, because of
population growth, they are more numerous than when planning began. In spite of this the domestic savings rate is still very
low. Using Planning Commission data – which may not be
accurate but, if anything, are likely to be biased upward – it is
argued that private investment in directly productive non-
agricultural activities is about 1 to 3 per cent of G.N.P. Even if
there is a substantial error in the estimate the plan strategy
can only be considered a very modest success.

Income inequalities have not ensured markedly high rates
of private savings – they have mostly led to privilege: the
ho using boom is largely confined to urban areas and the wealthy

classes; imports of photographic equipment and supplies were five million rupees per annum during the First Plan, whereas they were running at an annual rate of 14 million rupees in 1964/5; imports of passenger motorcars were 12·6 million rupees per annum during the First Plan, whereas they soared to an annual rate of 72 million rupees in the first nine months of 1964/5 [22; 24]. In contrast, according to information published in the *Pakistan Observer*, only 75 million rupees were allocated by the government to assist the victims of the May 1965 cyclones and floods which killed nearly 13,000 people and made 500,000 homeless.

This entire social and economic system, and the planning exercise which is its manifestation, is supported and sustained by foreign assistance. A former member of Harvard's Development Advisory Service practically concedes this. He says: 'It is ironical but true that the strongest prop of the planning enterprise in Pakistan is the nation's continued dependence on foreign aid' [38, p. 78]. The assertion of the Planning Commission that '. . . a liberalised economic system is highly conducive to accelerated capital formation and economic growth . . .' is not consistent with the facts [31, p. 123]. Pakistan's economic performance has depended heavily on capital imports and this dependence is increasing. The volume of external assistance requested for the Third Plan is 300 per cent higher than that obtained during the First, and the proportion of total imports financed by aid is growing as well.

The authorities are obviously pleased that 'excluding consumer goods imported under P.L. 480 programme, consumer items constitute only about 12 per cent of total imports' [31, p. 9]. Yet the implication of this is that the planned substitution of imported consumer goods by privileged local producers has introduced a strong pro-consumption, anti-saving bias into the economy, i.e. the output mix in the industrial sector is not consistent with a high savings policy [cf., for example, 13]. If consumer demand is not maintained at a high level Pakistan will have excess industrial capacity! There is little choice but to continue consuming locally produced 'Pakola', clocks, fountain pens and radios.

Private investment in tubewells in West Pakistan and the consequent expansion of output of raw cotton are perhaps the most encouraging recent developments in the country. Although the government did subsidise inputs and remove price controls, to a large extent the planners were lucky. Private tubewell installation was unanticipated and in fact is being resisted by the government's Water and Power Development Authority, which favours licensing controls. It would be difficult to attribute the buoyancy of agricultural investment directly to the government's initiative in this field, much less to its policy of redistributing income to urban areas. 'Emergency conditions' are said to have prevailed in agriculture at the end of 1959/60; that conditions today are not catastrophic is an unplanned blessing [30, p. 128].

One suspects that capital imports have substituted rather than supplemented domestic savings, although it is impossible to predict what would have happened if foreign assistance had not been available. In M. Haq's book [8] domestic savings are a residual derived by subtracting foreign aid from desired gross investment. Saving is also treated as a residual in the Third Plan. One can scarcely disagree with Power's statement, that 'it is fair to say that in Pakistan the mobilisation of domestic resources has never had first priority' [35, p. 418].

In the second half of the essay it is shown that the burden of foreign debt is rising rapidly and in view of the excessive optimism of the balance-of-payments projections of the Third Plan, the debt burden in 1969/70 is likely to be higher than is anticipated. The implication of the argument is that the social and economic system which has been created and sustained with the help of foreign assistance is not viable. Continued reliance on foreign loans and private foreign investment is quite likely to lead to a situation in which debt repayment obligations and repatriation of private capital persistently grow at a faster rate than exports. This means that a growing proportion of current earnings of foreign exchange will be required to service foreign capital. The squeeze on foreign exchange earnings can only be avoided if (i) export earnings and import substitution grow at a phenomenal rate, or (ii) the trend in foreign assistance is reversed in favour of more grants; or (iii) foreign debts are incurred to service past loans so that capital imports grow at an accelerating rate; or (iv) the foreign debt is repudiated and foreign firms are nationalised.

The panacea for all development problems in Pakistan has been 'more aid'.[1] Even such a sensitive analyst as John Power, who recognises that 'foreign aid can serve to forestall as well as encourage the social and institutional changes that are required', finally joins the chorus of domestic and foreign economists and insists that 'Pakistan must continue to rely heavily on external financing of its development effort' [36, pp. 193, 207].

An alternative strategy would place reliance on the mobilisation of domestic resources – both rural and urban – through such programmes as (i) the acquisition of large land holdings and their consequent control by the State; (ii) the consolidation of fragmented holdings and the formation of co-operatives; (iii) the full mobilisation of overt and seasonal unemployed labour on rural investment projects and low-cost housing – in an institutional environment in which those who contribute their effort receive the fruits thereof; (iv) the establishment and management of state industrial enterprises[2] operating under maximum efficiency and maximum investment principles; (v) the full use of the state's powers of taxation and control including an agricultural land tax; greater coverage, fewer exemptions and higher rates of personal income tax; higher corporation taxes; additional import controls; restrictions of the export bonus scheme and its substitution by direct controls on exports; and in some cases additional sales and other indirect taxes; (vi) a substantial increase of outlays on rural education.[3] Almost all of these measures would tend to increase both equity and domestic savings.

[1] Perhaps most extraordinary of all in Fei's 'demonstration' that— assuming high rates of population growth and everything else constant— Pakistan will experience 'sudden death' if she fails to acquire the minimum foreign aid [5, p. 56]. One would have thought that by now it was generally recognized that the whole process of development consists of turning constants into variables.

[2] This does not imply that existing private enterprises would necessarily be nationalized or even that certain sectors would be reserved for the state. It does imply, however, that P.I.D.C.-established enterprises would not be turned over to private interests.

[3] Half the Central Government's current 'expenditures are on defence. The Third Plan proposes to spend 127 per cent more on armaments than on education. Annual per capita expenditure on education will be less than 6 rupees and almost none of this will be spent in the countryside.

Foreign aid may not, in practice, be used to encourage reform, because the way in which resources are mobilised is not independent of the institutional organisation of society. Foreign assistance is largely a transaction between governments of wealthy societies (plus international agencies operating for them) and the government of an underdeveloped country. The latter, as with all governments, usually reflects the balance of power in the society and hence is likely to have an anti-reform, pro-*status quo* bias. Under these conditions aid may only strengthen the forces opposing change – regardless of whether the contributing countries want change or not. In its simplest form the argument is as follows: development requires economic reforms; economic reforms are impossible without institutional changes; foreign aid tends to strengthen institutions and thereby inhibit change; hence aid tends to retard development. If the hypothesis is correct the implication is that foreign assistance is most likely to be effective in fostering development only after (or during the period when) the necessary reforms have been (or are being) introduced, and not before.

REFERENCES

[1] Adil, A., 'Economic Development and an Egalitarian Society' – a paper read at the R.C.D. Colloquium on 'Common Problems of Economic Growth', Karachi, June 1965.

[2] Beringer, C. and Ahmad, I., *The Use of Agricultural Surplus Commodities for Economic Development in Pakistan* (Karachi: Pakistan Institute of Development Economics, Jan. 1964).

[3] Chowdhury, A. H. M. N., 'The Weight of Tax Revenue in the Pakistan Economy', *Pakistan Development Review*, III, 1, spring 1963, pp. 98–117.

[4] Falcon, W. and Gotsch, C., *Preliminary Comments on Private Investment in Agriculture* – memorandum (Karachi: Planning Commission, 22 Jan. 1965).

[5] Fei, J. C. H., *An Analysis of the Long-Run Prospects of Economic Development in Pakistan* (Karachi: Pakistan Institute of Development Economics, Apr. 1962.)

[6] Glassburner, Bruce, 'The Balance of Payments and External Resources in Pakistan's Third Five-Year Plan', *Pakistan Development Review*, v, 3, autumn 1965, pp. 496–524.

[7] Habibullah, M., *Pattern of Urban Savings; A Case Study of Dacca City* (Dacca: Dacca University, 1964).

[8] Haq, M., *The Strategy of Economic Planning* (Karachi: Oxford University Press, 1963).

[9] Hashmi, S. S., *Main Features of the Demographic Conditions in Pakistan* – mimeographed (Karachi: Central Statistical Office, 1963).

[10] Hussain, S. M., 'Export Potential of Fine Rice from Pakistan', *Pakistan Development Review*, iv, 4, winter 1964, pp. 665–706.

[11] Ibrahim, A. R., 'The Pains of Economic Development' – a paper read at the R.C.D. Colloquium on 'Common Problems of Economic Growth', Karachi, June 1965.

[12] Jafri, S. S., 'The Role of Private Foreign Investment' – a paper read at the R.C.D. Colloquium on 'Common Problems of Economic Growth', Karachi, June 1965.

[13] Khan, A. R., 'Import Substitution, Export Expansion and Consumption Liberalisation: A Preliminary Report', *Pakistan Development Review*, iii, 2, summer 1963, pp. 208–31.

[14] Krotki, K. J., 'Population Size, Growth and Age Distribution: Fourth Release from the 1961 Census of Pakistan', *Pakistan Development Review*, iii, 2, summer 1963, pp. 279–305.

[15] Lewis, S. R., 'Aspects of Fiscal Policy and Resource Mobilisation in Pakistan', *Pakistan Development Review*, iv, 2, summer 1964, pp. 261–83.

[16] Lewis, S. R. and Khan, M. I., 'Estimates of Noncorporate Private Saving in Pakistan: 1949–1962', *Pakistan Development Review*, iv, 1, spring 1964, pp. 1–50.

[17] Lewis, S. R. and Soligo, Ronald, 'Growth and Structural Change in Pakistan's Manufacturing Industry, 1957 to 1964', *Pakistan Development Review*, v, 1, spring 1965, pp. 94–139.

[18] Mohammad, G., 'Private Tubewell Development and Cropping Patterns in West Pakistan', *Pakistan Development Review*, v, 1, spring 1965, pp. 1–53.

[19] Mohammad, G., 'Some Physical and Economic Determinants of Cotton Production in West Pakistan', *Pakistan Development Review*, III, 4, winter 1963, pp. 491–526.

[20] Oshima, H. T., 'Share of Government in Gross National Product for Various Countries', *American Economic Review*, June 1957.

[21] Pakistan, Central Statistical Office, *Census of Manufacturing Industries, 1959–60* (Karachi: Central Statistical Office, 1962).

[22] Pakistan, Central Statistical Office, *Foreign Trade Statistics of Pakistan* (Karachi: Central Statistical Office, various issues).

[23] Pakistan, Central Statistical Office, *National Sample Survey (Third Round), 1961* (Karachi: Central Statistical Office, 1963).

[24] Pakistan, Central Statistical Office, *Statistical Bulletin* (Karachi: Central Statistical Office, various issues).

[25] Pakistan, Department of Marketing Intelligence and Agricultural Statistics, *Crop Statistics of Pakistan* – mimeographed (Karachi: Department of Marketing Intelligence and Agricultural Statistics, June 1964).

[26] Pakistan, National Income Commission, *Interim Report* (Karachi: Manager of Publications, Sep. 1964).

[27] Pakistan, *Pakistan Economic Survey, 1964–65* (Rawalpindi: Economic Advisor to the Government of Pakistan, May 1965).

[28] Pakistan, Planning Commission, *Growth Model for the Pakistan Economy* (Karachi: Planning Commission, Mar. 1965).

[29] Pakistan, Planning Commission, *The First Five-Year Plan (1955–60)*, vols 1 and 2 (Karachi: Manager of Publications, May 1956).

[30] Pakistan, Planning Commission, *The Second Five-Year Plan (1960–65)* (Karachi: Manager of Publications, June 1960).

[31] Pakistan, Planning Commission, *The Third Five-Year Plan (1965–70)* (Karachi: Manager of Publications, May 1965).

[32] Pakistan, *Preliminary Evaluation of Progress during the Second Five-Year Plan* (Karachi: Manager of Publications, March 1965).

[33] Pakistan, State Bank, *Liability on Foreign Loans and Credit*, Statement xxxii, Dec. 1963 (Karachi: State Bank).

[34] Pakistan, State Bank, *Pakistan's Balance of Payments* (Karachi: State Bank).

[35] Power, J. H., 'Development Strategy for Pakistan', *Pakistan Development Review*, iii, 3, autumn 1963, pp. 414–23.

[36] Power, J. H., 'Industrialisation in Pakistan: A Case of Frustrated Take-Off?', *Pakistan Development Review*, iii, 2, summer 1963, pp. 191–207.

[37] Shoaib, M., *1965–66 Budget Speech* (Rawalpindi: Government Press, 14 June 1965).

[38] Wilcox, C., 'Pakistan', in E. E. Hagen (ed.), *Planning Economic Development* (Homewood, Illinois: Richard D. Irwin, Inc., 1963).

[39] Zelnik, M. and Khan, M. R., 'An Estimate of the Birth Rate in East and West Pakistan', *Pakistan Development Review*, v, 1, spring 1965, pp. 64–93.

APPENDIX: TABLE APP. 1

REAL OUTPUT AND PER CAPITA INCOME 1949/50—1964/5

(1959/60 prices)

Year	G.N.P. at factor cost (1)	Agricultural output (2)	Total population (3)	Rural population (4)	G.N.P. per capita (5)	Rural income* per capita (6) col. (2) ÷ col. (4)
	(Rs. million)	(Rs. million)	(Rs. million)			(Rupees)
1949/50	24466	14668	79	71·0	311	207
1950/1	25078	14859·7	80·8	72·4	312	205
1951/2	25705	15052·9	82·7	73·8	313	204
1952/3	23648	15248·6	84·6	75·2	314	202
1953/4	27007	15446·8	86·5	76·6	315	202
1954/5	27908	15654	88	78·0	316	201
1955/6	28606	15857·5	90	79·7	316	199
1956/7	29321	16063·6	92·1	81·3	316	198
1957/8	30054	16272·4	94·2	83·0	317	195
1958/9	30805	16482·9	96·4	84·6	317	195
1959/60	31439	16753	99	86·3	318	194
1960/1	32946	17339·4	101·6	88·2	326	197
1961/2	34744	17946·3	104·2	90·1	334	199
1962/3	35929	18574·4	106·9	92·0	342	202
1963/4	38637	19224·5	109·7	94·0	351	205
1964/5	40525	19895	112	95·9	360	207

Sources: Col. (1): 1949/50–1959/60:[31]. Applying a 2·5 per cent growth rate to missing years. 1959/60–1964/5:[32].

Col. (2): [31]. Applying a 1·3 per cent annual increase up to 1959–60 and a 3·5 per cent increase thereafter.

Col. (3): [31]. Applying a 2·3 per cent rate of increase over first ten years and a 2·6 per cent rate from 1959/60.

Col. (4): [31]. For estimates at five-year intervals, interpolation in between.

Col. (5): [31]. Applying a 0·2 per cent rate over first ten years and a 2·5 per cent rate from 1959/60.

*Rural income per capita is understated to the extent that the output of cottage industries is excluded from our calculations. Unfortunately, virtually nothing is known about the size and rate of growth of small-scale manufacturing; so we have been forced to omit it entirely.

PART TWO

Stagnation and Growth in Agriculture

Stagnation and Growth in Agriculture

Commentary

BETWEEN 1947 and 1959 the rate of growth of agricultural production in both wings of Pakistan was substantially less than the rate of demographic increase. Indeed, in the first dozen years after independence agriculture was stagnant. What little growth was achieved – approximately 1·1 per cent per annum – was due to an increase in the area under cultivation rather than to a rise in yields associated with improvements in techniques. In the Second Plan period, however, agricultural growth accelerated sharply, and this acceleration continued during the Third Plan.

According to official sources the annual rate of growth of agriculture was 1·4 per cent in the First Plan, 3·4 per cent in the Second and 4·5 per cent in the Third.[1] The acceleration that occurred in the first half of the 1960s was reported to have been spread equally between the two wings. Falcon and Gotsch, two agricultural experts working at the time with the Harvard Development Advisory Service, claim that '... the rural sector in the East as well as the West grew remarkably during the Second Plan.[2]

No one denies that the agricultural sector of West Pakistan did become transformed in the early 1960s, as a result of investment in tubewells by the larger farmers, improved irrigation, greater use of fertilizers and other changes in cultivating

---

[1] Government of Pakistan, Ministry of Finance, *Pakistan Economic Survey—* 1969–1970, p. 2.

[2] W. P. Falcon and C. H. Gotsch. 'Lessons in Agricultural Development—Pakistan', in G. F. Papanek, ed., *Development Policy: Theory and Practice*, Harvard University Press, 1968, p. 288.

practices. Scepticism was expressed about the reported performance in East Pakistan, however. Griffin wrote as follows: 'Jute and rice are grown in East Pakistan; jute output declined; rice output increased enormously. Yet we know that neither the area cultivated nor the use of unconventional inputs rose very much, so – at least on the surface – it is very difficult to explain the reported increase in rice yields'.[1]

Falcon and Gotsch did not share this scepticism. They fitted a trend line to six observations and concluded that in East Pakistan total agricultural output was growing at 3 per cent a year and rice production was increasing 3·4 per cent a year, nearly two-thirds of which was due to a rise in yields. Referring to Griffin they said, 'It has sometimes been implied, usually without supporting evidence, that the reported growth in East Pakistan rice production during recent years represents nothing more than statistical manipulation'.[2] 'This measured growth [of 3·4 per cent a year in rice production] was a definite reality, not a mere statistical manipulation'.[3] Moreover, this spectacular success is attributed to 'a number of bold government policy actions in agriculture'.[4]

Unfortunately for our two Harvard advisers, their trend equation measured the effects not of bold government policies but of the weather.[5] Two swallows may not make a spring, but Falcon and Gotsch leaped to the conclusion that six observations in a region notable for its volatile agriculture make a trend! Their trend-estimating technique is a good example of statistical manipulation and special pleading by interested parties.

A more detached view is taken by Swadesh Bose in Chapter 2. Examining the period 1960/1 to 1967/8 he shows that the trend rate of increase of rice production in East Pakistan was only 1·7 per cent a year, i.e. exactly half that claimed by Falcon and Gotsch and substantially less than the rate of increase of population, which may be nearly 3 per cent per

[1] See Chapter 1 above.
[2] Op. cit., p. 298.
[3] Op. cit., p. 299.
[4] Op. cit., p. 300.
[5] This has since been admitted by Falcon and Gotsch in private correspondence.

annum now in the East wing. Bose estimates that total agricultural production in East Pakistan is growing about 2·1 per cent a year.

In West Pakistan, in contrast, agricultural output is growing 4·6 per cent a year, and major crops are increasing even faster, viz. 5·5 per cent per annum. It is here that a 'green revolution' has occurred. The revolution, particularly in its early stages, was a revolution in water and fertilisation. It was not until quite recently that the much heralded new plant varieties became important. In fact, at the moment only the new wheat variety, Mexi-Pak, is widely used, although the improved I.R.R.I. rice seeds are spreading rapidly.

The latest development in West Pakistan's agriculture is the rapid introduction of tractors on the large farms. In 1967 there were 17,000 wheel-type agricultural tractors in use, about 15,000 of which were privately owned. The number of tractors has been rising by over 10 per cent a year. Unlike the other elements in the 'green revolution', tractor mechanisation is a substitute for, rather than a complement to, labour and it is being used by the large farmers to reduce their labour force. (According to Bose, the average size of farm on which tractors are used is 267 acres.[1]).

It is a matter of current dispute whether tractor mechanisation should be encouraged. There certainly is not any doubt that it is being encouraged. At one stage the cost per tractor horsepower was lower in Pakistan than in the United States![2] At present, farmers can obtain imported tractors at the low official exchange rate plus 25 per cent in additional taxes; this purchase can be financed with inexpensive credit, viz. 7 per cent interest, repayable over a long period.

The advocates of tractors claim they are essential for the modernisation of West Pakistan's agriculture. Moreover, they solve the problem of labour and bullock shortages which occur

[1] S. R. Bose, 'The Green Revolution, and Agricultural Employment Under Conditions of Rapid Population Growth: The Pakistan Problem', paper presented to the Near East/South Asian Employment Conference in Katmandu, 6–9 July 1970, p. 16.

[2] S. R. Bose and F. H. Clark II, 'Some Basic Considerations on Agricultural Mechanization in West Pakistan', *Pakistan Development Review*, autumn 1969, p. 284n.

at the peak season when wheat harvesting, threshing and land preparations for the next crop must all be done at the same time. On the other hand, the critics point out that tractors are profitable to private farmers only because the exchange rate is overvalued and capital is underpriced. A social benefit-cost calculation would indicate that tractor mechanisation is a poor use of scarce resources.[1] As regards shortages during the peak season, they can be overcome by mechanising threshing and thereby releasing men and bullocks for land preparation.

Hiromitsu Kaneda, in Chapter 3, places the discussion of mechanisation in the broad context of an agricultural development strategy for West Pakistan. Both logic and the historical experience of Japan and the United States can be used to argue that tractor mechanisation is premature. West Pakistan suffers from a shortage of good land and water, not labour. The objective of policy, therefore, should be to increase yields, not output per worker. Yet 'there is no evidence that tractor-mechanisation *per se* will increase yields; output per worker will rise only by causing unemployment'. Thus there is a danger that West Pakistan's agriculture, which made undoubted progress in the 1960s, will take a wrong turn in the 1970s.

If present policies continue of subsidising fertilisers and tractors and maintaining a high support price for wheat, it is possible that eventually the increase in supply of foodgrains in West Pakistan will outstrip the demand. At current prices Pakistan cannot export wheat, and given the unequal distribution of income and lack of purchasing power of the poor, the need for food cannot be translated into a demand for food. In these conditions, the 'green revolution' is likely to lead not only to unemployment (as a consequence of mechanisation), but also to increased inequality in the distribution of land (as large farmers increase their holdings in order to spread the fixed costs of machinery) and impoverishment of smallholders (when the price of wheat inevitably falls). Thus unless policies change very quickly, the 'green revolution' may well become yet another example of growth and inequality in Pakistan.

[1] S. R. Bose and E. H. Clark II, 'Some Basic Considerations on Agricultural Mechanization in West Pakistan', *Pakistan Development Review*, autumn 1969, p. 284n.

2 East-West Contrast in Pakistan's Agricultural Development

SWADESH R. BOSE*

INTRODUCTION

MANY of the recent writings on economic development emphasise the key role that agriculture must play in the development process. Yet success stories of development are few, and the agricultural bottleneck remains a difficult problem in most of the underdeveloped countries and areas with traditional peasant agriculture. Pakistan's earlier agricultural stagnation and recent growth presents both a comparison and contrast with the situation in many other countries.

Agriculture in Pakistan in the twelve or so years after independence was virtually stagnant. Only since the beginning of the 1960s did production increases in agriculture outstrip population growth. The annual compound rate of growth rose from 1·2 per cent in the earlier period to 3·2 per cent in the 1960s. Agricultural exports increased rapidly and rural private investment accelerated. An understanding of the causes of this recent growth is clearly important for Pakistan's future development and may also provide lessons for other countries and areas in South Asia.

The stagnation of agriculture in the 1950s was common to both East and West Pakistan. The recent progress has, however, been largely confined to West Pakistan which with the 1968 wheat harvest appears to have made a remarkable breakthrough in agriculture. The picture in East Pakistan is much less encouraging and may be interpreted as still largely one of stagnation, although some observers have expressed contrary

* An earlier version of this paper was presented to the International Economic Association Conference on Economic Development in South Asia (Kandy, Ceylon, 1–12 June 1969).

views and some others have suggested that it also is at the
threshold of an agricultural revolution.

On the basis of the experience during the Second Plan
Period (1959/60–1964/5), several studies [Falcon and Gotsch
1966; Papanek 1967] concluded that agricultural growth out-
stripped population growth in both provinces although the
performance was relatively better in West Pakistan. The conclusion about West Pakistan is strengthened, but that about
East Pakistan is undermined, if the same statistical series as
used by these earlier studies are extended to 1967/8 and the
base year changed from 1959/60 to 1960/1. It is then found
that in West Pakistan during the 1960s value added in agriculture and in major crops grew at 4·6 per cent and 5·5 per
cent per annum respectively, while the corresponding growth
rates in East Pakistan were 2·1 per cent and 2·2 per cent[1]
(Table 2.1).

TABLE 2.1

RECENT AGRICULTURAL GROWTH IN PAKISTAN
1960/1 TO 1967/8

Value added (in 1959/60 prices)	West Pakistan	East Pakistan	All Pakistan
		(per cent per annum)	
Total agriculture	4·6	2·1	3·2
Major crops	5·5	2·2	not estimated
Output			
Rice	5·3	1·7	,,
Jute	—	2·6	,,
Wheat	4·5		,,
Cotton	6·8		

* Based on least square estimate of b in the equation: $\log Y = a + b$ time.

Source: Value added from Government of Pakistan, C.S.O., and Government of East Pakistan, *Economic Survey of East Pakistan* 1967/8. Output from
Pakistan Statistical Year Book 1967 and *Pakistan Economic Survey 1967/68.*

Because of weather-induced variations in production, particularly in East Pakistan, estimates of growth based on short

[1] Using the same method the corresponding growth rates during 1959/60
to 1964/5 were estimated at 3·8 per cent and 4·9 per cent for West Pakistan
and 3·0 per cent and 3·2 per cent for East Pakistan [Falcon and Gotsch
1966].

periods can hardly be made with assurance. But it is fairly certain that the relative performances of agriculture was much poorer in East Pakistan. Given the population growth rate of approximately 3 per cent in the region, a 2 per cent agricultural growth rate can hardly be considered as indicative of a radical change from the earlier state of stagnation. Output of rice – which constitutes about 70 per cent of total crop production in East Pakistan – increased at an even lower rate of 1·7 per cent per year, and the target of self-sufficiency in foodgrains by 1969–70 cannot be fulfilled. Thus, the optimism about agricultural growth in East Pakistan expressed by some analysts appears to be largely unfounded.

In West Pakistan production of the major crops which account for about two-thirds of total agricultural production showed consistent increases during the 1960s except in 1965/6 and 1966/7, the former being a year of severe drought. In 1967/8 there was a big leap in wheat and rice production, which exceeded any previous year's output. Still larger crops are expected this year and the prospects of a food deficit region becoming self-sufficient in foodgrains by 1969/70 are very bright.

It is, therefore, important for future development policy to investigate why the success story of West Pakistan has not been repeated in East Pakistan, and how far it is due to differences in natural, environmental factors or to the limitations of institutions and policies. This paper is a preliminary analysis of the major causes of the contrast in recent agricultural growth in East and West Pakistan. An attempt is made to indicate the implications of the recent experience for the country's prospective development.

MAJOR FACTORS EXPLAINING EAST-WEST DISPARITY IN AGRICULTURAL GROWTH

The monsoon rice-jute agriculture of riverine East Pakistan is basically different from the irrigated wheat-cotton-rice agriculture of West Pakistan, particularly in regard to water availability. However, an explanation of the sharp contrast in recent development may be sought in the relative achievement of increased use of improved inputs and techniques suited to different natural conditions, the relative efficacy of public investment and policies and the response of farmers to opportunities for innovation in the two provinces.

The physical requirements for agricultural development may generally be considered to be improved farming techniques with proper and adequate use of such inputs as water, fertilizers, pesticides, improved seeds, and proper facilities for storage, transportation and marketing. The adoption of these innovations in techniques and input-use by large numbers of farmers depends on their knowledge, willingness and ability to do so. Therefore, in addition to effective public investment for development of rural infrastructure – roads, large-scale irrigation, etc. – which is beyond the technical and financial capacities of individual farmers, there is a need for proper institutions and agricultural policies to encourage farmers to adopt innovations.

Extension services may disseminate knowledge of improved techniques to farmers to make them aware of the opportunities open to them. It is reasonable to assume that farmers' behaviour is economically rational and that their willingness to innovate and invest depends on expected rewards. Adequate marketing facilities, reasonably attractive and stable agricultural prices and a land tenure system which allows farmers to retain the larger part of any additional output are necessary for making such rewards attractive. Availability of inputs and credit is also essential to ensure that adoption of new techniques by willing farmers is not frustrated through lack of inputs and finance. These elements constitute an integrated programme for agricultural development.

The recent agricultural breakthrough in West Pakistan appears to be largely explained by considerable progress in fulfilling these conditions. A number of observable changes in the use of inputs necessarily associated with improvements in farming techniques took place in West Pakistan during the 1960s. Field availability of irrigation water increased, use of fertilisers and improved seeds expanded, and plant protection covered larger areas. While it is very difficult, if not impossible, to measure precisely the individual importance of these various factors, there can be little doubt that the combination of water, fertiliser and improved seeds largely account for the recent remarkable growth. In this regard government measures, especially incentive policies and extension services, appear to have played a very important role in the adoption of these innovations by farmers – mostly large farmers.

The situation in the case of East Pakistan agriculture is radically different. There the increase in rice output has been associated with an increase in *Aus* and *Boro* rice acreage, and some increase in yield of *Aman* and *Boro* rice. The acreage expansion has partly been due to increased winter irrigation and coastal embankments and partly due to cultivation of some marginal land as a result of heavy population pressure. The small yield increases are difficult to explain, and may be considered the combined effects of fertilisers, pesticides, improved seeds and increased use of labour. But the progress in irrigation, fertiliser use, plant protection and use of improved seeds has been poor. Farmers' response to the use of improved inputs and techniques has not been encouraging. As we shall see, inadequate government measures bear some responsibility for the failure of farmers to innovate.

WATER RESOURCES DEVELOPMENT AND USE

(i) *West Pakistan*
Water is and will continue to remain a very important constraint on agricultural production in arid West Pakistan. Measures which raise the productivity of water in agriculture and increase the supply of water are, therefore, of great importance. Most of the province receives inadequate rainfall to sustain crops. About 80 per cent of agricultural production of West Pakistan comes from the Indus Basin where agriculture depends on the world's largest irrigation canal system, which was established long before independence. The rest of the region's output is produced by rain-fed agriculture, mainly in the north. Because of an inadequate supply of water less than half of the cultivable area (27 out of 73 million acres) in the Indus Basin is now being cropped. The cropping intensity is about 100 per cent on average.

Practically throughout the basin the canal system has been designed for much lower cropping intensity than the land is capable of supporting. Crop production has almost everywhere expanded to the limits of the canal irrigation system except in newly developing command areas served by Taunsa, Guddu and Ghulam Mohammad Barrages. Over the vast areas of the older parts of the system the area cropped has gone beyond the proper limit of the water supply [I.B.R.D. vol. 5, 1966]. The main constraints of the present system are that the amount of water available to the cultivators is too variable and inadequate to sustain optimum crop production. Moreover, problems of waterlogging and salinity have been caused by a long period of seepage of water into the ground from the canals and the thin spreading of water on land with poor drainage. Therefore the key problems of water use in West Pakistan are storage, ground water irrigation, and treatment of waterlogging and salinity.

The Indus Basin 'replacement' projects, parts of which have just been completed, e.g. Mangla Dam and reservoir, will increase storage and augment water supplies of the canal system. However, it has not yet affected the field availability of water. Salinity Control and Reclamation Projects (SCARP) have already made some progress. More importantly, in many parts of the canal system a rapid advance is being made towards the exploitation of the vast ground water acquifer underlying the plains, and this is of great value for crop production and can also reduce the hazards of waterlogging and salinity.

Even a decade ago individual farmers could not do much to supplement the wager supplies from the public canal system. The traditional Persian wheels well known to the farmers were not good enough for large-scale irrigation. Surface water supply from the canal system also did not increase appreciably in the first decade after independence. The installation of tubewells by farmers to supplement the water supply from the canals is a very important development of the 1960s. From a very modest beginning in the 1950s the number of tubewells installed has accelerated to over 6000 per year [Ghulam Mohammad 1965]. By 1965 there were over 31,000 tubewells and at present there are estimated to be over 60,000.

This development has increased considerably the field availability of irrigation water. In 1960 the whole of Indus Basin received 59 million acre-feet of irrigation water from all sources [WAPDA 1964]. Out of this, 55 million acre-feet were from canals, 0·3 from private tubewells, 2 from public tubewells and about 1·7 from Persian wheels. In 1965 the total field availability increased to about 68 million acre-feet, of which 58 came from canals, 5·3 from private tubewells, 2·7 from public tubewells and 1·7 from Persian wheels [I.B.R.D., Vol. 5, Page 15]. Thus in the first half of the decade private tubewells contributed 5 out of 9 million acre-feet of additional irrigation water. Since 1965 the availability of irrigation water from sources other than private tubewells has not increased much while private tubewells have nearly doubled their capacity, thus enlarging further their contribution to increased water supply.

Since irrigation water is a key input with a high marginal productivity, especially in certain critical periods, the great surge in tubewells is an important contributing factor to recent agricultural growth in West Pakistan.

Several factors may explain the rapid increase of tubewells in the 1960s. The rather simple technology of tubewell installation and operation began to be disseminated to farmers and small business firms in the 1950s through a government programme of sinking a small number of mechanical tubewells for private farmers [Ghulam Mohammad 1965]. Later the public tubewell programme of WAPDA (Water and Power Development Authority) also spread this knowledge. Moreover, installation and operating costs of tubewells declined in the 1960s. This was partly due to a gradual improvement in efficiency of the Department of Agriculture and of private firms in installing wells. More importantly, there was a increased availability of materials for tubewells at lower prices as a result of import liberalisation. This was underwritten by liberal foreign aid, particularly large imports of steel through commodity aid. Foreign aid appears to have played a crucial role.

As electric power was made available by government to increasingly numerous rural areas, costs of tubewells were substantially reduced. Investment as well as operating costs of electric tubewells are much lower to farmers [Ghulam Mohammad 1965 and I.B.R.D. vol. 5] because of the substantial subsidy on electricity given to agricultural consumers [G.W.P. 1967].

Demonstrated profitability was a major factor in the rapid development of tubewells. The support price of agricultural products raised and stabilised the expected value of any increased crop production. The financial return-cost estimates [Ghulam Mohammad 1965; Tipton and Kalmback, WAPDA, 1965 and others] show that tubewells are a highly profitable investment. The initial investment cost of the typical tubewell of one cusec in delivery is between Rs. 6000 and Rs. 9000, and the investment payout period is less than two years.

While the earlier surveys [Ghulam Mohammad 1965] found that tubewells were being installed mostly by large farmers having 25 or more acres, a more recent survey [Clark and Gaffar 1968] has established that a considerable proportion of tubewells are being installed by smaller farmers, sometimes in partnership. The finance for investment is being obtained partly through institutional and other borrowing but more importantly from own savings out of current income. This suggests that knowledge of income-augmenting opportunities, through increased investment may increase farmers' willingness to save in spite of rather low incomes.

Tubewell farmers increased cropping intensity, used more fertilisers, changed cropping pattern in favour of higher value crops and increasingly adopted other practices to raise yields [Ghulam Mohammad 1965].

(ii) *East Pakistan*

In East Pakistan most of the agricultural land is submerged under water by flooding and monsoon rainfall in the summer, while there is hardly any traditional system of irrigation in the dry winter. In some years excessive flooding results from inadequate drainage or severe overflows from rivers. Effective use of water in East Pakistan, therefore, involves flood control and drainage in the summer and irrigation in the winter.

The possibility of cropped acreage expansion through winter irrigation should be viewed in the proper perspective. Land use is already very tight. The extensive margin has virtually been reached. The cropping intensity is also among the highest in the world. According to a recent estimate (by East Pakistan Directorate of Agriculture, 1962–3), of the net cultivable area of 21·5 million acres about 16·6 million and 15·1 million are under crops during *aman* season (roughly August to December) and *aus* season (April to July) respectively, and 5·1 million acres are under crops during *boro/rabi* season (roughly December to March). A considerable part of the cultivable area not cropped during *aus* and *aman* seasons is either too flooded during monsoon or has inadequate surface water. Moreover, until the adoption of sophisticated fertilisation practices, some land should be kept fallow for parts of the year [Hendry and Hpu 1964]. Thus, except during *boro/rabi* season there is not much scope for increasing acreage under crops.

Even to make an addition of 20–25 per cent (about 8–10 million cropped acres, mainly in the dry season) to the total cropped acreage and thus to raise overall cropping intensity to over 200 per cent does not appear to be easy. In many areas, supplementary surface water for winter irrigation may not be available. In such areas, which are mainly monocultural, increases in cropping intensity is dependent largely on ground-water development through deep tubewells and, in some cases, also on intensive use of fertilisers because of poor soil [Rashid 1964]. However, no serious efforts have yet been made to increase the knowledge of East Pakistan's hydrology. Little is known about the acquifer potential and the extent of recharge.

Notwithstanding the possibilities of such irrigation, the extremely tight land use seems to imply that planning for agricultural development has to rely more on increased yields per season than on further increasing cropping intensity. Irrigation may, however, not only raise cropping intensity but also, as West Pakistan experience shows, promote rapid intro-duction of yield-raising inputs and farming practices.

At present two broad types of irrigation and water control measures are being tried: (1) flood irrigation, small-scale flood protection, tubewell irrigation, coastal embankments and drainage by WAPDA (Water and Power Development Authority) and (2) low-lift pump irrigation by A.D.C. (Agri-cultural Development Corporation).

Dry season irrigation through low-lift pumps depends on the availability of surface water (of rivers) within a distance of one mile at most. Such area is about 4·5 million acres of which 2 million acres are already getting water through seepage or otherwise. Pumping out large quantities of water from the rivers increases the danger of saline water penetration from the sea. It has been estimated by experts that within the safety limit only about 1·3 million acres can be irrigated by pumps

[Professor Thijsse, 'Preliminary Comments on Hydrology of East Pakistan', quoted in Hendry and Hpu 1964]. As against this potential the number of pumps has increased from 1367 in 1960–1 to about 6600 in 1967–8 and the corresponding irrigated area increased from 32 thousand acres to 400 thousand acres. In addition, the area irrigated by WAPDA surface water and tubewell projects has reached 172 thousand acres in 1967–8 out of a total command area of these projects of 322 thousand acres [G.E.P. 1968]. By 1969/70 it is planned to increase the area irrigated by pumps to over 1 million acres and that by other means to about 0·7–0·9 million acres. The low-lift pumps which are concentrated in the central regions and are seasonally operated are expected to increase the *boro* rice acreage, and WAPDA irrigation may result in one extra crop – *aus* followed by transplanted *aman* and some increased quantities of *rabi* crops.

Not only has the expansion of irrigation facilities been small, the programme also has failed to generate a response from farmers. Most pumps are now owned and operated by the A.D.C., which hires them out to farmers at rates involving 50 per cent subsidy. In the case of tubewells installed by WAPDA, and on a pilot basis through an expansion of the Comilla approach,[1] it has been reported that farmers are not eager to obtain irrigation water although a nominal price much lower than the cost is charged for water.[2] This is in sharp contrast to the great demand for irrigation water and the surge in tubewell installations by farmers in West Pakistan.

It seems that the prospects of tubewell and low-lift pump programmes depend on the quality and size of the extension service for educating farmers in proper ways of using irrigation water and thus generating the demand for pumps or wells, and the ability of government (or other) agencies to install and maintain them in increasing numbers. Availability of requisite finance is essential if farmers are to own and operate them in

[1] This name is given to the rural development programme conducted on an experimental basis by Pakistan Academy for Rural Development, Comilla.

[2] Certain tubewells also are reported to have become dry due to inadequate recharge. This underlines the point that there is no substitute for proper technical studies to acquire hydrological knowledge.

large numbers. Moreover, farmers cannot be expected to make an investment unless it is highly rewarding. Therefore, the demonstration of profitability of irrigation and spread of knowledge of necessary farming methods and cropping pattern on irrigated land are also essential for generating adequate response from farmers.

Another major factor hindering progress is the much greater poverty of most farmers in East Pakistan. Private tubewell development in West Pakistan was pioneered by large farmers having 25 acres and above, who constitute 8 per cent of total number of farmers and operate 42 per cent of total farm area (Table 2.2). The participation of medium and small farmers

TABLE 2.2

SIZE DISTRIBUTIONS OF FARMS IN EAST AND WEST PAKISTAN

Size of farms (acres)	East		West	
	Per cent of farms	Per cent of farm area	Per cent of farms	Per cent of farm area
Less than 5	78	43	49	10
5 to under 12·5	19	38	28	22
12·5 to under 25	2·5	14	15	26
25 and above	0·5*	5	8	42
Average farm size (acres)	3·5		10·1	

* Approximately.

Source: Adapted from *Pakistan Census of Agriculture*, 1960.

in this development came later. In East Pakistan only 3 per cent of farms are of 12·5 acres and above and cover 19 per cent of farm area; farms of 25 acres and above are less than 1 per cent of the total and cover about 5 per cent of total farm area. Although the average gross production value per acre in East Pakistan is considerably higher than that in West Pakistan, the differences in size distribution of farms indicate that the number of well-to-do farmers who may have the means to make a sizeable investment on their own is very small. This underlines the much greater need for credit in East Pakistan not only for water development but for purchase of other inputs as well.

The share-cropping system under which a considerable proportion of land is cultivated in East Pakistan may be another hindrance. The largely absentee owners of share-cropped land do not make investments for irrigation or drainage, and take no interest in improving farming practices. The share croppers usually retain half of the produce, bear all costs of production but have no right of occupancy to the land. Even if they have the means they can hardly be expected to make investments for irrigation or any land improvement. The use of improved current inputs by share-croppers also may not be very attractive unless the financial return over cost of such inputs is very high.

Tenants' rights to land are no greater in West Pakistan. Share-cropping also exists, and the (*hari*) tenants of Sind area operate under greater difficulties. But particularly in the Punjab area, where the surge in tubewell development occurred, owner-cultivation is more important; and even for tenanted and share-cropped land the owners have shown genuine interest in agricultural development and made investment in agriculture to increase their income.

FERTILIZER USE

(i) *West Pakistan*
The use of fertilisers in West Pakistan steadily increased during the 1960s except in 1965/6 when there was a fall from the previous year's level due to import reduction following the 1965 war. Its use increased from 31,000 nutrient tons in 1960/1 to 116,000 in 1966/7, and to 193,000 in 1967/8 (Table 2.3). Although the rate of increase is impressive, the quantity used is still rather small. The limiting factor is the availability of fertilisers. There is a widespread black market in fertilisers, which are sold to farmers at prices involving a 35 per cent subsidy.

Recently fertiliser distribution facilities have expanded as a result of adding private trade channels to the network of government agencies. However, the supply limitation remains the bottleneck; demand continues to increase, partly because larger doses can be applied profitably by farmers as more water and improved seeds become available.

Fertiliser response factors (tons of output per ton of nutrient)

TABLE 2.3

FERTILIZER DISTRIBUTION IN PAKISTAN IN
RECENT YEARS

Year	Quantity (in thousand nutrient tons)	
	West	East
1960/1	31	24
1964/5	87	45
1965/6	71	54
1966/7	116	77
1967/8	193	115

Sources: East Pakistan A.D.C.; West Pakistan A.D.C.; *Economic Survey of East Pakistan 1967/68.*

have been found to be high on farm trials. In the early 1960s it was estimated to be 4 for cotton, 8 for rice, 9 for wheat and 6 for oilseeds [Falcon and Gotsch 1966, based on Wahab 1965]. With the introduction of improved seed varieties the response factor has further increased e.g. to about 16 for Mexican wheat. Clearly, therefore, fertiliser use has contributed to recent growth and is a very important factor for further increases in crop yields and output.

(ii) *East Pakistan*
In East Pakistan the use of this key input increased from 24,000 nutrient tons in 1960/1 to an estimated 115,000 tons in 1967–8 (Table 2.3). This means that the average dose of fertilisers per cropped acre is still less than 6 lbs compared with over 10 lbs in West Pakistan.

There has been in the past an over-emphasis on making farmers use nitrogen in the form of urea. Exclusive use of nitrogen can eventually lead to reduction in yield, and urea if applied in improper doses and at wrong times can burn the crop. These evil effects actually took place in East Pakistan and led the farmers to resist fertilisers. Since 1963/4 efforts have been made to promote the sale of phosphates to offset these effects [Hendry and Hpu 1964].

Another problem has been that those farmers who used fertiliser applied only a small quantity per acre – on average 22 lbs per acre (mostly urea), i.e. roughly one tenth of the recommended dosage [Rahim 1963]. Such low levels of fertiliser use do not raise yields significantly and therefore farmers do not feel encouraged to repeat the experiment.

Although the demand for fertilisers has not yet reached a high level, in spite of a 50 per cent subsidy, it has been found that considerable potential demand is frustrated because of inadequate stocks and a poor distribution network which has not been capable of supplying fertilisers in the right areas and at the peak demand season (August to October) [Mears and Hpu 1964].

It is reasonable to maintain that a satisfactory increase in fertiliser use by farmers in traditional agriculture can hardly be expected without the fulfilment of certain necessary conditions.

By and large, farmers in East Pakistan have not been exposed to fertiliser use. Their primary concern before accepting fertilisers will be to weigh the potential gains from their use in present conditions against the additional risks that they have to bear. The most important additional risk is that in case of a crop failure he will lose the capital (own or borrowed) invested in fertiliser. Obviously this risk is greater the higher the probability of a crop failure. The probability of a crop failure is greater on monsoon land which is rain-fed and subject to occasional excessive flooding, as in East Pakistan, than on land reliably irrigated, such as tubewell farms in the Indus Basin. Hence, in this respect the farmers in the Indus Basin may be more easily persuaded to use fertilisers than those in East Pakistan. Hence the need for eliminating or reducing the probability of crop failure due to excessive flooding, to which we shall return later.

Knowledge about how much extra effort is needed to obtain and apply fertilisers, and what changes in cultivation practices are required to realise the full benefits of fertilisation is also important to the farmers. This underlines the need for easy availability of fertilisers at the right time and in the right composition, and the dissemination of knowledge to the farmers about the best fertilisation rates and practices.

Thirdly, for adopting new innovations the farmers have to be assured of a reasonably predicatable financial return-cost ratio not unduly affected by price fluctuations. This underlines the importance of stabilisation and support of output prices.

Finally, when all but a few very large farmers are too poor to finance the purchase of needed inputs in any given year for even a very high expected return next year the need for making credit available assumes great importance.

The relatively less satisfactory progress in fertiliser use in East Pakistan may largely be explained by poor extension work, inadequate credit, inadequate winter irrigation, and failure to reduce risks of crop failure. Institutional credit facilities provided only a small part of the limited credit which was available to finance desired investment and current inputs [Khan 1963]. The number and quality of personnel in the extension service in East Pakistan definitely compares very unfavourably with that in West Pakistan. In East Pakistan the basic extension workers (Union Agricultural Assistants) are small in number, inadequately trained in improved agricultural practices, and poorly paid and motivated [Hendry and Hpu 1964; Mears and Hpu 1964]. These workers and Thana Agricultural Officers are often transferred from one location to another in less than six months [Ferguson 1963]. Such frequent shifting of professional personnel hampers sustained efforts necessary for rural development.

IMPROVED SEEDS AND PLANT PROTECTION

(i) *West Pakistan*

The use of improved seeds is potentially another important means to raise crop yields, as has been shown by the yields of Mexican wheat and I.R.R.I. rice varieties in West Pakistan.

The role of improved seed varieties was probably marginal in the first half of this decade. The quantity of improved seeds distributed in West Pakistan in this period was small, being only 31,000 tons in 1964/5 for all major crops (Table 2.4). For many crops the base stock of improved seeds was small or nil, government efforts for multiplication and distribution of good seeds were inadequate. In this period farmer to farmer transfer of good local varieties of seeds was more important than the government's seed distribution programme.

In the second half of this decade, with the introduction of imported seed varieties, particularly of wheat and rice, the role of seeds has become very important. The planned distribution of improved seeds of major crops for 1967/8 was 128,000 tons, including 40,000 tons of Mexican wheat seed and about 2000 tons of I.R.R.I. (International Rice Research Institute) rice. The area under Mexican wheat increased from 0·25 million acres in 1966/7 to 2 million acres in 1967/8. The yield of Mexican wheat is over 25 maunds per acre, or double the yield of local varieties. Thus, improved seeds may have accounted for nearly 1 million tons of the total wheat production of 1967/8.

TABLE 2.4

DISTRIBUTION OF IMPROVED SEEDS OF MAJOR CROPS

Year	East Pakistan	West Pakistan
	(000 tons)	
1961/2	3	—
1964/5	9	31
1965/6	8	56
1966/7	6	38
1967/8[a]	12[b]	128[c]

[a] Planned.
[b] including 2 of IRRI rice.
[c] including 40 of Mexican wheat.

Sources: *Mid Plan Review of Third Five-Year Plan 1965–70*, and *Economic Survey of East Pakistan 1967/68*.

Through local multiplication of imported seeds and larger imports the acreage under these higher yielding varieties is expanding rapidly. This season (1968/9) about 4 million acres are under Mexican wheat. In 1969/70 it is expected to cover 7 million acres, or over 55 per cent of wheat acreage. I.R.R.I. rice acreage, although relatively small, is increasing rapidly, and West Pakistan is proving to be one of the best areas in the world for rice cultivation.

Plant protection is another important means of increasing yields. In the opinion of agricultural experts, it raises the yields of various crops by 10 to 20 per cent. The extent of cropped acreage covered by plant protection measures increased in West Pakistan in the 1960s. In 1964/5 about 5·5 million cropped acres, or about one sixth of the total were covered by these measures.

(ii) *East Pakistan*

In East Pakistan no major improvements have been made in local seed varieties nor has any appreciable progress been made in the use of imported ones. Only the use of some relatively improved local varieties has increased (Table 2.4). Even such local varieties have considerable potential. As one author notes about the two most important rice crops [Rashid 1964]: '. . . the improved *aus* and shail transplanted *aman* varieties yield 20 per cent more than the majority of local varieties'. But such improved local varieties have not yet spread widely enough to make an impact on total crop production.

The use of imported I.R.R.I. paddy seed varieties is still largely at the experimental stage; one variety (I.R.R.I.-8) was tested and found to produce high yields under controlled irrigation with adequate application of fertilisers and pesticides. Small quantities of this seed distributed to farmers for *boro* and early *aus* cultivation in selected irrigated areas in 1967/8 did not in many cases produce satisfactory results owing to inadequate fertiliser use, crop disease and, in some cases, destruction of early plantings by cold weather. Such selected irrigated areas being actually and potentially small in East Pakistan, it is very urgent to evolve new paddy varieties to suit the different local conditions in the more important *aus* and *aman* seasons. Development of such seeds from I.R.R.I. varieties or through domestic research will help to remove a major obstacle in the way of rapid increases in rice production.

As regards raising yields through plant protection, East Pakistan has made little progress; only about 2·4 million cropped acres were covered by plant protection in 1964/5. East Pakistan's climate is highly favourable for rapid growth of crop insects and diseases. Even under normal conditions of incidence of crop pests there is a loss of 10–50 per cent of crop output [G.E.P. 1968]. The losses are much greater in years of serious outbreaks. High-yielding seed varieties, especially I.R.R.I., are generally much more susceptible to insects and pests. In order to exploit the potentialities of improved seeds, much greater progress in plant protection than has been achieved in recent years is needed.

NCENTIVE POLICIES AND FARMERS' RESPONSE

Identification of the major physical factors largely responsible for recent production increases in agriculture is useful for assessing the key physical requirements for future development. The improved physical inputs have, however, to be used by many farmers before the output increases can be realised. Therefore, an understanding of why farmers in West Pakistan quickly adopted the innovations and farmers in East Pakistan failed to respond satisfactorily is important for future agricultural policies in Pakistan, and is likely to be instructive for other countries in South Asia. Some explanatory factors have already been mentioned in the preceding section. The role of public investment in agriculture and price incentives will be discussed here.

(i) *West Pakistan*

Large and effective public investment in rural infrastructure and extension services, and policies of incentives to farmers created an economic climate which helped the quick adoption of innovations by many West Pakistan farmers. Three major steps were taken to provide incentives to farmers: (a) reduction of export duties; (b) price decontrol and price support to major grain crops; and (c) input subsidy.

Export duty on cotton was gradually reduced from Rs. 115 per bale (392 lbs) in 1958 to Rs. 25 by 1964/5. This had a direct impact on raising the absolute and relative price of cotton received by growers, and contributed greatly to the remarkable growth in cotton output.

In early 1960, direct controls on prices and movement of wheat were abolished in West Pakistan and a buffer-stock system was introduced. Compulsory procurement was replaced by voluntary sales by farmers to government. Government guaranteed farmers a minimum price of Rs. 13·50 per maund and a ceiling price of Rs. 16 per maund.[1] Government decided to intervene in the market when price fell below the minimum and release stocks when price rose above the ceiling.

[1] The guaranteed minimum price was raised to Rs. 17 per maund in 1967 and lowered to Rs. 15 in 1969. The ceiling price was raised to Rs. 17·50 per maund in 1966 and lowered to Rs. 15·50 in 1969.

In the early 1960s only a small proportion of these stocks came from wheat procured by government through support operations, because the government did not undertake vigorous procurement in this way. The bulk of these stocks came from an expanded supply of wheat (1·5 million tons per year on average) under P.L. 480, which played a crucial role in the success of wheat price decontrol and stabilisation policies. Contrary to earlier apprehensions about the damaging effects of P.L. 480 supplies on domestic output growth, the experience has been that in a deficit situation these were successfully used to stabilise prices and provide incentives to those who sell their surpluses. Stable prices of wheat also provided incentives to small farmers to shift from subsistence wheat production to higher value cash crops.

In 1967, for the first time, government fixed support prices for maize and groundnuts at Rs. 14·50 and Rs. 20per maund respectively.

Large subsidies are given on such inputs as irrigation water, fertilisers, and seeds. Plant protection service was provided free; and only since 1966/7 has government decided to recover 25 per cent of the cost of pesticides.

The response of farmers in West Pakistan, particularly large farmers, has been remarkable. Therefore, it is questionable whether input subsidies particularly on fertilisers and seeds are any longer necessary or desirable to provide incentives when output prices are supported at high levels.

Using the fertiliser response factor of each of the major crops obtained on farm trials [Wahab 1965] and the prices[1] of major crops and subsidised fertiliser price it has been estimated that the average financial return – cost ratio for fertiliser is greater than 4:1 [Falcon and Gotsch 1966]. This makes investment in fertiliser use very attractive to farmers. The existence of a black market indicates that a somewhat lower financial return–cost ratio would not make such investment unattractive.

Fertiliser subsidy is a major financial burden and amounts to around 15 per cent of the development allocation for agriculture. A part of this subsidy compensates for the high costs of domestic production but the internal subsidised price is somewhat below import price. The removal of the 35 per cent

[1] As used by the National Income Commission for 1959/60.

subsidy would reduce the return–cost ratio to between 2·5 and 3, which may still be sufficiently appealing. Moreover, with the expansion of improved seed varieties the fertiliser response factor is increasing. The response factor in the case of Mexican wheat varieties is reported to be 16 compared with 9 for the indigenous varieties. Even at the newly fixed support price of Rs. 15 per maund of wheat, and subsidised fertiliser price of about Rs. 900 per ton, the financial return–cost ratio would be over 7:1 for Mexican wheat.

It seems that elimination of fertiliser subsidy is highly desirable. It would reduce the increasingly large financial burden on the government and increase its capacity for price support policies and other aspects of the agricultural development programme. This will not eliminate the attractiveness of fertilisers to farmers. Nor will it discourage expansion of domestic fertiliser production in a growing market.

(ii) *East Pakistan*
Since the proportion of large farmers is very small and the knowledge of improved agricultural practices very poor, development efforts in East Pakistan require a much greater participation of government through public investment, extension work and encouragement of farmers' co-operation. Major reliance on market incentives is unlikely to generate satisfactory response from farmers.

The relatively poor quality of the extension service in East Pakistan has already been mentioned. Public investment in agriculture and irrigation has been much smaller in East Pakistan. At current prices it is estimated to have been Rs. 150 million in East Pakistan and Rs. 285 million in West Pakistan in 1959/60, and Rs. 210 million and Rs. 386 million respectively in 1964/5. [Papanek 1967]. In addition, during 1964/5 Rs. 910 million was spent on Indus Basin works in West Pakistan [Ibid.]. In East Pakistan public investment was supplemented from 1962/3 by a Rural Works Programme financed through P.L. 480 wheat supplies. While this programme provided considerable employment and income to rural labourers, its contribution to development of rural roads, drainage and embankments, and through these on agricultural production, is hard to establish.

The policy of agricultural price support and stabilisation has also been much less successful in East Pakistan.

Export duty on East Pakistan's jute was reduced rather late. Only in 1964 was it reduced from Rs. 20 to Rs. 10 per bale (400 lbs). The wholesale jute to rice price ratio increased and jute production in the following year also increased significantly. However, the specific effects of this reduction in duty are not clear, partly because of the nature of export demand and lack of knowledge about the prices received by farmers. Apart from demand conditions, the failure in stabilisation of rice price has its adverse effects on jute production.

The policy of compulsory procurement of rice from farmers at low prices was abandoned in East Pakistan in the 1960s, and replaced by voluntary sales by farmers to government. The procurement price of paddy was raised from Rs. 12·50 to Rs. 17/– per maund in 1967, and that of coarse rice fixed at Rs. 26·28 per maund. The prices at which rice could be purchased by consumers have not yet been stabilised within a narrow range. Thus while large farmers were given an incentive to increase production for sale, small farmers were provided with no incentives to shift from subsistence rice production to production of other valuable crops. So far the higher procurement price has not resulted in any significant increase in rice production. There appear to be no signs of eliminating the rice deficit in the near future and reducing imports, which averaged 0·1 million tons per year during the 1960s.

Large subsidies on such inputs as irrigation water, fertilisers and seeds are also given in East Pakistan, and plant protection is provided free. However, for reasons discussed earlier, the incentives of input subsidies have not generated satisfactory farmers' response in East Pakistan. Nonetheless, continuation of such subsidies in East Pakistan appears to be necessary to reduce risks of financial loss to farmers through crop failure and thus to encourage them to use these inputs and associated farming practices.

Need for reducing risks of crop failures
But more importantly, public investment in flood control and drainage is necessary to reduce the risks of crop failures in East Pakistan. Fluctuations in East Pakistan's agricultural

production in the past can be traced in part to severe flooding beyond the limits of normal expectations by farmers or to inadequate drainage which creates local flooding conditions after very heavy rains. Well over 50 per cent of cultivated land is affected by such severe flooding, mainly resulting from an overflow of the river Brahmaputra. In 1962/3 production fell sharply, owing to severe flooding in several areas, while in 1963/4 absence of severe flooding was an important factor contributing to a bumper crop.

The apprehension of excessive flooding and consequent crop failure very greatly increases the element of risk and uncertainty, and reduces the willingness to use improved agricultural inputs. The variance of past yields due largely to flooding is overwhelmingly important in farmers' decision-making.

Flood control and drainage is important not only because it can prevent reduction in output resulting from excessive flooding. This by itself would be a large benefit which may justify the admittedly large investment required for controlling floods, especially in the worse affected areas which lie on both sides of the Brahmaputra. The improvement in farmers' income resulting from protection of crops will also increase their capacity to invest for agricultural development. But more importantly, with the reduction of risk of crop failure, farmers would be more willing to adopt new innovations and make investment in new agricultural inputs to raise output and income. The much needed responsiveness of large numbers of farmers will be more likely to come in an improved economic climate of reduced risk.

CONCLUDING REMARKS

Lessons for Future Development

The recent remarkable agricultural development in West Pakistan has been the result of the combination of increased water, fertilizers, and improved seeds. The quick adoption of these innovations by farmers has been helped by large and effective public investment in rural infrastructure, reasonably competent extension services, and incentives. As a result, West Pakistan is likely to achieve self-sufficiency by 1969/70, and will have to begin to resolve problems of agricultural development beyond this objective. It will be necessary to increase and improve storage and marketing facilities, and adopt policies which may lead to a greater diversification of agricultural production in conformity with the pattern of demand at home and prospects of exports abroad. Wheat, for example, cannot be exported without a large subsidy, since the domestic support price (Rs. 15/– per maund) is much higher than the world market price (Rs. 11/– per maund). West Pakistan's comparative advantage may lie in other crops, such as cotton, rice and fruits.

The powerful combination of water, seeds and fertilisers also clearly indicates that for a considerable period in the future agricultural development in West Pakistan can be promoted without recourse to more capital-intensive and labour-displacing techniques, such as large scale use of tractors, which is now being encouraged by government through implicit subsidies. A policy of mechanisation would result in an intra-agricultural misallocation of scarce capital in the face of an actual or prospective farm labour surplus. Returns would be much higher and sustained agricultural growth can be assured if the same capital were used to augment the supplies of water, fertilisers, pesticides, and improved seeds, and spread further these successful innovations to small farmers. This is difficult but necessary for continued agricultural development. Problems of distribution of improved seeds and fertilisers will be more complex. The requirements of credit will greatly increase. Moreover, since tubewell installations for very small individual farms are not economic, there will be need for co-operation among small farmers or development of public tubewells to supply water.

The demonstrated high profitability of these inputs and their successful use by a large number of farmers suggests that subsidies on inputs in West Pakistan should be reduced and then eliminated. Agricultural price support and stabilisation policies can in future provide adequate incentives to farmers. The large amounts now spent on such subsidies may be used for other purposes, including expansion of credit to small farmers to enable them to purchase these inputs.

East Pakistan's very sluggish agricultural growth is explained by the poor progress in winter irrigation, fertilisation, plant protection and use of improved seeds, and by the lack of flood control and effective water use in summer.

The main factors limiting the programme of increased use of improved inputs have been the size and quality of the extension service, financial inability of most farmers to purchase these inputs, and the risks of crop failure due to natural calamities. These obstacles cannot be eliminated by price incentives. The use of improved inputs, particularly new varieties of higher-yielding seeds, requires controlled irrigation at particular times and avoidance of excessive flooding during monsoon. While the knowledge of the required water control and farming methods may be disseminated through better extension services, the risks involved in growing crops on monsoon land subject to recurring excessive flooding acts as a great deterrent to adoption of these innovations and investments in improved inputs by farmers.

A real breakthrough in East Pakistan's agriculture would require effective measures to reduce the risks of crop failure through excessive flooding. But so far agricultural development policy in East Pakistan has not faced this problem squarely. This is partly due to the dominant short-run view that since monsoon crops are subject to hazardous floods, the target output in the next five or so years can be achieved mainly through winter irrigation. While such short-run achievement may be possible, major flood control and effective water use in summer appears to be a necessary condition for sustained agricultural development in East Pakistan.

REFERENCES

[1] Falcon, W. P. and Gotsch, C. H., 'Agricultural Development in Pakistan: Lessons from the Second Plan Period', Bellagio Conference, mimiographed (Cambridge: Harvard University, 1966).

[2] Ferguson, B. R., *A Report of the Operation of a New Extension System for East Pakistan*, mimeographed (Karachi, U.S., A.I.D., 1963).

[3] Ghaffar, M., Mohammad, A. and Clark, E. H., II, 'Size of Holdings of Private Tubewell Owners', Research Report no. 69, mimeographed, Pakistan Institute of Development Economics, Karachi.

[4] Ghulam Mohammad, 'Private Tubewell Development and

Cropping Patterns in West Pakistan', *Pakistan Development Review*, spring 1965.

[5] Government of East Pakistan, *Economic Survey of East Pakistan 1967–68* (Dacca: Planning Department, 1968).

[6] Government of West Pakistan, 'Programme for Attainment of Self-Sufficiency in Food During Third Plan (1965–70)' (Lahore: Planning and Development Department, 1967).

[7] Hendry, J. B. and Hpu U, 'East Pakistan Agriculture During the Third Five Year Plan: Estimates of Possible Performance of Selected Major Crops' (Dacca: Harvard Advisory Group, 1964).

[8] I.B.R.D. (International Land Development Consultants), Programme for the Development of Irrigation and Agriculture in West Pakistan, vol. 5, annexe 7–Water Supply and Distribution, 1966.

[9] Khan, M. I., 'The Development of Institutional Agricultural Credit in Pakistan', *Pakistan Development Review*, spring 1963.

[10] Mears, L. and U Hpu *The Role of Fertilizer in Increasing the Growth Rate of Production of Major Crops in East Pakistan During the Third Plan*, mimeographed (Dacca: Harvard Advisory Group, 1964).

[11] Papanek, G. F., *Pakistan's Development: Social Goals and Private Incentives*, (Cambridge: Harvard University Press, 1967).

[12] Rahim, S. A., *Diffusion and Adoption of Agricultural Practices* (Comilla: Pakistan Academy for Rural Development, 1963).

[13] Rashid, H., 'Outline of a Proposed Strategy for Increased Agricultural Growth During the Third Five Year Plan', mimeographed (Dacca: East Pakistan Planning Department, 1964).

[14] Wahab, A., 'Fertilizer Trials in Farmers' Fields', 1965.

[15] WAPDA (Water and Power Development Authority) (Tipton and Kalmbach, Inc.,), *Salinity Control and Reclamation Programme* No. 4, Upper Rechna Doab, West Pakistan, 1965.

[16] WAPDA (Harza Engineering Co.), *Programme for Water and Power Development in West Pakistan through 1975*, 1964.

3 Economic Implications of the 'Green Revolution' and the Strategy of Agricultural Development in West Pakistan

HIROMITSU KANEDA*

I. INTRODUCTION

THE short-stemmed varieties of wheat and rice imported from abroad and the increased use of fertilizers have dramatically enlarged the potential for rapid increases in the agricultural output of West Pakistan. This recent breakthrough in food-grains production is sometimes referred to as the 'green revolution'. Because of the generally favourable conditions in West Pakistan in regard to irrigation water and solar energy, and of the unusually favourable weather in 1967/8 in particular, the 'green revolution' is spreading very rapidly. It is high time to focus our attention on some of the economic implications of the new developments in agriculture.

Recent agricultural growth in West Pakistan has been the result of improvements in the production relationship in the agricultural sector. However, the relationship between land and man in agriculture and that between agricultural production and other economic activities tend to be neglected in the current discussions of the ways in which the country may sustain the recent growth performance. Having identified the sources of growth in the agricultural sector during the 1960s, some expound the virtue of further improving the production relationship by introducing an extensive mechanisation programme in the agriculture of West Pakistan. The engineering criteria used

* An extended version of this chapter was first published in the *Pakistan Development Review*, summer 1969. The author wishes to thank Bruce F. Johnston and Frank C. Child for many valuable suggestions during the course of this study. He is also grateful to Robert D. Havener and Jerry B. Eckert of the Ford Foundation.

in such arguments are seemingly flawless. And it is attractive to state that, after water and biological-chemical technology has been introduced, mechanical-engineering technology should follow to promote further improvements in the basic production relationship in agriculture.[1] However, the choice of techniques, the ways in which the factors of production are to be combined, and the phasing-in of new technologies cannot be determined solely on the basis of mechanical-engineering criteria. There are other questions which call for economic analysis focused not only on the production relationship in agriculture *per se*, but also on the marketing and distribution systems and on the relation between agriculture and non-agricultural sectors of the economy.

The opportunities created by the 'green revolution' present some challenging economic issues besides the mechanisation question. A rapid increase in agricultural output and the consequent increase in the marketable surplus of agricultural products are expected to overwhelm the processing, warehousing, distribution, and marketing systems that exist today. The rapid achievement of self-sufficiency in food-grains will bring a very sharp reduction in the P.L. 480 programme in Pakistan and in the generation of counterpart funds that the government has relied upon to finance a substantial fraction of its development programme. A rapid increase in cash income for the agricultural sector will call for a re-examination of the system of agricultural taxation as well as the entire strategy of economic development. The problem of a stagnant agriculture has been primarily on the supply side; now that agriculture has experienced a rapid increase in productivity it must face an increasingly difficult problem of expanding effective demand to match the growth of supply. The euphoria of the present situation cannot, itself, sustain the view that there is unlimited demand for increased agricultural output. The prospects for

[1] The phrase 'biological-chemical technology' refers to agricultural technology bound up with the biological growth process of farm products and yield-increasing chemicals such as fertilisers, pesticides and herbicides. The phrase is used in contrast to 'mechanical-engineering technology'. As will become clear in the text of the paper below, 'biological-chemical technology' is more divisible, quicker in payoff, and primarily yield-increasing in contrast to 'mechanical-engineering technology' that is in general 'lumpy', slow in payoff, and primarily labour-displacing.

international as well as domestic marketing have to be seriously explored.

In this paper I shall deal with a few of these problems. My immediate concern is the question of tractor mechanisation in West Pakistan. I shall deal with other problems in the context of this main theme but only to the extent that they are relevant to the theme. First, the economic implications of West Pakistan's demographic characteristics will be analyzed in order to give perspective to the agricultural development of the province. Attention will be focused on the relationship between the land-man ratio and the output trend in the agriculture of West Pakistan. Next, the question of tractor mechanization in West Pakistan will be examined from the standpoint of economic efficiency and the choice of strategy for agricultural development. Finally, I shall present some basic considerations for an alternative strategy of the agricultural development of West Pakistan in view of the further progress of the green revolution.

II. DEMOGRAPHIC CHARACTERISTICS OF WEST PAKISTAN

As in other countries, industrialisation in West Pakistan has been accompanied by a decline in the relative share of the agricultural labour force in the total labour force. The 1961 Census shows that the share of agriculture was 59·3 per cent of the total labour force, declining from 65·1 per cent in 1951. During the ten years between the two decennial censuses, however, the agricultural labour force grew at the compound annual rate of 2·0 per cent and the non-agricultural labour force at 4·6 per cent, while the total labour force grew at the rate of 3·0 per cent per annum. Consequently, the absolute number of the agricultural labour force in West Pakistan increased from approximately 6·2 million in 1951 to 7·6 million in 1961.

On the basis of the assumption of constant fertility and declining mortality, experts at the P.I.D.E. estimate that the population of West Pakistan will rise at the annual rate of 3 to 4 per cent in the coming decades. If fertility is assumed to remain constant until 1970 and then decline linearly by 30 per cent to the period 1980/5, the effect of this minor change in fertility is minimal with respect to growth rates. The growth rate of population in West Pakistan will then fluctuate between 2·9 per cent to 3·1 per cent per annum [2].

Given the high rate of population growth (which implies a high growth rate of the total labour force), and the very large share of the agricultural labour force in the total, it will be a long time before the absolute size of the agricultural labour force starts declining. According to the calculations carried out by Jerry B. Eckert, if the share of agricultural labour in the initial year is 59·3 per cent (as observed in 1961), with the total labour force increasing at 3 per cent and non-farm employment growing at 4·6 per cent per annum, it would take about fifteen years for the share of agriculture to decline to the level of 50 per cent and more than thirty years for the absolute size of the agricultural labour force to begin to decline. Table 3.1 represents a hypothetical pattern of growth of the labour force on the basis of the parameters observed during the decade of 1951 to 1961.

The table shows that the projected labour force in agriculture is expected to increase by 2·4 million over its 1968 level before it begins to decline absolutely. It is of vital importance, therefore, to realize that the agricultural labour force in West Pakistan will continue to increase in absolute size and to account for the bulk of the labour force for some time (several planning periods) to come. Absorption of the rapidly increasing labour force into productive employment is, rightly, one of the most urgent policy issues facing the economy. Since relatively capital-intensive investment is inevitable in building up the infra-structure and in expanding large-scale manufacturing indus-tries, agriculture has a special role to play as the most important 'self-employment sector'; it must not only retain the current level of the agricultural labour force but also absorb residual increases in the total labour force in excess of those finding employment in the nonagricultural sectors of the economy.

Man–Land Ratio and Output in the Agriculture of West Pakistan
During the period between 1951 and 1961 the agricultural labour force in West Pakistan grew at the annual rate of 2 per cent. The cropped area in West Pakistan, on the other hand, increased at about 0·7 per cent per annum. Consequently,

TABLE 3.1

PROJECTED LABOUR FORCE BY SECTOR:
WEST PAKISTAN SELECTED YEARS

Year	Total	Labour force (in thousands) Non-agricultural	Agricultural	Share of agricultural labour force (%)
1951 (Census)	9,507	3,319	6,188	65·1
1961 (Census)	12,763	5,193	7,570	59·3
1965	14,359	6,211	8,148	56·7
1968	15,685	7,104	8,581	54·7
1969	16,154	7,429	8,707	53·9
1970	16,637	7,769	8,868	53·3
1974	18,717	9,293	9,424	50·4
	(50 per cent non-agricultural)			
1975	19,276	9,718	9,558	49·6
1980	22,334	12,156	10,179	45·6
1985	25,878	15,205	10,673	41·2
1990	29,984	19,019	10,964	36·6
1992	31,803	20,800	11,002	34·6
	(Agricultural labour force begins to decline)			
1993	32,753	21,753	11,001	33·6

The assumed constants are as follows:
  Share of agricultural labour force (1961): 59·3 per cent
  Compound growth rates (1951–61):
    Total labour force   2.99 ,,
    Nonagricultural labour force   4·58 ,,
    Agricultural labour force   2·02 ,,
Source: computed by Jerry B. Eckert.

the land area available per worker in agriculture declined
substantially during the decade.

Table 3.2 presents agricultural labour force, planted acreage,
and gross crop production in West Pakistan during the period
between 1951 and 1964. It is easy to derive relative changes in
planted acreage per worker and in gross crop production per
acre from the information presented in the table. The results of
such derivations are shown in the following tabulation:

PERCENTAGE CHANGES IN ACREAGE PER
WORKER AND OUTPUT PER ACRE, WEST
PAKISTAN, SELECTED YEARS, 1951–64

Changes in	1951–5	1955–61	1961–4
Acreage per worker	none	−10·3%	−2·1%
Output per acre	none	4·2	9·2

The stagnation of agricultural production during the 1950s is attributable to the worsening land–man ratio which was not fully compensated for by the slow increase in output per acre. In contrast, the celebrated performance of agriculture during the second-plan period is the result of the expansion in planted acreage almost paralleling the growth of the agricultural labour force and a rapid expansion of yields per acre (real output per acre per year).

TABLE 3.2

AGRICULTURAL LABOUR FORCE, PLANTED ACREAGE AND GROSS CROP PRODUCTION, WEST PAKISTAN, 1951–64

Year	Agricultural labour force (million)	Acreage planted under crops[a] (million acres)	Gross crop production[a] (Rs. million in FY 1960 prices)
1950–52	6·188[b]	24·69	4105
1954–56	6·620	26·58	4385
1960–62	7·570[b]	28·39	4870
1964/65	8·148	29·12	5587

[a] Crops included are as follows: rice, wheat, bajra, jowar, maize, barley, gram, sugarcane, rapeseed, mustard, sesamum, linseed, cotton and tobacco.
[b] Census figures for the mid-year, 1950/1 and 1960/1, respectively.

If we are to measure the performance of agriculture in West Pakistan in terms of output per worker, the years between 1951 and 1955 should be characterized as those of virtual stagnation, the first-plan period as the period of retrogression, and only the second-plan period may be termed a successful period. The encouraging performance during the second-plan period took place largely as a result of water-resource development, in which private tubewells were particularly important. Additional supplies of water from tubewells increased both the cropping intensity and crop yields.

III. SOURCES OF PRODUCTIVITY GROWTH IN AGRICULTURE

In analysing the basic production relationships and in

assessing the productivity performance of agriculture, it is convenient to consider the following identity:

$$O = L \times \frac{A}{L} \times \frac{O}{A}$$

where O denotes output in agriculture, A planted acreage, and L stands for workers gainfully employed in agriculture. The output per worker is then given by the product of the two ratios on the right-hand side of the identity, namely, planted acreage worked by a unit of labour and output per acre. The identity states that, in incremental terms, an increase in output of agriculture results from an increase in any one of the three terms on the right-hand side so long as such an increase is not offset by adverse effects on the other terms.

It is clear that there are many ways in which factors of production can be combined to achieve a certain level of output. For any given set of factor prices different techniques of production (i.e. different combinations of factors) can be arranged in order of increasing unit cost of production. For any given price of the product this is also the order of decreasing profitability. It follows, therefore, that given factor and product prices it is profitable to adopt and use the method of production which minimises per unit of cost of production. Economists would call this method of production the most efficient. Thus, from the economist's point of view, that a certain operation is performed more 'efficiently' in the engineering sense, be it in fuel-energy conversion, body weight-energy conversion, or in the power-draft-speed relationship, does not necessarily mean it is a more efficient operation than other alternatives. Economic discussions of the choice of technique are couched crucially in terms of the relative prices (opportunity costs) of the substitutable factors of production.

Where a particular factor is relatively abundant, the price of that factor is low, and vice versa. Because of market imperfections and systems of discriminating subsidies and taxes, prevailing costs of the factors of production do not reflect their opportunity costs with any accuracy in developing economies. Nonetheless, it is undebatable that the economically most efficient technique is that which employs a relatively larger amount of abundant resources and economizes on the use of scarce resources. In other words, the criterion of economic efficiency dictates that output per unit of scarce resources be maximised by combining abundant resources as much as is economical with a unit of scarce resource.

If land is in ample supply and labour is scarce, the primary emphasis of agricultural development may be on an increase of acreage per worker, thus raising the output of each worker in the sector. On the other hand, if labour is abundant and land is scarce, the basic theme in the growth of agricultural productivity will be an increase in yields per acre to enhance the output per unit of available land.

Although it is often impossible to distinguish clearly the effect of an innovation in agriculture, it is convenient to associate loosely mechanical-engineering technology with an increase in acreage per worker and biological-chemical technology with a rise in yields per acre. Then, we may state that the emphasis of agricultural development in a land-rich, labour-poor economy will be primarily on mechanical-engineering innovations, and that the basic theme in a land-poor, labour-abundant economy will be on biological-chemical innovations. In case both land and labour become the constraints for the growth in agricultural production, both acreage per worker and yields per acre are proper targets for improvement. Expansion of output per acre and acreage per worker will increase agricultural output even under conditions of declining agricultural labour force and reduced acreage available for farming.[1]

[1] It is common knowledge that machines and implements save labour required for any specific operation. Proponents of tractor-mechanisation, however, would emphasize the yield effect rather than the labour-displacement effect when faced with a situation characterised by an abundant supply of labour. One of the most important of the favourable effects of mechanical power and implements on better yields is the so-called 'timely preparation of seedbed'. Of course, timeliness in seedbed preparation is less critical on irrigated lands than on rain-fed areas, which have to rely on the moisture retained in the soil for the growth of crops. However, it is often argued that the time element in seedbed preparation becomes of crucial importance on irrigated lands if there is pressure to achieve multiple cropping. In West Pakistan the most binding constraint on increasing the intensity of cropping is the availability of additional supplies of water, rather than mechanical power *per se*.

TRACTOR MECHANISATION IN
WEST PAKISTAN

The Private and Social Profitability of Tractor-Mechanisation

Generally speaking, tractor-mechanisation has progressed in countries where the land–man ratio is extremely favourable and where economic development has reached the phase in which a large quantity of accumulated capital per man would make the productivity of labour high and capital cost cheaper relatively to the cost of labour. As we have seen, the land–man ratio in Pakistan is expected to worsen rather than improve and, given the dimmed prospects for massive foreign assistance and the increasing population, capital accumulation per man will be slow in the foreseeable future. Nonetheless, it is clear that the tractor population in private hands has increased substantially, particularly in West Pakistan. There are indications that in the Punjab a number of large landowners are setting up management units of 150 acres or more as they obtain tractors. On such farms the number of hired workers has been drastically curtailed as compared with the situation before the introduction of tractors and implements.[1] There are reports, moreover, that self-propelled combine harvesters are being purchased by some of these landowners.

A number of important factors explain this phenomenon. The Government of Pakistan made it clear that the move towards self-sufficiency in food requirements is one of the specific objectives for agriculture in the Third Plan. The government has promoted new farming techniques by its policies concerning the prices of inputs and outputs which enhance farm profits. On the input side the most prominent have been the subsidies on fertilisers, pesticides and water rates. Important also have been the government measures to grant tax and tariff exemptions to the imports of agricultural investment goods and to license imports at the artificially low official rate

---

[1] Reports indicate, furthermore, that even the tenants are being moved off the land. Although rights of tenants are protected by law, if the landlord introduces a mechanisation programme on his farm and cultivates the land himself, tenants can be removed by legal process. This is another instance of divergence between private profitability (for landlords) of tractor mechanisation and its social profitability (for the economy as a whole).

of exchange. On the output side, a key feature of government policy has been price-support schemes on some commodities in order to provide an incentive to farmers by giving them the prospects of a more predictable income. Floor prices, which the government guarantees by purchasing in the regular commercial markets when necessary, are established for wheat, rice, maize and groundnuts. These policy measures have been quite successful in accomplishing the immediate task for which they were intended. The use of fertilisers has continued to expand and output of foodgrains has increased. However, they have also introduced a peculiar price structure which has tended to distort real economic calculations for the agriculture of Pakistan.

According to a study by Oddvar Aresvik, assuming the world import price of wheat at 12·70 rupees per maund (the average for 1960/1 to 1964/5), the f.o.b. Karachi price of wheat for export from West Pakistan would have to be about 11·00 rupees per maund. Counting the handling and transport charges necessary for wheat exports, therefore, the price on the farm level would have to be much lower (8·00 rupees per maund) [1]. Given the official exchange rate, there is no doubt that the domestic price of wheat is substantially higher than the world price. The support price is double the price 'justified' by the world market. In other words, the 'justifiable' price of wheat, in this sense, is one-half of the current support price.

On the other hand, the substantial exemption of agricultural capital goods from tariffs and taxes means that tractors and machinery can be obtained at the official exchange rate for the price prevailing in the world market. It is evident that in terms of the quantity of output to pay for a given input, Pakastani farmers pay only about one half the amount of wheat which the world farmers have to pay for a tractor of equal design and power. Tractor-mechanisation in Pakistan becomes a profitable if not economical proposition. In Pakistan's capital-poor economy, capital equipment is obtainable at a cheaper price in terms of output than in capital-rich economies, whereas the economic measure of relative scarcity should indicate the contrary for the economy as a whole. This paradox reflects a situation in which a relatively cheap input (labour) is being replaced by a relatively dearer input (capital). The prices artificially maintained by government measures thus make the private marginal productivity of investment in tractor-mechanisation considerably higher than its counterpart abroad (in capital-rich countries) and its social marginal productivity at home.

Microeconomics of Tractor-Mechanisation and its Implications
Despite all that has been said in the government's policy pronouncements and the assertions made about the yield-increasing effects of mechanisation, one is struck by the paucity of data in West Pakistan on this subject. The available data on costs and incomes comparing the mechanised farm operations and bullock-power operations, such as those appearing in the report of the First Machinery Conference and Exhibition held in Lahore during early March 1967, appear to rely exclusively on a study by M. S. Gill reported in 1962.[1] According to this report, the increase in yield per acre in the case of tractor farming, as against bullock-power farming, amounts to five maunds of maize and four maunds of wheat (about 25–30 per cent).

[1] The study [6] refers to experiments performed during 1952–4. Lacking in detailed data which formed the basis of various tables presented by Gill, it is not possible to use the results for the purpose of meaningful economic calculations. The total cultivation charges per acre with the use of different tractors and bullocks are ranked in the report. However, the acreage on which these operations were performed is not given. It is common knowledge that on smaller plots of land, less expensive power (draft animals and small tractors) is economical and that in larger acreage the reverse is true. It is also reported that among various farming systems, as defined by the author, the so-called 'direct mechanised farming' used the maximum amount of manual labour per year. Unless the cropping intensity is increased, or the number of operations (say weeding, fertilising, etc.) in cultivation of a single crop is made larger, or both, it does not make sense to say that the input of labour was larger under mechanised farming than under bullock farming. This particular set of data serves to point out what the author intended, namely, that machines do not necessarily displace labour under the given situation in Lyallpur in 1952–4. Of course, however, it cannot be used for the purpose of demonstrating that machines use more labour per single operation required in growing of crops, nor that 'direct mechanised farming' is the economically most efficient method of combining resources. The same is true with the report on yield performance of mechanised farming and bullock farming as discussed in the text. For the purpose of strict comparison only the motive power should be different in the two situations, given other conditions approximately equal.

Except for the possibility of increasing the intensity of cropping and, therefore, increasing *yield per acre per year*, it is not obvious that tractor mechanisation *per se* has much of an effect on yield (per acre per crop) as compared with animal draft power. Experiments in Japan indicate that yield per acre does not increase from mechanisation *per se*. These results seem to be confirmed by experiments at the International Rice Research Institute. Moreover, the availability of water is the most binding constraint in West Pakistan's agriculture for increasing the intensity of cropping.[1] Increases in the cropping intensity with or without tractors become possible only if additional supplies of water can be made available.

It is certainly true that good seedbed preparation, weed/pest control, and uniform planting depth assume much greater importance with the new varieties and heavier fertiliser applications. However, these operations can be accomplished by more economic combinations of factors. Ultimately, the answer depends on how well land preparation and other operations are carried out by animal-drawn equipment and small power machines in Pakistan, whose development, improvements, and diffusion among the farmers may well be as effective as all-out tractor-mechanisation of Pakistani farms.

Total cost incurred in crop production consists of the following items: (i) cost of the use of land and other fixed assets on land; (ii) costs of the current inputs, such as seeds, water, fertiliser, pest control, etc.; (iii) cost of power equipment and machinery; (iv) cost of labour. It is safe to assume that the magnitude of the first two items would be approximately the same, irrespective of type of power used in producing a single crop. The last two items could depend on the field operations required and, crucially, on acres covered as well as on the type of soil.

---

[1] The cropping intensity (as defined as the percentage of the holding cropped) of the farms with tubewells exceeds that of the non-tubewell farms by a substantial margin. Ghulam Mohammad reported that in the Multan and Montgomery districts the non-tubewell farmers had an average cropping intensity of about 99 per cent, whereas the tubewell farmers had a cropping intensity of about 131 per cent. In the Gujranwala district, the intensity of cropping was about 115 per cent in the case of non-tubewell farmers and about 146 per cent in the case of tubewell farmers [7, pp. 25–6].

Cost of the use of farm machinery consists of charges for depreciation (by use and by obsolescence), interest payments on investment (regardless of whether the money invested was borrowed or not, since the funds could have been used otherwise and yielded returns), other fixed charges (such as housing, taxes and insurance), and variable costs which depend on the actual use of the machinery (e.g. repairs, costs of fuel and oil). Since fixed charges are large for large machinery, comparative costs of the use of machinery per acre between different size machines depends on the acreage on which they are operated.

According to an experiment carried out at the Central Agricultural Experiment Station of Japan in 1963, the minimum acreage, the 'threshold-acreage', required to make the use cost of a 35 h.p. tractor equal to that of a 15 h.p. tractor, was between 25 and 30 hectares. For a larger acreage the use cost of a 35 h.p. tractor declines more rapidly than the smaller one but, unless farm size exceeds 50 hectares, it does not come down to the level of the use cost involving smaller machinery and animals in the customary method of cultivation. Because 'large-scale' or 'medium-scale' mechanisation requires a large quantity of investment, the cost of machine use per hectare with mechanised farming is greater than that in the customary methods of cultivation.

However, the Japanese experiment found that the direct cost of production per hectare in mechanised farming was less than that of the customary method, owing mainly to the saving in the cost of labour involved. For a larger tractor the 'threshold acreage' in this case was between 10 and 15 hectares and that for a smaller tractor was less than 10 hectares. Because of the decrease in yield by mechanised farming, the Japanese experiment found that the use of a 35 h.p. tractor gives greater returns (value of output minus cost) than the customary method only when the operating acreage is more than 30 hectares, and that the use of a 15 h.p. tractor was not justifiable under the circumstances.

It is to be noted that the calculation was made on the basis of the Japanese price structure of the wage rate and the cost of capital. It goes without saying that the ratio between the market prices of labour and capital is higher in Japan (especially in the 1960s) than in present-day Pakistan. And, therefore, if one is to use the market (in the sense of 'shadow' or 'accounting') prices of capital and labour for Pakistan, the 'threshold acreage' for the use of a larger tractor is expected to increase. It is a well-known proposition that when the opportunity cost of labour is low and the rate of interest is high, the threshold acreage will be large and labour-using and capital-saving techniques will be optimal.

According to the agricultural census of 1960, only 8 per cent of the farms in West Pakistan exceeded 25 acres (of cultivated land). Since there were 37·2 million acres of cultivated area and 4·86 million farms, on the average only 7·6 acres of cultivated area was available per farm. If we add the reported cultivable waste of 24 million acres, and assume that the number of farms remained constant, total land area available per farm would be 12·7 acres.

Accordingly, the Government of West Pakistan has been advised recently to pursue a programme of rapid tractor-mechanisation especially for farms holding more than 25 acres. On the average, these large farm-owners operate 54 acres. Given the present structure of output and input prices in Pakistani agriculture, these large farmers may very well be able to reap private profits from tractor-mechanisation. We have seen, however, that the present price structure is the product of artificially inflated prices of output and similarly deflated prices of farm machinery. The question regarding the future price structure, therefore, has to deal squarely with the probable future prices of agricultural products. If the output prices were to decline, or more precisely, if the relationship between capital cost and labour cost in terms of output prices should move against capital, the 'threshold acreage' will have to rise above the level now being assumed for private profit-ability of tractor-mechanisation.

Economic Implications of a 'Bi-Modal' Pattern of Agricultural Development

The 'bi-modal' pattern of agricultural development being recommended, where the programme of mechanisation is to be concentrated on the farms with more than 25 acres of cultivated area, calls for serious thinking in the perspective of Pakistan's agriculture and economy. There are both international and domestic dimensions in this subject regarding the output and the inputs of the agriculture of Pakistan.

Because of the favourable conditions in West Pakistan regarding the availability of irrigation water and abundance of solar energy, and of the unusually favourable weather in 1967/8 in particular, the 'green revolution' seems to have spread most rapidly in West Pakistan. However, the dwarf varieties of Mexican wheat and the dwarf varieties of rice developed by the International Rice Research Institute are being made available to other developing countries in Asia, and their impact is just beginning to be felt. In Pakistan a supply shortage of the new seeds and limited availability of fertilisers severely limited planting until the 1967/8 season. But Pakistan was not an isolated example. According to the 1968 annual report of the I.B.R.D., India and the Philippines showed a rapid expansion in acreage planted to the new varieties of wheat and rice during the past season. Good progress in introducing the new seeds is also reported in Afghanistan, Ceylon, Indonesia, Malaysia and Turkey. It can be reasonably expected that a growing number of countries in Asia and elsewhere will soon feel the impact of the so-called 'miracle seeds'. There is no question that these countries are as anxious as Pakistan to achieve self-sufficiency in foodgrains. The spread of the 'green revolution' to many countries, thus diminishes the prospects of a long-run expansion of grain exports from Pakistan, and the poor quality of grain processing here severely limits the possibility of expanding the export markcts (except for the traditional basmati rice) in the near future.[1] The monetary return from the potential increases in grain production in Pakistan depends crucially on effective demand. Inasmuch as 70–80 per cent of Pakistan's population are members of self-supplying farm households, the growth of domestic demand for purchased foodgrains is severely limited. Increase in effective

---

[1] See a study on this problem by J. Norman Efferson [3]. One of Efferson's conclusions is that 'most of the medium-grain rice now being produced in West Pakistan is of such poor quality that it will not be accepted in world markets'. Facilities for handling wheat are physically different from those handling rice but they are not much different in quality standards. In fact, the consensus of experts in this field is that Mexi-Pak wheat, as prepared here, cannot be given even the lowest commercial grading in the international market.

demand, commensurate with the growth in potential supplies of foodgrains, therefore, is very questionable.

It is indeed difficult to imagine the problem of a foodgrain glut in a country characterised by chronic under-consumption and hunger in recent years. However, the maintenance of a government-guaranteed price of foodgrains will become increasingly difficult as the marketed surplus of foodgrains increases. In anticipation of the excellent 1968 wheat crop and a fall in wheat prices after the harvest, the government announced its intention to purchase 'at least 5 lakh tons of wheat' in order to prevent the prices from falling below the support level. At this time, it is not known whether purchase of that much wheat was enough to guarantee the floor price after harvest. It is worth noting, however, that government purchases would cost 231·9 million rupees for 5 lakh tons. This amount is about equal to the public-sector development expenditure on education and training for all Pakistan during the 1966/7 period.

The 'bi-modal' pattern of agricultural development will not only create a subsector of agriculture which is large-scale and capital-intensive but would also promote commercial sales of output more than the growth in total output. If effective demand cannot be expected to increase as rapidly, and/or if the government cannot purchase all that is brought to the markets over and above the absorption by regular commercial channels, the prices of foodgrains must decline below the favourable level existing now. Consequences of such a development are not difficult to imagine. The great bulk of the farmers left out in the programme will face a decline in their net incomes due to the worsened terms of trade for their small marketable surpluses. Large farmers will find that in order to cut the costs of operation per acre their operating acreage has to be further expanded and their operations made more commercially oriented. Expansion of acreage would take place, in the absence of effective legal restrictions, so long as mechanical engineering economies of scale outweigh managerial diseconomies of large-scale operation. The economic logic of this process is simple but hard. Once investments are made on fixed assets (such as tractors), the short-run cost function becomes 'lower' than the long-run cost function. Since fixed costs are costs forgone in the

short run, it does not affect the short-run supply of output.
Prices of the product can fall to the levels that cover only
variable costs and not fixed costs. The impact of such a situation
can be disastrous to small farmers whose total costs are largely
variable.

A vicious circle of the large getting larger and the small
getting smaller will set in until the rural population is polarised
into the large, rich farmers and small, poor farmers. The
tragedy is not only that the small will suffer, as they will suffer,
but that the small will have nothing to look forward to despite
the apparently promising future with the dawn of the 'green
revolution'. The undesirable effects of massive grain imports
from developed countries (say, under the P.L. 480 programmes)
will be reproduced in the domestic scene. The only difference is
the change in the actor who plays the role of surplus exporter
and, more importantly, in the use of funds generated into the
hands of the new large supplier. The agricultural sector is very
lightly taxed. Of course, this means that the mobilisation of
increased cash incomes in the hands of large farmers becomes
difficult, if not impossible. Despite certain undesirable effects,
the foodgrain imports provided Pakistan with needed foodgrains as well as the counterpart funds that the government has
relied on to finance a substantial fraction of its development
programme.

V. BASIC CONSIDERATIONS FOR THE
STRATEGY OF AGRICULTURAL DEVELOPMENT
IN WEST PAKISTAN

Beyond Self-sufficiency in Foodgrain Production
The goal of recent agricultural policy in Pakistan has been
self-sufficiency in foodgrain production. Measures ranging
from input subsidies to output price-support programme have
all been designed and executed for the purpose of substituting
domestic production for the import of foodgrains. The development of tubewell irrigation since the second-plan period and
the more recent 'green revolution', however, have ushered in a
new situation. One can confidently state that the substantial
increase in yields obtainable by the progress of the 'green
revolution' will make it possible for the mass of the nation's

farmers to achieve satisfactory increases in output and solve the problem of foodgrain deficits within a short period of time. As a consequence, it is now necessary to re-examine the basic orientation of the agricultural policy of the country.

Since the foodgrain is one of the cheapest sources of calories, it is only natural that emphasis has been placed on the rapid increase in its output when there is a widespread shortage in food energy intake. Simply eliminating the foodgrain deficits, however, does not provide a final solution to the food problem of the country. There is a whole range of other problems of which those in the areas of production and marketing stand out.

In the sphere of production, there is an increasingly difficult problem of producing an improved output mix to provide the nation with a more nutritional diet. Pakistan's deficits in high-quality proteins, edible oils, vegetables, fruits and sugar are obvious even today. As the pattern of food consumption changes in response to an increase in per capita income or in response to improvements in education and communication, the over-whelmingly large proportion of calories currently derived from starchy staples in Pakistani diets will have to decline. Effective demand for 'protective foods' that are rich in vitamins, minerals and high-quality proteins, such as fruits, vegetables, meats and dairy products, will surely increase. If Pakistan were to dissipate valuable foreign exchange on imports of these food items, the attainment of self-sufficiency in foodgrains and the consequent 'savings' of the scarce resource would lose much of its meaning.

Diversification of Pakistan's agriculture is rightly the next order of business; policy measures should be designed to change the cropping patterns to bring forth this result. As the rapid spread of new varieties of rice and wheat has shown beyond any doubt, farmers respond strongly to the comparative net cash return of various crops. The major determinants of the net profitability being the physical yield per acre and the price per unit of output, a new set of comparative yield performance and a new set of relative prices among crops have to be developed. The current system of support prices needs re-examination and determined efforts to improve yields of crop other than rice and wheat are called for.

The improvement of food storage, processing and distribution systems in Pakistan is as important as increasing production. It is said that losses caused by microorganisms, insects, rodents and other factors amount to some 10 to 15 per cent of the output of foodgrains. Reduction of such losses by better storage facilities is an immediate necessity. As the marketable surplus of farm products increases, and as the proportion that perishable commodities occupy in total farm output increases, the problem of adequately handling farm products after harvest becomes increasingly important. Improved food protection practices should be made available at reasonable cost to the farmers. The improvement of marketing systems assumes a unique importance, furthermore, if the emphasis is placed on the production of crops which will provide the farmer with the largest cash return. A price-incentive scheme can work only if it is coupled with a highly developed marketing system.

The improvement of food storage, processing and distribution systems in Pakistan will require a substantial amount of foreign exchange and will be costly in terms of domestic resources. In view of the pressing need for improving these facilities and for strengthening the existing facilities which supply farm inputs, the priority currently given to tractor-mechanisation in West Pakistan should be carefully re-examined.

Selective Mechanisation

Mechanical engineering technology in agriculture can embrace a wide range of different configurations involving motive power, machines, and implements. There are many ways in which one may classify mechanical engineering technology in agriculture. Most important from our point of view, however, are the following two types of distinctions: (i) 'mechanisation' as applied to each specific operation, and 'mechanisation' as applied to several or all of the farm operations; (ii) "mechanisation' as introduced into a given socioeconomic organisation of agriculture and calling for minor adjustments, and 'mechanisation' calling for a highly sophisticated organisation and cooperation not easily introduced into a given situation.

The first distinction recognises the many different operations related to growing and harvesting of crops, such as levelling of land, irrigation/drainage, ploughing, seedbed preparation, planting and fertilising, crop protection, harvesting, and preparation of products. Machines and implements can be designed specifically for a limited number, or for many, or all, of these operations. Aside from implements relying on human or animal power, tubewells, low-lift pumps and power threshers are examples of machines used specifically for limited tasks, as are Japanese power tillers, dusters and sprayers. On the other hand, the development of the tractor and the so-called power take-off, together with the development of various implements, make possible the more direct and widespread application of engine power to many different operations. In the United States the total cultivation processes came under the aegis of mechanical power; also the harvesting processes and many post-harvest operations became thoroughly mechanised with the advent of the self-propelled combine harvester. Nonetheless, it should be clear that a tractor is by no means the only way to mechanise agriculture. Mechanisation of selected processes of cultivation and post-harvest operations, as in the case of Japan, may prove to be more beneficial for the agriculture of Pakistan given the circumstances it faces now and in the decades to come.

The increase in size and specialisation of farms has been one of the most significant changes in farm structure and organisation associated with the adoption of tractor-mechanisation in the United States. Modern equipment and machines are so expensive in many instances that it is advantageous for the farmer to develop larger farms and enterprises (i.e. to specialise) to make full use of the new resources and to hold down unit costs. The typical relationship between acreage and unit-cost is a curve that shows a steep decline in costs until utilisation reaches about one fourth to one half the maximum possible with the machine and, thereafter, a very moderate reduction in costs with greater use. High costs per acre or per hour with limited use reflect, of course, the fixed charges unrelated to the actual use of the machine. Introduction of larger machines and implements, therefore, necessitates large management units, output standardisation, and uniform cultural practices, which call for highly sophisticated organisation and co-operation. Organisational problems loom as large as technical problems, solution of one not necessarily guaranteeing the solution of the other. Smaller-scale mechanisation programmes embracing machines for a few selected operations would be much easier to introduce into the given organisation of agriculture without the necessity of a wholesale substitution of 'modern' for 'traditional' practices. It also has the advantage of involving the bulk of the nation's farmers in the process of agricultural innovation.

Emphasis on Divisible, Farm-resource Augmenting Inputs

Biological and chemical innovations that have brought forth the 'green revolution' are, by their very nature, neutral to scale. They can, therefore, be incorporated into the existing institutional framework of Pakistani agriculture without drastic adjustments. Small-scale peasant farms can adopt these innovations with relatively minor adjustments in contrast to technical innovations involving tractors and combines. Undoubtedly, this aspect of recent innovations has contributed to the very rapid diffusion of technology in the Punjab as elsewhere. The benefits of the 'green revolution' have not been limited to a few large farmers. As with the recent private tubewell development in the Punjab, many small farmers are taking advantage of the development.

Tubewell water, new seeds and increased applications of fertilisers, which dramatise the 'green revolution' on the input side, are basically complementary to the farm resources of labour and land. By making it possible to grow more crops, more lucratively, per acre of cultivated area, these inputs have increased the use of labour on farms as well as the incomes of farm workers concerned. In contrast to investments in tractors and combines, which are fundamentally labour-displacing, investments in inputs such as seeds, fertilisers and even tubewells are much more conducive to augmenting the income of the bulk of the nation's farmers. Emphasis on these inputs, furthermore, would retard the polarisation of the rural population and land holdings, and make it possible for the mass of the nation's farmers to achieve satisfactory increases in output at modest costs in terms of scarce resources of capital and foreign exchange.

Much can be done to 'make animals more effective by improving the equipment they power' [5, p. 24]. It is often said that the farmer's reluctance in accepting improved animal-drawn equipment is evidence of the inertia existing in the present situation and that a drastic improvement, such as tractor mechanisation, is needed for breaking this situation. In view of the progress of private tubewell development and the green revolution and the increasing rewards they offer, we may expect the majority of farmers to accept voluntarily new technology developed in this area. The development and diffusion of the mouldboard plough, various harrows, the seed-cum-fertiliser drills, all of which are animal-drawn equipment, and knapsack power sprayer-cum-duster, hand weeders and small stationary threshers, are highly desirable. These kinds of equipment can remove bottlenecks and increase the economic efficiency as well as engineering efficiency of the agriculture of West Pakistan.[1]

Interrelationship between Agriculture and Non-agricultural Sectors
The economic relation between agriculture and non-agricultural sectors involves exchange of products, flows of productive factors, and diffusion of ideas. Typically, an underdeveloped economy is fragmented, heterogeneous, and lacking in the cohesive forces emanating from adequate transportation and communication systems. Although they are not obvious under these circumstances, the intersectoral flows of products, productive factors, and ideas characterise a two-way relationship between agriculture and industry.

The importance of each sector for the other is appreciated first by looking at exchange of products. On the one hand, there is the interdependence of sectors through direct intermediate deliveries; both sectors buy products as intermediate inputs for further production from each other. Obvious examples are cash crops, such as cotton, jute and sugar on the agricultural output side and machines, implements, fertilisers and pesticides on the industrial output side. On the other hand,

[1] The 'problems of success' revealed by the recent developments in the agriculture of West Pakistan are nowhere more visible than in the harvesting and post-harvest operations. If indeed a bottleneck exists in the crop-production processes, it is more likely in harvesting and post-harvest operations than anywhere else. The delay involved in field preparation for the next crop is as much a result of 'inefficient' threshing operations as that of the 'inefficiency of bullock cultivation. Moreover, the loss of grains involved in the traditional threshing operations is appalling: Giles reports that losses, from the maturity of the grain in the field onward, are estimated by experts at 25 per cent [5, p. 30].

each sector is a source of effective demand for the final products of the other. It is important to have consistency and compatibility in industrial planning; it is equally important to recognise this interdependence and to exploit positive intersectoral relationships that promote rapid economic development.

A broad-based agricultural development is essential for creating a domestic market for the developing indigenous industries. A conscious effort to develop agricultural technology will foster domestic industries and will return a handsome reward. It is appropriate here to recall one such example in the recent experience of West Pakistan. In reference to the spontaneous, private development of tubewells during the second-plan period, W. P. Falcon and C. H. Gotsch observed that [4, p. 12]:

> These 25,000 (tube) wells represented an initial investment on the order of Rs. 250 million, a sum thought impossible in West Pakistan's traditional agriculture. Moreover, this investment was an important stimulus to the small-scale machine industry. Whole streets in such cities as Multan, Lyallpur, Lahore, Gujranwala, Sialkot, and Daska have been devoted to the manufacture of pumps and engines, and the skill, ingenuity, and training demonstrated in these shops have been impressive.

There is undoubtedly a similar opportunity for a rapid expansion of indigenous production of improved farm implements. The emphasis on selective mechanisation would, as in the case of tubewells, nurture indigenous industries catering directly to the agricultural sector of the country. The development of such industries, in turn, would make it possible for the farmers to acquire the machines and implements at increasingly favourable terms, encouraging further use of such inputs. It would be a clear mistake to minimise this type of positive interaction between agricultural and industrial development by using large amounts of capital and foreign exchange for tractor-mechanisation. The progress of the 'green revolution' has increased the attractiveness of investments in improved farm implements. Investments of this type will grow, the alleged inertia and reluctance of the farmer notwithstanding, unless aborted by large-scale, heavily subsidised imports.

VI. SUMMARY AND CONCLUSIONS

In summary, let us recapitulate some of the highlights of the paper.

1. Given the present share of the agricultural labour force in the total labour force and the growth rate of the total labour force of 3 per cent per annum in West Pakistan, even if non-agricultural employment grew at the very high rate of 4·6 per cent per year, the absolute number of the agricultural labour force will continue to grow for several decades to come.

2. On the other hand, in view of the fact that the marginal capital labour ratio is expected to increase (owing to the need for capital-intensive investments in infrastructure and in large-scale manufacturing industries), the economy's ability to absorb a growing labour force into productive non-agricultural employment will be limited.

3. In contrast to the decade of the 1950s, the output increasing effects of the tubewells in the second-plan period and the 'green revolution' of the more recent years have shown, without doubt, distinctive alternatives to tractor mechanisation for a rapid agricultural development in West Pakistan. These alternatives are inexpensive in terms of the scarce resources of capital and foreign exchange. Moreover, they increase output without displacing the employed labour force in agriculture, thus enabling the mass of the nation's farmers to share satisfactory increases in output.

4. 'The world food and agriculture situation is now in a stage of transition and hope'. The 'miracle' seeds and the increased application of fertilisers are spreading all over the world. In view of the poor quality of foodgrain processing, marketing and distribution systems, and the grave uncertainty regarding the world markets for Pakistani foodgrain exports, the prospects for earning foreign exchange by exporting the surplus grains are at best problematical.

5. The economic argument against rapid tractor-mechanisation in West Pakistan is as follows:

(*a*) It uses more of the nation's scarce resources and reduces the use of the abundant resource.

(*b*) Since water is the limiting factor in West Pakistan, the strategy that maximises output per unit of water (or per unit of irrigated acreage) is the most economical strategy. We do have well-known technology in this regard, thanks to the tubewell development and the green revolution.

(*c*) There is no evidence that tractor-mechanisation *per se* will increase yields; output per worker will rise only by causing unemployment.

(*d*) Tractor-mechanisation will not 'earn' foreign exchange, nor 'save' it.

6. A rapid tractor-mechanisation programme will create social and political problems.

(*a*) Given the economic-demographic characteristics of West Pakistan, it is important for the agricultural sector to absorb the residual increase in the labour force over and above those finding employment in the non-agricultural sectors.

(*b*) The pervasiveness of the green revolution cannot take place with tractor-mechanisation. Polarisation occurs in the ranks of the farming population because of the impossibility of maintaining support prices. The large will get larger, the small will get smaller.

(*c*) Tractor-mechanisation is an error from which it is difficult to recover because of the nature of short-run fixed costs associated with investment in tractors and creation of bottlenecks elsewhere.

7. Tractor-mechanisation diverts capital from other vitally needed areas. There is no overemphasising the fact that capital is needed in building up infrastructure, education and transportation systems. Even within the agricultural sector it is of vital importance to increase the provision of water and bio-logical-chemical inputs, such as fertilisers and pesticides. The fact that imported foodgrains feed the urban population rather than the rural in West Pakistan has geared the marketing and distribution systems to handling imported foodgrains exclusively. In Pakistan the marketing system, grading and processing procedures as well as transportation and storage facilities remain antiquated – a situation tolerable so long as the marketable surplus of agriculture remains meagre. The situation in West Pakistan has now changed. A rapid increase in output has now raised the marketable surplus and taxes the facilities for handling it. Attacks on these problem areas will compete for the scarce resources of capital and foreign exchange.

8. Capital formation in agriculture should most appropriately be in the form of small-scale, divisible, easily adaptable units to (*a*) remove bottlenecks, (*b*) involve the bulk of the nation's farmers, and (*c*) generate employment opportunities in agriculture. Instead of tractors and combines, serious attention should be paid to the machines designed for selected processes of farm operation, such as threshers, winnowers, sprayers, engines and pumps as well as improved animal-drawn implements.

9. The strategy of emphasising agricultural inputs of the type outlined in point 8 above will also generate investment opportunities for local industry and, therefore, employment opportunities also in that sector. This, in turn, will have beneficial effects on the agricultural sector by providing it with inputs at increasingly favourable terms and encouraging the use of them.

10. There is a pressing need to plan for changes in cropping patterns by shifting attention to crops such as cotton, pulses, oilseeds and sugarcane and by re-examining the structure of output prices.

Water is still the major constraint for the full realisation of the agricultural potential for this area. Despite the remarkable increase in the number of tubewells and the expansion of surface water supplies, many farms cannot yet realise the full benefits of the 'green revolution'. There are reports that the acreage of water-consuming crops, such as rice and sugarcane, is held back and even that the acreage planted under these crops has been ploughed under because of the shortage of water. Moreover, in many regions the needed fertiliser is not available at the right time. The recent growth in fertiliser consumption is indeed impressive, but the amounts being distributed come nowhere near the level required for the optimum performance of the agricultural sector. In short, there is ample scope for *further exploiting well-known techniques and factor combinations* for the benefit of the agricultural development of West Pakistan. Further development of the farm implement and tubewell industries, improvements in the seed/fertiliser distribution systems, investment in marketing and storage facilities – all of these things – may cost as much as tractor-mechanisation and may even press available domestic and foreign developmental resources to the limit. The returns to be reaped from such investment, however, would not only be more widespread, they would exceed by far that which is possible by tractor-mechanisation.

REFERENCES

[1] Aresvik, Oddvar, *Possible Export Price for Wheat*, mimeographed memorandum to Mr M. K. Bakhsh, ex-Minister for Food and Agriculture, Government of West Pakistan, 1968.

[2] Bean, L. L., Khan, M. R. and Rukanuddin, A. R. *Population Projections for Pakistan, 1960–2000*: monographs in the Economics of Development, no. 17 (Karachi: Pakistan Institute of Development Economics, 1968).

[3] Efferson, J. N., *Prospects for Expanding Export Markets for West Pakistan Rice*, mimeographed (Lahore: Planning Cell, Agriculture Department, Government of West Pakistan, 1968).

[4] Falcon, W. P. and Gotsch, C. H. *Agricultural Development in Pakistan: Lessons from the Second-Plan Period* mimeographed (Cambridge: Harvard University Economic Development Series, Report no. 6, 1966).

[5] Giles, G. W., *Toward a More Powerful Agriculture* mimeographed (Lahore: Planning Cell, Agriculture Department, Government of West Pakistan, 1967).

[6] Gill, M. S., 'Economics of Farm Mechanisation', *West Pakistan Journal of Agricultural Research*, vol. i, 1, Dec., 1962.

[7] Mohammad, Ghulam, 'Private Tubewell Development and Cropping Patterns in West Pakistan', *Pakistan Development Review*, v, 1, spring 1965.

Industry and Trade

Industry and Trade

Commentary

IN PREVIOUS sections of this book references have been made to the quasi-autarkic nature of Pakistan's industrialisation. In this section, Part Three, we have included several papers which analyse the effects of government controls over foreign trade on the nature and efficiency of the industrialisation process. No single set of economic policies has been more important in influencing the character of the industrialisation programme than the controls over foreign trade. There are three major aspects of the policy of trade control: the promotion of extreme and highly non-uniform rates of protection, the use of direct quantitative controls on imports through a detailed licensing scheme and the maintenance of an overvalued rate of exchange for the rupee.

Before analysing how these devices were responsible for widespread misallocation of resources in industry and other sectors, it is useful to consider the reasons and motives for adopting such controls. It is frequently suggested by the critics of these policies that direct controls are instituted by the governments of underdeveloped countries in the mistaken belief that they would promote the economic and social objectives that the governments set out to achieve. There is a tendency to regard these governments as slaves of some obsolete economic doctrine and to accuse the authorities of misinterpreting the arguments of economic theory. Thus, it is argued by the critics, the demonstration of theory that static comparative advantage in a free market does not usually provide the best answer to the problem of resource allocation in a developing economy is misinterpreted by the government as a recommendation to reject the market and the principle of comparative advantage entirely and to create, by arbitrary controls on trade, a system of incentives which has no correspondence to social priorities.

There are several reasons why such an explanation of the behaviour of the government does not appear plausible. For well over a decade, economists, local and foreign, in Pakistan and elsewhere, have been waging a crusade to liberate government from 'their habits of thought' and the 'slavery of obsolete doctrines'. But the government has retained the whole irrational system of controls largely intact.[1] Thus, to argue as above is to take the view that the process of learning is unimaginably slow, that the policymakers continue to fail to understand the real working of their policies despite intensive instruction by technical economists. This, in our opinion, is to grossly underestimate the intelligence and ability of the government and those who make its economic policies.

Rather than resorting to stupidity and irrationality on the part of the political leadership as an explanation, while attributing to them an imaginary set of objectives, it seems much more satisfactory to try to explain the behaviour of the government by referring to realistic objectives that might in fact have been pursued. At the time of political independence, Pakistan had no industry worth mentioning. Agriculture contributed more than two-thirds of domestic product and nearly all exports. The movement for Pakistan was led by an élite of Muslim landlords, traders and businessmen of India. This élite saw the opportunity for industrialising and modernising the nation through private enterprise, and this was attractive to them because it would ensure their leadership of the economy. The élite had no difficulty in getting their ideas accepted by a government which had come to rule in a country that was created on the basis of religious nationalism. The independence movement did not embody a commitment to any specific pattern of social and economic organisation.

The policy of the government from the beginning has been

---

[1] There have, of course, been changes in the methods of control and on occasion these have been hailed by the critics as significant steps toward 'liberalisation'. As we shall see below, such changes did not result in a significantly more rational system for identifying relative priorities.

one of utilising all its policy instruments to promote rapid industrialisation under the ownership and control of the emerging capitalist class. This strategy implied the need for rapid increase in the profits and assets of the new industrialists. The strategy was not based on the assumption that there was a correspondence between the objective of maximising the interest of this small group and the social objectives of maximising real national product, i.e. national product evaluated not at distorted market prices but at some sensible set of prices reflecting relative social scarcities, and ensuring its reasonable distribution at the margin. To the extent that the social objective was inconsistent with the narrow objective that the government pursued – and we shall see that they have been inconsistent – the former was sacrificed.

Given the financially weak position of the emerging capitalists at the time of independence, it was impossible for them to attain rapid industrialisation in a competitive, free market environment without massive assistance from the government. The decision that industry should be owned by the private sector and supported as much as necessary by the government was taken early and everything else followed as a natural consequence. Indirect monetary and fiscal measures could not be used effectively in a largely unmonetised economy; they were not powerful enough to effect a sufficient resource transfer to industry or to provide a large profit incentive to industrialists. Hence increasing reliance had to be placed on more direct methods of obtaining these objectives.

The major problem was, of course, to obtain a surplus for capital formation. The emerging entrepreneurs had very little capital of their own. Domestic credit institutions were undeveloped and could not effectively mobilise a sufficient amount of savings. Foreign assistance was not available in the early years after independence. The tax base was very narrow, in part because the capitalist sector was virtually non-existent. Moreover, one could not obtain a surplus by taxing the wealthy because this would make it even more difficult to foster industry through private enterprise. Thus the primary need was for a powerful mechanism which would extract a surplus from the economy and channel it into the hands of the emerging industrialists. Inevitably, agriculture was the sector which was called upon to generate such a surplus, since it accounted for a very large proportion of total economic activity.

Once a surplus was extracted, the next step was to protect the emerging industrialists from foreign competition.

Given the extremely simple economic structure of Pakistan, most of these objectives could be achieved by adopting a set of direct controls on foreign trade. The major elements of these controls were the maintenance of a highly overvalued rate of exchange for the rupee and the rationing of foreign exchange among capitalists through direct licensing. The sale of foreign currency at an overvalued rate of exchange for domestic rupees is equivalent to a tax on the producers of exportables – the poor agricultural farmers. The sale of import licenses at the official rate of exchange to traders and investors constituted a corresponding subsidy to the capitalists. The high premium at which imported consumption goods were sold in a domestic market starved of goods created the necessary surplus and directed it into the hands of the new capitalist class. This class was further strengthened by a policy of underpricing capital and maintaining a low cost of imported equipment and material. In addition, an incentive of high profits for investment was provided by the high protection granted to domestic manufacturing industries.

Rough quantitative measurements of the rate of 'primitive capital accumulation' have been made for Pakistan. These estimates indicate that nearly all investment in the manufacturing industries and perhaps a bit more (i.e. all investment and some of the consumption of the capitalists as well) was financed in this way. Assuming exports account for 7 per cent of G.D.P. and the rate of overvaluation is only a modest 50 per cent (i.e. 5 rupees exchange officially for $1 while in reality they should exchange for 67 cents), the rate of 'primitive capital accumulation' would be 3·5 per cent of G.D.P. in terms of domestic currency values. In the early post-independence period this would have been equi valent to approximately 6 per cent of agricultural production. Considering the regressive nature of the entire system, the burden on the poorer farmers could have been over 10 per cent of their income. The government could not have hoped to raise anything like this through direct or indirect taxation of agriculture.

It is true, of course, that the agricultural sector does not consist of a homogeneous group of income earners; within agriculture there are politically powerful landlords who could be expected to resist government measures which implied heavy concealed taxation on them. To understand how the burden of resource transfer was shared within agriculture, one must examine the regional question. Most of the primitive capital accumulation was made possible by extracting a surplus from East Pakistan. This arose quite 'naturally' because East Pakistan accounted for a larger share of exports than the West and a greater proportion of agricultural goods in total exports. Much of the surplus mobilised in the East, however, was transferred to West Pakistan. This was a result of the policy of distributing import licenses against the East's foreign exchange earnings to the traders and capitalists located in the West. Thus the resource transfer from agriculture to industry was intimately associated with a resource transfer from East to West. In East Pakistan landlordism ceased to exist after 1950 and the pattern of land distribution since then has been highly equitable. No privileged group in the East was hurt as a result of extracting a surplus from agriculture; it was the poor who suffered. In West Pakistan the distribution of land ownership was and still continues to be highly unequal. One would expect, therefore, that many privileged people in this wing would have been hurt. But in fact this did not occur. The big landlords were able in part to escape the effects of government policy and in part they were compensated for its effects. Quite a few big landlords entered industrial activities and benefited directly from the system of controls. In addition, there were significant subsidies to agriculture which could only be obtained by the richer farmers. For example, large farmers could obtain imported tractors at the overvalued rate of exchange; electric power for tubewells was subsidised, as was irrigation water; and in more recent years wheat farmers have benefited from price supports. In the 1960s the agricultural sector of West Pakistan contributed very little to the resource transfer, and the large landlords may have contributed nothing. Indeed they benefited enormously by the decision to postpone land reforms.

At the start of the last decade there appeared to be a trend in

Pakistan to replace several of the direct trade controls by somewhat more indirect ones. Quite a few economists, particularly foreign advisers, were ecstatic. At last their wise advice was being accepted! These economists regarded any small step towards greater use of the market in determining prices, however imperfect the market might be, as a major improvement. This judgement appears to have been reached without considering the relative rationality or efficiency of the two systems for allocating resources. Many observers believed simply that if at least one more price were determined by market supply and demand (however directly controlled these conditions might be) resource allocation was bound to improve; they did not consider whether the resulting set of prices conformed more closely to relative scarcities. Yet if one examines the period before and after the supposed 'relaxation' of controls one finds that in most cases there was a substitution of one form of direct control for another, usually more complicated one. The new controls were no less arbitrary than the old ones. Moreover, the motive for the change in the method of economic management seems to have been the same !as that which prompted the adoption of the original controls a decade earlier.

The most highly praised decontrol measure has been the adoption of the export bonus scheme. A number of exports were granted a bonus in the form of import entitlements (bonus vouchers) which could be sold in the market. A selected number of commodities could be imported against these vouchers. It is hard to understand why this was considered a great step towards a competitive market solution when the lists of commodities on which a bonus was allowed, the number of commodities which could be imported under the scheme and the rates of bonus were all determined directly, and in detail, by administrative decisions. The rates of bonus and the resulting rates of protection were highly discriminatory and arbitrary. There does not seem to be any basis for the belief that the new system resulted in a structure of relative prices significantly more rational than the one that prevailed under the régime of widespread import licensing.

Why was it necessary to make the changes? The brief answer is that the kinds of controls that were adequate for achieving a particular objective when the economy was relatively primitive were no longer suitable to promote the same objective at a time when the economy had become more complex and diversified. By the end of the 1950s a significant amount of industrialisation had taken place and the share of manufactured goods in exports had begun to rise. At this point the overvalued rate of exchange began to affect the export of manufactured goods as well. Yet a straightforward devaluation was not acceptable to the industrial capitalists because this would have reduced the net transfer of resources to them from the rest of the economy and made them pay the scarcity price for their imports of capital equipment and intermediate goods. In order to enjoy the best of both worlds, it was necessary to invent the complicated but more flexible régime of direct controls known as the export bonus scheme. This enabled the government to discriminate between sectors and activities by introducing a large number of exchange rates. Under this scheme exports of manufactured goods were entitled to a generous bonus. Later after capitalist farming spread in West Pakistan and started to produce an exportable surplus, a few agricultural items also were put on the bonus list. Most agricultural exports, however, especially those originating in East Pakistan, continued to receive payment at the unfavourable official rate. The industrialists and a handful of rich farmers in West Pakistan continued to import capital goods and intermediate supplies at the official rate of exchange. Part of the trader's profit that previously accrued to the licensed commercial importers was transferred to the producers of manufactured exports. This represented an income transfer from one rich group to another, and in fact the transfer often stayed within the family, since the same individuals were registered as two separate companies.

While the industrialisation programme that was encouraged by the controls on trade proved highly profitable to the private capitalists, it imposed tremendous loss on the society. One aspect of this loss, viz. the relative neglect of agriculture, has already been discussed. There is another consequence, however, that must be mentioned: increased inequality.

The income distribution effects of controls have also been unfavourable. This is largely because the sector that was discriminated against – agriculture – happens to be by far the poorest sector of the economy. Within agriculture, the smaller peasants seem to have been hit harder than the big landlords, since the latter were able to benefit relatively more from the programme of subsidising inputs and, of course, from the postponement of land reforms. The policies which led to a deterioration in the distribution of income were not neutral with respect to the two wings. The impact was much greater in the East. This was a consequence of the fact that East Pakistan was much more dependent on agriculture than the West. The East was also substantially poorer, yet it was from this region that resources were transferred in order to create industrial wealth in the major cities of the Punjab and Sind.

Resource misallocation was not confined to penalising agriculture and subsidising industry. The trade controls also led to a considerable distortion of *intra-industrial* priorities. It is this aspect of the control system that is discussed in great detail in three of the papers reprinted below in Part Three.

Both the earlier régime of complete import licensing and the present one of a partial export bonus scheme have resulted in non-uniformity of protection between various industries. Sectoral priorities within the industrial sector have become completely obscured, and the market prices and private profit incentives produced by the control system constitute a poor guide for the efficient allocation of investment. Capacity has been installed for the production of commodities in which the country does not have a comparative advantage – even after allowing for such things as infant industries and externalities. This is shown most dramatically in Soligo and Stern's paper, in which they argue that if outputs and inputs are valued in terms of world prices, some of the privately profitable industries in Pakistan actually make a negative contribution to value added. That is, they reduce national income absolutely. Nurul Islam finds that the degree of international competitiveness among Pakistan's industries varies considerably, and many suffer from a large comparative disadvantage. Gordon Winston shows how trade and exchange controls lead to many forms of waste in industry, including the wasteful use of foreign exchange and capital and the creation of excess capacity.

The intra-industrial misallocation of resources is not limited to the choice of wrong sectors. A related waste of very great importance is associated with the choice of wrong techniques of production. This results from the effects of trade controls on relative factor prices. In Pakistan, a large amount of capital equipment is imported from abroad. The rate of exchange is substantially overvalued and most of the equipment is imported by the actual users at very low rates of duty and sales tax. In consequence, the cost of capital to investors has been lower than its social cost. Moreover, there has been a policy of keeping the interest rate on bank loans low. In this way strong incentives were created for entrepreneurs to choose highly capital-intensive techniques from among the available alternatives. Furthermore, the low cost of capital has meant that the private cost of excess capacity was much lower than the social cost. As a consequence, the capital-labour ratio in many industries in Pakistan is higher than in countries in which labour is far less abundant.[1] The high degree of capital-intensity not only has resulted in the wasteful use of very scarce capital, it has also reduced the rate of expansion of employment in large-scale industry and thereby contributed to the growing inequality in the distribution of income.

[1] See A. R. Khan, 'Capital-Intensity and the Efficiency of Factor Use: The Case of Pakistan', *Pakistan Development Review*, summer 1970.

4 Tariff Protection, Import Substitution and Investment Efficiency

RONALD SOLIGO and JOSEPH STERN*

' . . . The important substitution effort will have to be intensified, particularly in capital goods and intermediate products, like base metals, chemicals, petroleum products and non-metallic minerals . . . The scarcity price of foreign exchange should be appropriately reflected to the economy so that there is an incentive to use less foreign exchange and more domestic resources. This will call for a revision in the present tariff policy. . . .' [11. p. 35].

' . . . The second important element in the [balance of payments] strategy is to develop an import pattern which will encourage savings and investment and extend the import substitution effort to a much wider front' [11, p. 79].

I. INTRODUCTION

A chronic deficit in the balance of payments is a problem which plagues almost all developing countries. In Pakistan, as in other countries, the development plans have contained a two-pronged approach to the problem: to increase exports and to reduce the need to import through a process of import substitution. Exports have been encouraged by giving numerous concessions and subsidies to the exporting firms[1] but the best known and most successful of the export-promotion schemes is the bonus-voucher system.[2]

* An extended version of this chapter originally appeared as an article in the summer 1965 issue of the *Pakistan Development Review*. The authors are indebted to Professor Nurul Islam, Dr Bruce Glassburner and Mr Asbjorn Bergan for their comments and suggestions, which have considerably improved the study.
   [1] For a detailed description of the export-promotion schemes which have been pursued in Pakistan since Partition, see [2].
   [2] For a description and analysis of the bonus-voucher scheme, see [1] .

Industrialisation has been pursued behind a wall of tariffs and import licensing which has provided generous incentives for the establishment in Pakistan of import-substituting industries. Within this framework of high protection to domestic industries and stiff barriers to foreign competition, manufacturing industries in Pakistan have indeed grown at a rapid rate [6; 13]. Pakistan's Third Five Year Plan [11] has taken cognisance of the need to develop and extend the import-substitution effort and, what is more, to use tariff policies to achieve this end.

The impressive gains which have taken place in industrialisation under the protection of tariffs and licences have always been used to justify the tariff policy. Yet the complexities of the economic system are such that what appears to be beneficial may, when looked at from the viewpoint of the whole economy, be less of a gain than one is led to believe at first, and may even be a loss to the economy. The purpose of this study is to examine, in light of the available data, the effects of past protection on the efficiency of investment allocation and to make some estimate of the implicit protection given to domestic industries by the present tariff structure in the absence of quantitative controls.

As is pointed out in Section II, the present tariff structure may have been inoperative in the past because of other trade barriers. But with sufficiently increased liberalisation of imports, it could become a major variable in determining the pattern of resource allocation in the future. Given the obvious need for import substitution, if the target for reducing dependence on foreign aid is to be realised, and the role that tariff policy must play in this effort, there can be no doubt that a serious effort to understand the full implications of the present tariff policy is warranted.

II. BACKGROUND TO THE PROBLEM

Two factors make import substitution an extremely attractive development strategy. First, a policy of encouraging import-substituting industries will produce results quickly since it permits indigenous entrepreneurs to exploit existing markets rather than forcing them to develop new markets for domestically produced goods. Second, import substitution makes an obvious and direct effort to save foreign exchange by substituting imports of raw materials for final manufactures while simultaneously increasing domestic value added.

For a number of reasons, a policy of import substitution often favours the development of consumer-goods-oriented industries. First, the markets which exist in developing economies are primarily for consumer goods. There being little or no indigenous manufacturing initially, the market for intermediate or capital goods is small or non-existent. Second, consumer-goods industries, by and large, require less capital investment than other industries, and often less skilled manpower – two factors which tend to be scarce in under developed economies. Finally, in order to raise revenue for the public treasury and/or to economise on scarce foreign exchange by discouraging 'non-essential' imports, developing countries generally levy high import duties on consumer goods. Equivalent taxes are not usually levied on domestically produced consumer goods because such taxes would conflict with the policy of providing encouragement for domestic industries over imports. Domestic industry requires, at least initially, a subsidy to overcome lack of experience and capital. Such a subsidy is usually given in the form of high tariffs on competing imports with low taxes on domestic output and low tariffs on imported capital and industrial inputs.

It has been pointed out, first by Power [14] and Khan[4] and more recently by Radhu [15] that Pakistan's tariff structure has indeed given substantially more protection to consumer 'non-essential' industries than to intermediate and capital-goods industries. However, Lewis and Qureshi [5], and also Radhu [15], have argued that the relative profitability of investment in different industries is affected as much by other government policies such as import licensing and the export-bonus scheme as by indirect taxes, and that these other factors have probably outweighed the tariff-created profit differentials. Lewis and Soligo [6] have more recently analysed the available data on the production, imports, and exports of manufactured goods and have concluded that over the period 1954/5 to 1963/4, import substitution has been equally important in both consumer goods and investment- and related-goods industries. In terms of percentage rates of growth, investment and related-goods industries have grown faster than both intermediate- and consumer-goods industries. Intermediate-goods industries have apparently grown more rapidly than consumer-goods industries.

While the work done by Lewis and Soligo [6] shows that import substitution and growth of output have taken place more or less equally in consumer, intermediate and capital-goods industries, the question still remains: has import substitution proceeded too far in consumer-goods industries? Has Pakistan used her scarce capital efficiently?

Power [14] and Khan [4] have argued that import substitution in consumer goods is not always a good thing. So long as consumer goods must be imported, the extreme scarcity of foreign exchange acts as an effective constraint to the expansion of consumption. Once consumer-goods industries have been established domestically, the discipline enforced by the supply of foreign exchange is to some extent removed. As the indigenous production of consumer goods increases, consumption is 'liberalised' and savings do not increase as quickly as they otherwise might. Ultimately, the rate of growth in real income will be lower when import substitution in consumer goods is permitted.

A second possible danger of import substitution is pointed out by Johnson [3] who notes that:

> ... the excess cost of import substitution may be high, appreciably higher than is implied by the tariff rates or the excess of domestic over foreign prices. Progressive import substitution could therefore easily absorb or more than absorb the potential increase in real income that would normally accrue from technical improvements and capital accumulation, and permit a country to accumulate capital at a substantial rate without achieving a significant increase in real income or in real income per head.

Import substitution, in so far as it departs from the principle of comparative advantage, may saddle a country with high-cost industries which can only survive behind a high protective wall. In fact, these industries may turn out to be so inefficient that the amount of protection that has to be provided to them is greater than their contribution in terms of value added.

In order to examine the issue raised by Johnson we must compute the implicit subsidy given to manufacturing industries in Pakistan by means of the tariff structure. As a country's tariff structure normally extends protection to intermediate products and raw materials as well as to final goods, the tariff acts as both a subsidy and a tax on domestic production. The tariff on competing imports of an industry allows the producer to raise the price of his product and in this respect the tariff is a subsidy to domestic production. On the other hand, the tariff on competing intermediate and raw-material inputs allows the domestic suppliers of such products to raise their prices and in this sense the tariff is a tax on domestic production. The implicit subsidy is the amount of protection a producer gets from the tariff structure after allowing for the fact that tariffs act as both a subsidy and tax on domestic production. The residual obtained by subtracting this subsidy from the current value added in the industry measures the value added (the amount which could be paid to the domestic factors of production) if tariff protection were removed and assuming that foreign exchange was valued at its real opportunity cost.

If the new value added, computed in the above manner, is less than what would be necessary to pay capital and labour inputs their real scarcity price, we may conclude, excepting those cases in which the 'infant' industry argument is applicable, that investment in that particular industry is inefficient, at least at the margin. Real income could, therefore, be increased by transferring resources from this industry to some other industry where factors of production are receiving their scarcity price.

As we point out in Section III, the above exercise is only correct under certain assumptions about the relationship of domestic prices to foreign prices. While these simplifying assumptions do not in fact hold for Pakistan, our results are such that, together with what information is available about the divergence of reality from our assumptions, we can draw some revealing and interesting conclusions regarding the efficiency of past allocation of capital and of the relative rates of protection to domestic value added inherent in the present tariff structure.

III. METHODOLOGICAL FRAMEWORK AND
SOURCES OF DATA

As we have pointed out in the previous section, the purpose of this paper is to examine the available data from the viewpoint of drawing some conclusions about the efficiency of past investment and to evaluate the bias inherent in the present tariff structure as measured by the implicit subsidy given to domestic value added. Because of the disequilibrium in the market for foreign exchange and the distortion which results from import licensing, it is not possible to deal definitively with the issues we have raised. In order to show clearly what can be said about investment efficiency and tariff protection with the data at hand, we first analyse the data within the framework of a simplified model which embodies several restrictive assumptions. We then discuss what effect the relaxation of these assumptions will have on our results.

In what follows, we first develop a simplified model and then analytically relax the assumptions. This exercise will clarify the difference between what we would like to measure and what in fact we can measure with our data. In Section IV, where we present our results, we discuss what the relaxation of the assumptions would mean with respect to the data we have used.

What we wish to measure is the implicit subsidy which would be given to domestic industry as a result of tariffs, where in fact the tariff structure is a determinant of relative domestic prices. Under such conditions, the subsidy is measured for each industry by taking the difference between what domestic factors of production receive in that industry with the given tariff structure (i.e. value added with the tariff structure) and what these same factors could be paid if the industry was required to operate within a framework of free trade, that is, where output was sold at 'world' prices and, similarly, inputs were purchased at 'world' prices.

Suppose the input-output structure for the ith manufacturing industry is given by:

$$X_i = \sum_{j=1}^{n} X_{ji} + W_i \qquad (1)$$

where: X_i = gross value of output in domestic prices of ith industry at factor cost

X_{ji} = total deliveries from industry j to industry i measured in domestic prices

W_i = value added in domestic prices of ith industry.

In order to measure the difference between actual value added, W_i, and what would be paid to domestic factors in the absence of trade barriers, we make two simplifying assumptions:

(i) that the official exchange rate reflects the scarcity price of foreign exchange; and

(ii) that the domestic price of any commodity is equal to the world price of a competing import plus domestic taxes on imports. That is,

$$P_{di} = P_{wi} (1 + t_i) \qquad (2)$$

where P_{di} = the domestic price for commodity i;

P_{wi} = the 'world' price for commodity i, converted at the official exchange rate; and

t_i = the tariff rate on commodity i.

We define

$$V_i = Y_i - \sum_{j=1}^{n} Y_{ji} \qquad (3)$$

where Y_i = the gross value of output of industry i at 'world' prices;

Y_{ji} = the value of the interindustry deliveries from industry j to industry i, expressed in 'world' prices;

V_i = the amount which could be paid to domestic factors of production in industry i if the output were sold, and inputs purchased, at 'world' prices, all converted at the official rate of exchange.

Using assumptions (i) and (ii), we have the following relationship between the variables in equations (1) and (3):

$$X_i = Y_i (1 + t_i) \qquad (4)$$
$$X_{ji} = Y_{ji} (1 + t_j)$$

Substituting (4) into (3), we have:

$$V_i = \frac{X_i}{(1 + t_i)} - \sum_{j=1}^{n} \frac{X_{ji}}{(1 + t_j)} \qquad (5)$$

It should be noted that V_i does not measure the amount which could be paid to domestic factors of production after all trade barriers were eliminated and the economy were permitted to find a new equilibrium position in terms of the exchange rate, relative prices, and so on. Rather, V_i measures the payments to domestic factors which would be possible, given the existing technology, as represented by the input-output coefficients, and the existing opportunity price of foreign exchange. This concept of V_i is the appropriate one, since we wish to determine the relative efficiency of domestic industries with the present technology and exchange rate.

The subsidy implicit in the tariff structure would then be given by:

$$W_i - V_i \qquad (6)$$

To make interindustry comparisons, one should compare the absolute subsidy as measured by equation (6) with total value added. Hence, we define:

$$U_i = \frac{W_i - V_i}{W_i} \qquad (7)$$

where U_i measures the proportion of domestic value added in current domestic prices which is subsidised by the tariff structure and, in this sense, is a measurement of the implicit rate of protection given to domestic value added by the tariff structure.

Equations (5) through (7) would permit us to evaluate the impact of the tariff structure provided the assumptions made above are correct. Unfortunately, assumptions (i) and (ii) are not valid for Pakistan. It is well known and has been demonstrated by Pal [12] that at the official rate of exchange there exists a scarcity margin on imports. That is to say, the present official exchange rate overvalues the rupee. Because of excess demand for foreign exchange at the official exchange rate, the available foreign exchange is allocated by means of import licensing[1] with the result that the scarcity margin for imports and competing domestic output will be different for each commodity.

[1] See Naqvi [7] for a description of the import licensing system.

Very little is known about the scarcity margin aside from Pal's study. He found that the margin did vary from commodity to commodity but, on the average, the scarcity margin on consumer goods was the same as on investment goods. Pal was concerned only with prices of imported goods and, hence, his study throws no light on those cases where the import taxes are so high that competing imports are completely absent from the market. In those cases, or where there is an outright embargo on imports, the domestic price could well be below the c.i.f. price plus import tariffs. Unfortunately, there is no information to either support or refute this proposition. We are, however, inclined to believe that there is likely to be excess demand in all commodity markets and, that as a *minimum*, domestic price does equal c.i.f. price and import taxes. That is to say that *at best* the scarcity margin is zero. This assumption is maintained throughout what follows.

How would the relaxation of assumptions (i) and (ii) affect the results computed from equations (5) to (7)? First, let us assume that although there is disequilibrium in the foreign-exchange market, the scarcity premium is equal for all commodities. Such a situation would arise if foreign exchange were auctioned and no controls were imposed on the composition of imports.

If this were the case, the V_i, computed by Equations (5) to (7), would represent V_i at the true scarcity price of foreign exchange and not at the official rate of exchange. This would still be the appropriate measure of V_i since it measures V_i at the current opportunity cost of foreign exchange. Similarly, U_i, computed from this V_i, would be the 'correct' measure of the implicit protection, given to domestic value added by the tariff structure. If one wished to measure the rate of protection given by both the tariff and the overvalued exchange rate then one should deflate V_i by the extent of overvaluation. Suppose that S is the scarcity margin, then this would change equation (5) to

$$V_i' = \frac{X_i}{(1 + t_i)(1 + S)} - \sum_{j=1}^{n} \frac{X_{ji}}{(1 + tj)(1 + S)} = \frac{V_i}{(1 + S)}$$
$$(5')$$

and equation (7) to:

$$U_i' = \frac{W_i - V_i'}{W_i} = \frac{W_i - \left[\frac{V_i}{(1+S)}\right]}{W_i} \qquad (7'')$$

The extent of the subsidy involved, and hence the absolute value of U_i, is a function of the scarcity margin. However, if S is equal for all industries, the ranking of the industries by U_i is not affected by the value of the scarcity margin.

Let us now assume, as is in fact the case, that the scarcity margin is different for each commodity. Calculating V_i from equation (5) now gives the amount which would be paid to domestic factors of production taking into account the vector of scarcity prices of foreign exchange which prevail. That is, V_i would measure the amount which could be paid to domestic factors under a multiple-exchange-rate system where the exchange rate for each commodity is equal to the present official exchange rate plus the scarcity margin on that commodity.

The amount which could be paid to domestic factors at the current official exchange rate, if both tariffs and licensing protection were withdrawn, would be:

$$V'' = \frac{X_i}{(1 + t_i)(1 + S_i)} - \sum_{j=1}^{n} \frac{X_{ij}}{(1 + t_j)(1 + S_j)} \qquad (5'')$$

where S_i and S_j are the scarcity margins on the i-th and j-th commodity, respectively.

In what follows we have computed V_i and U_i using equation (5), and on this basis draw some conclusions about the relative ranking of V_i and U_i as if they had been calculated by equation (5'').

We feel that there is some justification for making the jump from equation (5) to equation (5'') because (*a*) the data we use give imported inputs at c.i.f. prices. This means that for these intermediate inputs we do not need to know either t_j or S_j to compute their value at world prices (at the official rate of exchange); and (*b*) domestic intermediate deliveries are predominantly either commodities which are also exported, such as raw cotton and jute, and for which the scarcity margin is zero, or services which cannot be traded in the international markets and, hence, for which 'world' prices are irrelevant.

The net result of (*a*) and (*b*) is that the proportion of intermediate inputs for which we need to know the value of the scarcity margin is small and that the bias in the value of V_i and U_i, computed on the basis of equation (5), is primarily determined by S_i, the scarcity margin on the output of the industry. Since Pal [12] shows that as a group the scarcity margin is the same for consumer goods and investment goods, our comparison of these two groups of industries, using U_i, is reasonable. Within groups, the ranking of industries on the basis of the computed V_i and U_i will differ from the 'true' ranking, that is to say the ranking which we would derive from our results if we had all the required data, depending on the extent to which the scarcity margins on the output of these industries differ.

Data on the interindustry relationships in Pakistan are available from the Tims-Stern input-output table prepared for the Planning Commission [10]. Explicit rates of tariff, t_i and t_j, have been derived from [15]. These estimates were modified in the following way.[1] First, Radhu's estimates are simple arithmetic averages of duties for all commodities within a group. Rather than accept these broad averages, we have (i) in the case of outputs taken the duties on only those commodities which are actually produced in Pakistan, and (ii) in the case of intermediate inputs, we have taken the rates of duty only on the specific inputs used in any given industry. Rates of duty on specific commodities have been taken from [9], while detailed information on composition of outputs and inputs for each industry is available from [8]. Secondly, Radhu's estimates include sales taxes in addition to import tariffs. Since we are working with output at factor cost, we have added the sales taxes only in those cases where domestic production is exempted from them. In those cases, the sales tax acts as additional tariff protection since it is levied only on competing

[1] We wish to express our appreciation to Mr Ghulam Mohammad Radhu for assisting us in revising some of the average rates of duty and for guiding us through all the manifold intricacies of the indirect tax structure. Although we have tried to take account of all the duties and taxes, inclusions and exclusions, the responsibility for any remaining errors rests exclusively with the authors.

imports. Finally, Radhu's data deal with the tariff structure as of 1962/3. We have incorporated the few changes in import duties and sales taxes which have become effective in 1963/4.

IV. ESTIMATES OF TARIFF PROTECTION AFFORDED TO VALUE ADDED

In this section, we discuss the significance of our computed U_i coefficients, compare them to other variables and parameters, and suggest some possible qualifications of our results.

We have computed U_i (the ratio of net subsidy from tariffs to value added) for some forty-eight manufacturing industries. These are shown in Table 4.1.

In three industries, grain milling, rice milling, and printing and publishing, the protection given to value added is negative, or, what is the same thing, the net effect of the tariff structure is to tax the output of these industries. This is not surprising in view of the fact that in all three cases the explicit rate of tariff protection given to the output of the industry is zero while tariffs are levied on inputs used in these industries.

In all other cases, U_i is greater than zero; that is, the rate of tariff on output is sufficiently high to more than offset the addition to cost which arises from the protection given to the suppliers of inputs. For these industries, the net effect of the tariff structure is to subsidise their value added; to permit them to pay a higher return to labour and capital than they would be able to pay if exposed to unfettered world competition.

There are considerable interindustry differences in the rates of protection given to value added. In general: (i) consumer goods are much more heavily protected than either intermediate or investment and related goods; (ii) within the consumer-goods industries, non-essentials, such as beverages and cigarettes, are much more heavily protected than essential industries such as grain and rice milling, salt and tea; (iii) textiles are the most heavily protected group of industries, although the protection is approximately the same for all components of the group; and (iv) the least protected industries are those producing heavy machinery, both electrical and non-electrical, and transport equipment other than motor vehicles and cycles. Fertiliser is also among the least protected group.

TABLE 4.1

IMPLICIT RATE OF PROTECTION OF VALUE ADDED

Consumer goods	U_t
(i) Food, beverage and tobacco	
Canning and preserving	3·11
Grain milling	−0·27
Rice milling	−0·10
Bakery products	1·21
Sugar	1·15
Edible oils and fats	2·02
Tea	0·45
Salt	0·78
Beverages (non-alcoholic)	1·08
Cigarettes	1·30
(ii) Textile, wearing apparel and footwear	
Cotton textiles	1·52
Woollen textiles	1·46
Silk and art silk	1·41
Knitting	1·30
Footwear	1·04
Wearing apparel	2·17
(iii) Other consumable goods	
Wood products (furniture)	1·84
Printing and publishing	−0·15
Leather goods	1·12
Soap, perfumes and cosmetics	0·64
Matches	0·92
Optical goods	0·31
Plastic hoods	0·77
Sports goods	0·48
Pencils and pens	0·39

Intermediate goods	U_t
Jute textiles	1·52
Dyeing and finishing	1·38
Thread and threadball	1·45
Saw milling	1·52
Tanning	2·11
Rubber products	0·81
Fertilisers	0·18
Paints and varnishes	0·46
Pharm., and chem., n.e.c.	0·33
Petroleum and coal products	1·01
Paper products	0·59

Investment and related goods	
Metal furniture	2·53
Non-metallic products	0·46
Cement	0·58
Basic metals	0·58
Metal products	0·98
Nonelectrical machinery	0·11
Sewing machinery	0·78
Electrical appliances	0·67
Electrical machinery	0·25
Other transport	0·33
Motor vehicles	3·96
Cycles	1·61

In twenty-three industries, the coefficient U_t is greater than unity. For these industries, the net subsidy received through tariff protection exceeds the total value added! These results are surprising, particularly because these industries are (i) primarily consumer-goods industries, and (ii) include very large industries (in terms of value added) such as cotton and jute textiles, sugar, tobacco, and coal and petroleum products.

What is the meaning of U_i greater than unity? From our definition of U_i, it is readily apparent that $U_i > 1$ implies that V_i is negative. From equation (7) we have:

$$U_i = \frac{W_i - V_i}{W_i}$$

or

$$U_i = 1 - \frac{V_i}{W_i}$$

V_i measures the amount which could be paid to capital and labour if output was sold and those inputs which can be traded were purchased at 'world' prices when converted at the official rate of exchange. A negative V_i means that the total cost of intermediate inputs valued at their 'world' prices, or at their domestic price, if they cannot be traded,[1] exceeds the value of output when expressed in 'world' prices. V_i could then be negative for two reasons: (i) intermediate inputs are used more inefficiently in Pakistan than in other countries. There may be more wastage of raw materials and services in Pakistan due to poor maintenance of machinery, inefficient quality control or lack of alternative uses for scrap, waste and some by-products because transport costs may be too high to permit these to be disposed off profitably. (ii) The price of domestically produced services, which cannot be imported, may be higher than the price of similar services in other countries. Electricity and motorised transport are two particular examples where cost per unit output is probably higher than in other countries.[2] If this be so, then our conclusions would indicate

[1] We assume that at the given supply, the current domestic price of these inputs is equal to their scarcity price.

[2] At least this is often alleged to be the case by industrialists. An international comparison of these costs, although not within the scope of this paper, would be extremely interesting and would throw considerable light on our findings. Although we have not attempted to make any international comparisons, we have made an interindustry comparison of these costs. The rank correlation coefficient between U_i and the cost of electricity, gas, water, and all other services was insignificant. Nevertheless, for some specific industries, the cost of electricity, gas, water, and services may be a contributing factor to the negative V_i.

that Pakistan should not invest in those industries which are intensive users of these inputs.

Whatever factors are the cause, a negative V_i is nevertheless surprising for it is equivalent to saying that the average revenue product of capital and labour is negative.

The data in Table 4.1 suggest that the following industries are cases of either over-expansion, premature investment, or of an infant industry:

    (i) all food, beverages, and tobacco except grain and rice milling, tea and salt;
   (ii) textiles, footwear and wearing apparel;
  (iii) leather and leather goods;
  (iv) wood and wood products;
   (v) motor vehicles, cycles and metal furniture.

Some of these industries may be genuine cases of 'infant industries' and our conclusions should be modified accordingly. On the other hand, looking at the list of industries in Table 4.1, it is clear that most of the industries with negative average product of labour and capital, that is with $U_i > 1$, are not likely candidates for the 'infant industry' argument. Most of the largest industries in Pakistan are in this group while many of the investment-goods industries which are relatively very small compared to other industries in Pakistan and to their counterparts in other countries have positive average product for capital and labour.

In terms of general categories of industries, investment has been either premature or over-extended, primarily in consumer-goods industries.

Power [14] and Khan [4] have criticised tariff, tax, import licensing and other policies which affect the pattern of investment on the grounds that they have permitted a too-rapid expansion of consumer-goods industries which in turn has led to 'consumption liberalisation', and reduced savings and growth in real income. Our results indicate that in addition to the effects on real income growth through reduced savings, the investment in consumer-goods industries has reduced growth in real income because, at world market prices, the marginal productivity of domestic capital and labour is below their opportunity cost and may even be negative.

Our data also indicate that the most productive use of capital in the future lies in the investment and related-goods industries. These industries have been able to survive, and indeed grow rapidly, with only relatively modest tariff protection. It is clearly in these industries in which Pakistan has a comparative advantage, which she should now go on to exploit. Our study, of course, has only compared the tariff protection given to different manufacturing industries. We have not compared the manufacturing sector as a whole with other sectors such as agriculture or mining. Our conclusions refer only to the relative profitability of different industries within the manufacturing sector. It may well be that investment in manufacturing as a whole is less productive than in other sectors.

REFERENCES

[1] Bruton, Henry J. and Bose, S. R., *The Pakistan Export Bonus Scheme* (Karachi: Pakistan Institute of Development Economics, 1963).

[2] Hecox, Walter E., *The Use of Import Privileges as Incentive to Exporters in Pakistan*, mimeographed Research Report 30 (Karachi: Pakistan Institute of Development Economics, June 1965).

[3] Johnson, Harry G., 'Tariffs and Economic Development', *Journal of Development Studies*, Oct. 1964.

[4] Khan, Azizur Rahman, 'Import Substitution, Export Expansion and Consumption Liberalization: A Preliminary Report', *Pakistan Development Review*, III, 2, summer 1963.

[5] Lewis, S. R. (Jr.) and Qureshi, S. K. 'The Structure of Revenue from Indirect Taxes in Pakistan', *Pakistan Development Review*, IV, 3, autumn 1964.

[6] Lewis, S. R. (Jr.) and Soligo, Ronald, 'Growth and Structural Change in Pakistan's Manufacturing Industry, 1954–1964', *Pakistan Development Review*, V, 1, spring 1965.

[7] Naqvi, Syed Nawab Haider, 'Import Licensing in Pakistan', *Pakistan Development Review*, IV, 1, spring 1964.

[8] Pakistan, Central Statistical Office, *Census of Manufacturing Industries, 1959–60* (Karachi: Manager of Publications, 1962).

[9] Pakistan, Ministry of Commerce, *Pakistan Customs Tariff* (Karachi: Manager of Publications, Feb. 1965).

[10] Pakistan, Planning Commission, International Economics Section, *Methodology of Estimating Import Requirements*, mimeographed (Karachi: Planning Commission, Mar. 1965).

[11] Pakistan, Planning Commission, *The Third Five-Year Plan, 1965–70* (Karachi: Manager of Publications, Mar. 1965).

[12] Pal, Mati Lal, 'The Determinants of the Domestic Prices of Imports', *Pakistan Development Review*, IV, 4, winter 1964.

[13] Papanek, Gustav F., 'Industrial Production and Investment in Pakistan', *Pakistan Development Review*, IV, 3, autumn 1964.

[14] Power, John H. 'Industrialization in Pakistan: A Case of Frustrated Take-Off?', *Pakistan Development Review*, III, 2, summer 1963.

[15] Radhu, Ghulam Mohammad, 'The Rate Structure of Indirect Taxes in Pakistan', *Pakistan Development Review* IV, 3, autumn 1964.

5 Comparative Costs, Factor Proportions and Industrial Efficiency in Pakistan

NURUL ISLAM*

THIS paper contains, in Section I, new and additional 'evidence on the comparative costs of manufacturing industries in Pakistan. Comparative costs in this context are defined as the ratios of ex-factory prices of specific domestic products to c.i.f. prices of closely competing imports. In Section II, we examine whether tariff rates are an adequate index of comparative cost ratios, i.e., in other words, whether the differences in the tariff rates reflect the differential cost structure of Pakistani industries. We also examine, in Section III, whether the available data provide any evidence on the relationship between the magnitude of cost disabilities of the Pakistani industries and their stage of infancy, i.e. whether and to what extent cost ratios decline with the growing up of infant industries. This paper also analyses in Sections IV and V how far comparative cost ratios can be used as a measure of the relative inefficiency of industries in Pakistan. How far, for example, do the high cost ratios of domesdic industries merely indicate that the Pakistani rupee is overvalued? How far are the cost ratios affected by or represent high profits of industries? An attempt is made to adjust for both the overvaluation of foreign exchange and the prevalence of abnormally high profits. Finally, in Section VI, we relate the comparative cost ratios of manufacturing industries to their factor intensities or their factor proportions in an attempt to explore whether relative efficiency is correlated with the relative

* An extended version of this chapter was published originally in the *Pakistan Development Review*, summer 1967. The author is grateful to Professor Marvin E. Rozen and Gordon Winston for helpful comments on an earlier version of this paper.

intensity of use of the different factors such as capital, labour, and skill.

I. EVIDENCE ON COMPARATIVE COST RATIOS

Pakistan's impressive achievement in the growth of the industrial sector has attracted a considerable amount of analysis, especially with respect to the pattern or strategy of industrialisation and the efficiency of the industrialisation programme. In this paper we attempt to analyse the comparative cost structure of Pakistani industries, based on a direct estimate of the costs of the individual manufactured goods and the c.i.f. prices of closely competing import products. The data are derived from the published and unpublished reports of the Pakistan Tariff Commission on 115 industries scattered over a 15 year period, i.e. 1951–66.[1] The analysis covers about 359 products. They in no sense, therefore, constitute a random sample from the manufacturing sector as a whole. The most important industries such as cotton textiles, jute textiles, woollen textiles and fertilisers are not included at all in this analysis since they have not been subject to investigation by the Tariff Commission. For the same reason there are also important omissions from within such industry groups as machinery, both electrical and otherwise, and transport equipment. The industries covered here, moreover, range over both the large-scale and small-scale manufacturing sectors. The difference in cost conditions between large and small firms is ignored in the analysis.

The total number of establishments or firms covered in the present analysis, excluding such industries as the coir goods industry, washing soap industry, leather footwear industry and bidi industry, where small firms predominate, is around 1164. This number, however, still includes a few small firms in a number of industries such as paints and varnishes, non-metallic mineral products, engine turbines, etc., which are included in the analysis. Since the number of establishments in the large-scale manufacturing sector as reported in the revised 1959–60

[1] All the data relating to cost ratios, unless otherwise specified, are from [9a]. The specific reports have not been cited and in some cases the reports have not been published so far. The cost data relating to sugar, cement and paper are taken from [3, pp. 121–8].

Census of Manufacturing Industries is about 3800, our coverage is quite large . . .[1]

The average cost ratios have been computed in three different ways for each of the time periods. Firstly, the simple averages of the cost ratios have been computed for the periods 1951–5, 1956–60 and 1961–6 respectively. Secondly, for each period, the individual industry ratios have been computed as a simple average of the cost ratios for individual products covered by an industry. The output data relating to individual products are not available; in fact, in the majority of the cases data relating to the value of output of an individual industry are not available, so that output cannot be used as weights. Accordingly, the number of products produced by each individual industry is used as weights to arrive at an estimate of the average cost ratio for all the industries in each of the time periods. Thirdly, an attempt was made to classify the individual industries into major groups, following the classification used by Pakistan Standard Industrial Classification, which is also used by the Pakistan Censuses of Manufactures. The cost ratios for these major groups have been computed by weighting the individual industry ratios by the number of products covered by them. But then in the next stage, the cost ratios of the major groups of industries are combined together by using as weights the values of gross output of each of the major groups of industries as given in the censuses. This average cost ratio is obtained for each period. The three sets of ratios are given below:

TABLE 5.1

COMPARATIVE COST RATIOS

	1951–5	*1956–60*	*1961–6*
		(Average values)	
(A)	1·56 (1·49)	1·40	1·83 (1·66)
(B)	1·65 (1·57)	1·62	1·83 (1·70)
(C)	1·56	1·33	2·16
			(median values)
	1·43	1·40–1·42	1·64–1·65

[1] Since data on the value of output of industries covered in this analysis are not available it has not been possible to estimate the proportion of total industrial output which the industries covered by the present study contribute.

The cost ratios are based on ex-factory prices without indirect taxes. The (A) ratios are unweighted, simple averages of individual industry ratios; (B) ratios are based on the number of products produced by each industry as weights; and the (C) ratios are based on the number of products as weights for deriving the cost ratios of each major industry group which are then weighted by the values of output of each major group of industry. Each of the three different systems of weighting has its own limitations. The best weights would have been the value of output of each individual industry to which a cost ratio relates. However, data on the value of output of each individual industry are not available. The first method, in fact, implies an equal weight to every ratio. To the extent that the relative numbers of products produced by different industries diverge widely from the relative outputs of different industries, the (B) ratios may contain a bias in favour of industries with a greater diversity of products. The (C) ratios are based on the appropriate weights in so far as the weights for the cost ratio of each major group of industry are concerned, even though the cost ratio for each major group suffers from the same limitation as that of the (B) ratios. The (A) and (B) sets of cost ratios are roughly comparable. The changes in the cost ratios of all the three sets between the different time periods are in the same direction. They all go down in the second period and go up in the third. The ratios within brackets exclude the extreme values above 3·00, of which there are about four to five items for the whole period. The ex-factory prices, on the average, are about 50–90 per cent higher than the corresponding c.i.f. prices in the different time periods whereas the median values of the excess of the ex-factory price over the c.i.f. prices range between 40–65 per cent.

The cost ratios of three out of 62 industries in the period 1961–6, two out of 29 industries in the period 1951–5, and five out of 24 industries in the period 1956–60 were less than one; this implies that they were highly competitive and their prices were less than the c.i.f. prices of competing products.

An attempt has been made to classify the industries into three groups, i.e. consumer goods, intermediate goods and raw materials, and capital goods; and to examine how the cost ratios differ between these three groups of industries.

The cost ratios are given below:[1]

TABLE 5.2

COST RATIOS (WITHOUT INDIRECT TAXES)

	Consumer goods	Intermediate goods	Capital goods
Simple average	1·58 (1·34)	1·78 (1·68)	1·70
Median value	1·40	1·58	1·62
Weighted average*	1·60 (1·43)	1·87 (1·77)	1·77

* The weighted average ratios used hereafter in this paper are based on the number of products relating to a particular industry.

The cost ratios computed by the different methods for consumer goods are consistently lower than those for the other two categories, whereas as between the intermediate and capital goods, both the weighted and simple average cost ratios of the former are higher than that of the latter. But the differences between the cost ratios of the two latter categories virtually disappear when the extreme values are omitted, as indicated in the above table . . .

The greatest number of consumer goods industries, i.e. 49 per cent of the total, have cost ratios between 1·00 and 1·50 and about 23 per cent have cost ratios between 1·50 and 2·00; in the case of intermediate and investment goods an almost equal percentage of industries, i.e. between 33 and 38 per cent, have cost ratios ranging between (*a*) 1·00 and 1·50 and (*b*) 1·51 – 2·00 respectively. About 20 per cent and 15 per cent respectively of the intermediate and capital goods industries have cost ratios between 2·00 and 2·50, whereas only about 8 per cent of the consumer goods fall in this range. The range of cost ratios derived above seem to compare well with the results of an earlier study.[2]

II. COMPARATIVE COSTS AND TARIFFS

A pertinent question relating to the measurement of comparative costs is whether and to what extent tariff rates measure

---

[1] The ratios within brackets exclude extreme values and are weighted averages, weights being the number of products in each industry.

[2] [6]. Unweighted averages in Table 5.3 are simple averages of cost ratios and weights used in the estimation of weighted averages are the values of imports of individual items or of the category of commodity to which the item belongs.

or fail to measure comparative costs. In a régime of quantitative restrictions the usual assumption is that tariffs underestimate the excess cost of the domestic product over the c.i.f. price of the competing imports. Therefore, the tariff rates on different commodities may not reflect the cost disadvantages of the producing industries.

Another hypothesis suggests that the excess of ex-factory prices (inclusive of indirect taxes) over landed costs (inclusive of excise and sales taxes) is a uniform percentage of landed costs for all commodities. Thus Soligo and Stern, in their analysis of effective protection, derive the world prices of the domestic products by deflating the domestic prices by tariffs alone, ignoring scarcity margins.[1] They assume that as a group the scarcity margin is the same for consumer goods and investment goods and that domestic prices are at least equal to the c.i.f. price of a competing import converted at the official exchange rate plus import duties. Thus where scarcity margins are positive, tariffs alone will understate cost disadvantage, and where scarcity margins are negative, the cost disadvantage of domestic industries will be overstated. The following analysis provides additional evidence on the overall magnitude, both positive and negative, of interindustry differences in scarcity margins.

TABLE 5.3

RATIO OF ACTUAL EX-FACTORY PRICE TO LANDED COSTS

Year	Equal to one No. of items	Below one		Above one	
		No. of items	Average ratio	No. of items	Average ratio
1951–5	—	9	0·75	22	1·29
1956–60	2	21	0·72	27	1·42
1961–6	5	47	0·75	120	1·47

In the majority of cases ex-factory price exceeds landed cost (67 per cent of the total number of items), whereas in 30 per cent of the cases it falls short of the landed cost. In a very few (about 3 per cent) they are equal. An ex-factory price below landed costs may imply either that for these products the

[1] [1, pp. 249–66].

tariffs are redundant, or that the domestic product fetches a lower price because of inferior quality. Even when rates are determined by the Tariff Commission, at a particular moment of time tariffs and quotas may be out of line with the divergence between the c.i.f. and the ex-factory price. Often these rates and quotas are fixed without reference to the Tariff Commission and hence without any reference to the divergence between the ex-factory price and the c.i.f. price of the competing product. Moreover, an industry which starts out with its ex-factory price being equal to or higher than the landed cost, both because of high profits as well as of high costs, may after a period not only reduce costs but also earn lower profits owing to increasing competition.

In many cases the available data on ex-factory prices relate to fair ex-factory prices rather than to actual prices. For the purposes of the estimate of scarcity margins, 'fair' prices have been used only when actual prices are not available so that the former provides additional evidence on the magnitude of scarcity margins. To the extent that fair prices are lower than actual prices, which is the case in the great majority of cases, excepting where firms were making losses, the corresponding scarcity margins are an underestimate of the actual scarcity margins. Sixty per cent of the items have positive scarcity margins varying between 43 and 73 per cent as seen below:

TABLE 5.4
RATIO OF FAIR EX-FACTORY PRICE TO LANDED COSTS

Year	Equal to one	Below one		Above one	
	No. of items	No. of items	Average ratio	No. of items	Average ratio
1951–5	1	23	0·80	40	1·43
1956–60	—	12	0·72	12	1·73
1961–6	—	6	0·65	13	1·43

Thus the general range of the positive scarcity margins in the case of both fair price and actual price are as high as 30–50 per cent above landed costs except for the period 1956/60, when the margin for 'fair price' went up as high as 73 per cent above the landed costs. In many cases, ex-factory prices are below landed costs by about 25–30 per cent . . .

III. COMPARATIVE COSTS AND INFANT INDUSTRIES

In a young industrialising economy, infant industries start out with high costs which, with the acquisition of skill and experience in terms of management and technical knowledge, are expected to decline over the years. Accordingly, cost ratios may be related to the age of the individual industries. It may be argued that an older industry, irrespective of its nature, benefits more from the growth of external economies and an industrial milieu. The cost ratios of the different industries on the basis of the number of years of their operation can be combined in a few limited number of broad groups as follows:

TABLE 5.5

No. of firms	No. of products	No. of years in operation	Comparative cost ratios	
			Unweighted	Weighted
41	131	1–5	1·54	1·61
25	112	6–10	1·61	1·65
23	49	11–20	1·46	1·61
2	4	21–30	1·34	1·34
2	12	31 and above	1·61	1·83

There does not appear to be any clear relationship between length of life and comparative cost ratios. However, the data presented above do not provide an adequate test of the hypothesis, partly because the composition of industries in different age groups is different and partly because the number of industries which have operated for a long period, i.e. above 20 years or so, is very small . . .

Our analysis, therefore, does not appear to provide a satisfactory or conclusive answer to the problem of the behaviour of cost ratios over time. Partly these comparisons are constrained because each industry group contains a large variety of products and activities whose cost behaviour over time may differ widely. An earlier analysis of the fifteen specific industries for which the cost ratios were reviewed by the Tariff Commission indicated an improvement in comparative efficiency in the course of ten to fifteen years. They covered abour forty individual products. For seven industries and sixteen products the cost ratios declined by 25 per cent to 60 per cent. The rest of the cost ratios declined by 5 per cent to 24 per cent [4, Table 3, p. 11].

An analysis of the cost ratios over time by itself may not provide an adequate test of the infant industry hypothesis. The cost ratios may turn unfavourable even when there is an improvement in efficiency and productivity in the domestic industry because the costs of competing imports may fall faster as a result of more rapid technological progress in the advanced countries. The problem is then one of the speed of technological advance in developed countries and a lag in the developing countries in the process of 'catching up'. This suggests that a more detailed analysis of the changes in the productive efficiency of domestic industries over time is necessary; this necessitates an identification of the changes in costs which are not due to (*a*) changes in wage rates, (*b*) profits, and (*c*) input prices over time, since it is an improvement in efficiency in the use of inputs through a learning process, as distinct from technological advance, that is involved in the infant industry argument. The improvement in efficiency in this sense should be compared with the c.i.f. prices which would have prevailed in the absence of technological advance. The statistical testing of a comparative cost analysis in a dynamic context of technological change thus confronts formidable difficulties.

IV. COMPARATIVE COSTS AND OVERVALUATION OF FOREIGN EXCHANGE

The comparative cost ratios in the preceding paragraphs have been obtained on the basis of the official exchange rate. To the extent that the Pakistani currency is overvalued, of which there is some evidence, comparative cost ratios greater than one really reflect the overvaluation of the currency, so that with an equilibrium rate of exchange all the cost ratios will be equal to each other and equal to one. The Pakistani rupee was devalued in 1955 and the fall in the average cost ratio between the periods, 1951–5 and 1956–60 may be partly traced to this fact, since with devaluation the c.i.f. price of imports in rupees increased.

One may, therefore, suggest that the comparative cost ratios should be corrected for the relative overvaluation of the currency. Study of the domestic prices of imports as well as analysis of the amount of subsidy implicit in the export bonus scheme suggests that the assumption of a 50 per cent overvaluation in the price of foreign exchange in Pakistan may be a reasonable one. It is not easy to estimate what would be the equilibrium rate of exchange in a free market with existing tariffs and domestic fiscal and monetary policies; supply and demand elasticities of exports and imports as well as that of demand and supply of domestic substitutes, etc., enter into the picture in a complicated way. The assumption of 50 per cent overvaluation may not be far out of line for use as an illustration, however. The adjustment in the comparative costs ratio for alternative estimates of overvaluation of exchange is easily done.

As a result of the correction for the overvaluation of exchange, the comparative cost disadvantage declines and the number of industries which have cost ratios below one and, therefore, are competitive are as follows:

TABLE 5.6

Cost ratios		Number of industries		
	1951–5	*1956–60*	*1961–6*	*Total*
Below one	17 (0·84)	14 (0·73)	26 (0·83)	57
Above one	12 (1·33)	10 (1·27)	36 (1·50)	58

For the period as a whole about half of the total number of industries appear to be competitive with imports while the other half have a cost ratio greater than one. The overall weighted cost ratios for the three periods after adjustment for the price of foreign exchange are 1·08 for 1951–5, 1·08 for 1956–60 and 1·21 for 1961–6. The weighted ratios for different groups of industries for the whole period are as follows:

Consumer goods	..	..	1·03
Intermediate goods	..	..	1·24
Capital goods	..	..	1·19

The consumer goods industries appear competitive whereas the capital goods industry is 19 per cent more expensive and intermediate goods industry 24 per cent more expensive than competing imports.

The correction of the cost ratios for the relative overvaluation of the currency, as shown above, is only partial in so far as it corrects the c.i.f. price of the competing imports in domestic currency and does not correct the import component of the domestic ex-factory price in domestic currency. The import component becomes more expensive in terms of domestic currency consequent on a correction for the overvaluation of foreign exchange. Data on the foreign exchange component of all the products are not available. In the case of only twenty-nine industries and their corresponding one hundred and seven products, the foreign exchange component (current requirements of imported raw materials and spare parts) is available and the result of adjustment for the value of foreign exchange is given below:

TABLE 5.7

COST RATIOS ADJUSTED FOR OVERVALUATION OF THE EXCHANGE RATE

	Unadjusted	Adjusted	Adjusted only for c.i.f. price
Consumer goods	2·29	1·66	1·53
Intermediate goods	1·82	1·45	1·20
Capital goods	1·79	1·33	1·33
Total	1·86	1·44	1·24

Thus the cost ratio for all industries declines from 1·86 to 1·44, i.e. about 23 per cent. It is important to mention that neither adjustment for the value of foreign exchange alters the ranking of the twenty-nine industries or three broad categories of industries, either in terms of the ex-factory price, or the foreign exchange component of the ex-factory price, or the comparative cost ratios.

V. PROFITS, MARKET STRUCTURE AND EXCESS CAPACITY

One important aspect of the analysis of comparative cost ratios on the basis of ex-factory prices is the extent to which the high ex-factory prices may be due to high profits or high factor prices in the relevant industries. If factor costs do not represent scarcity prices but contain large monopoly or rent elements due to institutional factors and the imperfections of markets, a high ex-factory price is not an index of comparative disadvantage or inefficiency but represents a transfer from the rest of the community to the factors employed in the industries concerned. The industrial wage for unskilled workers is generally presumed to be higher than the agricultural wage by more that what is accounted for by the costs of movement. Again, the wage rate is higher in organised industries than in unorganised, small-scale industries. Even larger firms in the same industry are found to pay higher wage rates than the smaller firms. One could argue that the kinds of labour employed in large- and small-scale industries or in large and small firms in the same industry are sufficiently different in terms of work, discipline and ability as to account for the wage differentials. These are issues on which conclusive answers are not yet available. There is some evidence, however, which permits at least a partial examination of how far excess profits may have contributed to the high ex-factory price.

The cost ratios discussed earlier include mostly actual ex-factory prices, which include abnormal profits, if any. In some cases, actual prices are not available and hence 'fair' prices are used for estimating the comparative cost ratios. The 'fair' prices are different from the actual prices in so far as the latter incorporate abnormal profits. The concept of normal profits expressed in terms of 'mark-up' over the cost of production which the Commission considers fair and reasonable has varied over the years. There are indications, however, in a number of reports that the mark-up permissible has increased over the years. In so far as the actual percentage of profit on invested capital which is allowed by the Commission in its estimation of fair price is concerned, it is not always mentioned in its earlier reports. During the fifties, the percentage of profit allowed on invested capital appears to be in the neighbourhood of 10 per cent in those cases where such a mention has been made, whereas in the sixties, when the reference to the rate of profit is more frequent, it has increased by gradual stages over the years to $12\frac{1}{2}$ per cent (1963), 15 per cent (1964), 19 per cent (1965), and 20 per cent (1966).

There are about 39 industries for which data on both fair and actual prices are available; they indicate the prevalence of abnormal profits in the sense that in these industries actual prices are higher than the fair prices to an extent varying between 8 per cent and 32 per cent [4, Table 7, p. 24]. A few have been found to be suffering losses. It is pertinent to point out, however, that abnormal profits earned by the firms under consideration may in fact be larger than what is reported, and reported losses may be misleading in so far as the firms succeed in either misreporting their costs or, in the case of direct investigations by the Commission, succeed in avoiding a careful scrutiny of the detailed cost data. The valuation of fixed assets on the basis of which the individual industries fix their actual rate of profit or the Commission fixes its fair rate of profit is in any case not an easy exercise. Thus the comparative cost ratios given below based on fair ex-factory prices may still contain elements of excess profits which are not related to the comparative efficiency of the industries concerned, with the result that the fair cost ratios may indeed be lower than what is indicated below:

TABLE 5.8

COMPARATIVE COST RATIOS*

	1951–5		1956–60		1961–6		1951–66	
	Actual	Fair	Actual	Fair	Actual	Fair	Actual	Fair
Consumer	1·39	1·53	1·25	1·62	1·83	1·48	1·62	1·30
goods	(19)	(36)	(15)	(10)	(45)	(11)	(79)	(67)
Intermediate	2·39	1·19	1·91	1·10	1·88	1·68	1·89	1·65
goods	(2)	(3)	(2)	(2)	(82)	(76)	(86)	(81)
Capital	2·24	1·60	1·67	1·96	1·82	1·66	1·82	1·70
goods	(12)	(27)	(30)	(14)	(34)	(12)	(76)	(53)
All goods	1·76	1·61	1·55	1·76	1·85	1·66	1·78	1·62

* The figures in brackets refer to the number of products.

The comparative cost ratios on the basis of fair ex-factory prices are generally lower than those based on actual ex-factory price. The fair cost ratio in some instances, especially during the period 1951–55 and 1956–60, is higher than the actual ratio. In some of these latter cases, of course, the firms may be making losses or the two sets of ratios may relate to different commodities. During 1961–6, the sample of industries covered under each set of ratios is much larger and the commodities covered in the two types of ratios are more comparable. Over the whole period 1951–66, the fair cost ratio is consistently below the actual cost ratio for all three categories.

If allowance is made for the fact that actual profits as reported by the Tariff Commission probably underestimate 'true' profits, the fair cost ratio, excluding excess profits, both recorded and unrecorded, would be even lower. The existence of very large profit margins, larger than 10–12 per cent over the cost of production and larger than 12–20 per cent over capital investment, is also indicated by additional evidence which is available on the profitability of industrial enterprises in Pakistan. A recent study of the balance sheets of public limited companies listed in the stock exchange shows that between 1959 and 1963 gross profits as a percentage of capital employed varied between 14 and 15 per cent. This was during the period when normal profits as allowed by the Commission varied between 10 and 12 per cent [7]. This is also very partial evidence and possibly is an underestimate.

Thus if allowance is made for (a) excess profits (to the extent of 10 per cent) and (b) scarcity price of foreign exchange or the overvaluation of the exchange rate (to the extent of 50 per cent), the aggregate comparative cost ratio is considerably reduced. Thus the cost ratio will be reduced by a factor of 65 per cent, i.e. all the products with cost ratios which are 1·65 and below will become competitive with the foreign product [7, p. 21].[1] The number of industries and products which have cost ratios below 1·50 and below 1·65 are given below. This generally indicates the change in the proportion of industries which become competitive when proper adjustments are made for the above two factors.

It appears that between 50 and 60 per cent of industries and between 40 to 54 per cent of the products become competitive as against about 10 per cent of the industries and 5 per cent of

[1] This estimate, however, does not make any adjustment for the foreign exchange component of the domestic product, which has the effect of raising the cost ratio. Making this double adjustment for overvaluation, where permitted by the data, would reduce the cost disadvantage by 23 per cent, and then all industries with cost ratios of 1·33 and below would be made competitive.

the products which are competitive in the absence of such adjustments.

TABLE 5.9

Years	No. of industries			No. of products		
	Below 1·50	*Below 1·65*	*Total*	*Below 1·50*	*Below 1·65*	*Total*
1951–5	17	21	29	49	68	99
1956–60	14	15	24	32	36	73
1961–6	26	32	62	57	87	179
Total	57	68	115	138	191	351

VI. COMPARATIVE COSTS AND FACTOR PROPORTIONS

As we have seen, there is considerable diversity in the comparative costs of different industries. A relevant question is whether the comparative costs of different industries can be related to and explained by the diversity in the characteristics of these industries in respect of technology and factor proportions. It is expected that in a labour abundant country like Pakistan more labour-intensive industries are likely to have lower cost ratios compared with the less labour-intensive industries. Data on labour costs as a proportion of ex-factory price are not available for all the industries under investigation. For a number of industries data are available on direct labour costs and not on indirect labour costs, which are part of the overhead cost, i.e. administrative as well as selling and distribution expenses.[1] A regression equation relating comparative cost ratios (Y) to the direct labour cost ratios (L) is shown below:

$$\text{Log } Y = 0 \cdot 252 - 0 \cdot 154 \log L$$
$$(0 \cdot 032)$$
$$R^2 = 0 \cdot 18$$

[1] [8]. In this exercise the comparative cost ratios and the labour cost ratios of the individual products are not combined to arrive at the average ratios for each industry. This increases the number of observations and improves statistical testing. There are differences, often significant, between the labour cost ratios of individual products in a given industry.

A double logarithmic regression gives reliable regression coefficients. The correlation is not very high but the regression coefficient is negative and statistically significant at the 5 per cent level, implying a reliable relationship between variations in the labour cost ratio and in the comparative cost ratio. A 10 per cent increase in the labour cost ratio causes a decline in the comparative cost ratio to the extent of 1·5 per cent.

Attempts to correlate comparative cost ratios to capital-output ratios are limited by a lack of direct data on the capital-output ratios of the specific industries under investigation. The Censuses of Manufacturing Industries in Pakistan provide data on the fixed assets, employment and wages and salaries by the major groups of industries. The comparative cost ratios which relate to specific individual industries may be grouped according to the classification of the major industry groups in the census. The capital-output ratios of the major groups of industries are then related to the cost ratios of the groups of industries. The capital/output ratios are available for 1959/60 and 1955. The former is related to the cost ratios for the periods 1961–6 and 1956–60, and the latter to the period 1951–5, respectively. The regression equations relating the cost ratios (Y) to the capital-output ratios (K) are given below:

$$\text{Log } Y = 0·078 + 0·003 \log K \quad (1951–55)$$
$$(0·049)$$
$$R^2 = 0·0038$$

$$\text{Log } Y = 0·195 + 0·021 \log K \quad (1956–60)$$
$$(0·075)$$
$$R^2 = 0·0092$$

$$\text{Log } Y = -1·175 + 0·704 \log K \quad (1961–66)$$
$$(0·0207)$$
$$R^2 = 0·87$$

The cost ratios and the capital-output ratios are positively correlated for the period (1961–6) and the correlation is highly significant. The higher the capital-output ratio of an industry, the higher is its comparative cost ratio. The magnitude of the relationship is also high, implying a 7 per cent rise in cost ratio in response to a 10 per cent rise in the capital-output ratio. However, for the other two periods, i.e. 1956–60 and 1951–5, the relationship between the cost ratio and the capital-output ratio, though positive, is not significant. The simple linear relationships are less reliable than what is shown in the above logarithmic equations.

The above two exercises tend to indicate that the industries which use more labour per unit of output and less capital per unit of output are more advantageously placed in respect of their comparative efficiency. Admittedly the evidence on the effects of differences in the capital-output ratio is not very conclusive, in part because in two of the three periods for which the hypothesis is tested the regression coefficients are not significant and also because of the general limitations of the data on which the exercise is based . . .

CONCLUSION

The manufacturing industries in Pakistan suffer, on the whole, from a high cost disadvantage *vis-à-vis* competing imports. The weighted average cost ratios vary between 1·50 and 1·90, i.e. the ex-factory prices are 50 to 90 per cent higher than the c.i.f. prices. Thirty per cent of the industries examined in this study have ex-factory prices 51–100 per cent higher than their corresponding c.i.f. prices; about 16 per cent of the industry have prices 100–200 per cent higher than the c.i.f. prices [4, Table 2, p. 8]. This range of the comparative cost ratios compares well with those obtained from earlier studies based on an analysis of the domestic prices of imported goods, allowing for the differences in the methodology and commodity composition of the two studies. Tariffs do not seem to provide an appropriate measure of either the absolute or relative cost disadvantage of the different industries in Pakistan. On the one hand, because of quantitative restrictions, there are positive scarcity margins over the landed costs of the competing imports for a great majority of the commodities examined here; on the other hand, there are many commodities for which the ex-factory price is below landed cost. For example, in 30 per cent of the cases, actual ex-factory prices and in 40 per cent of the cases, fair ex-factory prices fell short of landed costs. Positive scarcity margins usually vary between 30–50 per cent, except in one year when it rose to 73 per cent. In those cases in which ex-factory prices fall below the landed costs of competing imports, they are as much as 25 to 30 per cent lower.

As is well known and as is further corroborated by the present analysis, there is widespread under-utilisation of capacity, engendered partly by a lack of co-ordination between industrial investment licensing and the licensing of imports of raw materials and spare parts [4, footnote 18]. Even though excess capacity contributes to high cost in a particular industry there is no evidence that inter-industry differences in cost ratios are explained by the differences in excess capacity, which are substantial in almost all the industries.

High comparative cost ratios of Pakistani industries, however, do not necessarily measure the inefficiency of industrialisation in Pakistan to an equivalent extent, if allowance is made for (a) an overvaluation of the exchange rate and (b) the existence of high or excessive profits in many industries as a result of lack of competition. An adjustment of the c.i.f. price of the competing imports, as well as of the foreign exchange component of the ex-factory price, on the assumption of 50 per cent overvaluation, in the case of a sample of twenty-nine industries and one hundred and seventy products, shows that the aggregative comparative cost ratio declines from 1·84 to 1·44, i.e. by 23 per cent. If one adjusts only the c.i.f. price and not the foreign exchange component of the ex-factory price, 50 per cent of the industries under examination become competitive. Again, if allowance is made for the fact that the ex-factory price contains elements of excess profits, the comparative cost ratio will be further reduced by 10–11 per cent. When, however, both adjustments are made for overvaluation in the few cases when the data permit this to be done, the industries with a comparative cost ratio of 1·33 and below become competitive in the world market.

In so far as the growth of infant industries into adulthood is concerned, the evidence examined in this paper is quantitatively very small. The performance of only a few industries, about fifteen in all, has been reviewed by the Tariff Commission subsequent to the grant of protection by it. The evidence indicates an improvement in comparative advantage and a decline in cost ratios; an attempt to correlate the cost ratios with the length of the period of operation of the corresponding industry groups does not provide any conclusive, systematic, and consistent evidence relating to the development of infant industries. While there are a few cases of a fall in cost ratios with an increase in the number of years of operation and an accumulation of experience, it is not true for all, nor is there any evidence that the cost ratios are a smooth and continuously declining function of an increase in the number of years of operation. A satisfactory examination of this problem is, however, inhibited by the limitations of the data.

In so far as the differences in comparative costs among the individual industries are concerned, the industries with a higher labour-output ratio have a greater comparative advantage. However, the gain in terms of comparative costs resulting from the choice of industries with a higher labour cost does not appear to be appreciable. At the same time industries with a high component of skilled to unskilled labour tend to have high cost ratios, though the evidence on this is not conclusive. There is some evidence that industries with a high capital-output ratio also have a high comparative cost ratio. Contrariwise, the industries which have higher non-wage value added per employee, i.e. with a higher ratio of capital to labour, tend, however, to have lower comparative cost ratios, implying that, with a greater application of capital to labour, productivity of capital goes up and the cost disadvantage declines. However, it is necessary to point out that these conclusions are very tentative and need to be further verified on the basis of additional, more reliable and comprehensive data and for different samples of industries and different years.

REFERENCES

[1] Soligo, Ronald, and Stern, J. J., 'Tariff Protection, Import Substitution and Investment Efficiency', *Pakistan Development Review*, v, 2, summer 1965, pp. 249–270. See also Chapter 4 of this volume.

[2] Soligo, Ronald, and Stern, J. J., 'Some Comments on the Export Bonus, Export Promotion and Investment Criteria' *Pakistan Development Review*, vi, 1, spring 1966, pp. 38–56.

[3] I.B.R.D., *The Industrial Development of Pakistan* (Washington: I.B.R.D.,) 1966.

[4] Islam, Nurul, *Tariff Protection, Comparative Costs and Industrialisation in Pakistan*, mimeographed Research Report no. 57 (Karachi: Pakistan Institute of Development Economics, Jan. 1967).

[5] Stern, Joseph J., and Tims, Wouter, *Inter-Industry Input-Output Tables for Pakistan, 1962–63*, unpublished mimeographed report (Karachi: Pakistan Institute of Development Economics).

[6] Pal, M. L., 'Domestic Prices of Imports in Pakistan: Extension of Empirical Findings', *Pakistan Development Review*, v, 4, winter 1965.

[7] Baqai, Dr M., and K. Haq, 'A Study of Savings in the Corporate Sector in Pakistan, 1959–63', paper read at the Pakistan Institute of Development Economics Seminar on 'Current Economic Problems of Pakistan' held at Karachi, 28–30 Jan. 1967.

[8] Lary, H. B., *Exports of Manufactures by the Less Developed Countries* (New York: National Bureau of Economic Research Inc., June 1966).

[9] Pakistan, Central Statistical Office, *Census of Manufacturing Industries*, 1955 and 1959–60 (Karachi: Central Statistical Office).

[9a] Pakistan, Tariff Commission, *Reports*, various years (Karachi: Manager of Publications).

[10] Basevi, G., 'The U.S. Tariff Structure: Estimates of Effective Rates of the U.S. Industries and Industrial Labour', *Review of Economics and Statistics*, May 1966.

[11] Krueger, Anne O., 'Some Economic Costs of Exchange Control: The Turkish Case', *Journal of Political Economy*, Oct. 1966, pp. 466–80.

6 Overinvoicing and Industrial Efficiency

GORDON C. WINSTON*

MUCH of the corruption[1] in Pakistan industry stems from an unrealistic official exchange rate. The dollar sells for Rs. 4·75 in the official market but for two to three times that much in the free market, allowing handsome profits for those who can trade in both. This paper describes how corruption works through overinvoicing of capital equipment imports. Moral dimensions of the problem are ignored; the central question is how over-invoicing affects the allocation of investment and therefore the structure of industry – how (and by how much) over-invoicing changes the costs of capital to the men who make investment decisions.[2] The logic of the problem can be developed with simple equations but an understanding of overinvoicing and its consequences does not depend on algebra. The reader who finds equations more a hindrance than a help can omit them and still get a clear sense of the shape and magnitude of the problem.

* The original version of this chapter appeared in *Pakistan Development Review*, winter 1970.

[1] With an artificial exchange rate, the government establishes a set of prices that makes certain transactions highly profitable. At the same time, it establishes laws making those transactions illegal. We call it 'corruption' when people follow the government's *price* incentives instead of its contradictory *legal* incentives.

[2] The interested reader should also consult Bhagwati's excellent analysis of the statistical and financial problems created by faking of foreign trade declarations [1]. It is nicely complementary, both in generalizing the devices and incentives for faking invoices—over- and under-invoicing of imports and exports—and in analysing their impact on real and apparent balance of payments accounts. On the subject of this paper, however, Bhagwati does not touch.

For those unfamiliar with the system, overinvoicing works like this: an industrialist whose new factory has been sanctioned (i.e. approved officially) will arrange with a foreign supplier to sell him equipment at a fictitious invoice price, higher than the price he actually pays. Presentation of the partly fictitious invoice to the foreign exchange authorities entitles the industrialist to buy the full invoice amount of foreign exchange at the official rate of Rs. 4·75 to make payment. The portion of the invoiced amount that represents overpayment is then deposited by the supplier to the industrialist's account in a foreign bank and, because of the disequilibrium exchange rate, it can be sold for rupees at the higher black market rate. Therein lies the foreign exchange profit to the industrialist. The deception of overinvoicing, of course, is necessary because the government makes it illegal for anyone openly to trade foreign exchange between the official and black markets.

In Section I a way is devised to measure the incentive effects of overinvoicing by computing the financial – foreign exchange market – profits that reduce the real costs of capital equipment to the industrialist. The size of these financial profits is estimated for Pakistan to see if they are large enough to influence behaviour, since they will affect investment only if they are not trivial. In Section II, the impact of overinvoicing profits is expressed in terms of the effective exchange rate for capital imports that includes both tariffs and the subsidy of overinvoicing profits. Finally, in Sections III, IV and V, the simple analysis is extended and made more realistic by considering the price distortions that overinvoicing creates among capital goods and what these imply for industrial development and performance, i.e. foreign capital intensity, capital utilisation and employment and the growth of output.

The facts and estimates in this paper come from Pakistan, but the forces described apply to any underdeveloped country with an overvalued currency. Overvaluation creates the incentives to overinvoicing capital imports and competition among foreign equipment suppliers guarantees dissemination of the techniques of overinvoicing. So misallocation of investment due to overinvoicing of capital imports is one among the many development problems of distorted incentives created by an artificial exchange rate [2, 3, 11].

I. THE FOREIGN EXCHANGE PROFITS OF OVERINVOICING

In overinvoicing, a real transaction (the purchase of equipment)[1] is used as the vehicle for a financial transaction (the purchase of cheap dollars for resale in the black market). These are two sides of the same coin, of course, but it is helpful at first to separate them and look *only* at the financial transaction – at the profit earned through the purchase and sale of foreign exchange. It is important to note that we are completely disregarding any profit the industrialist may expect to earn on products made by the equipment. In order to see the magnitude and effects of the financial incentives alone we are explicitly ignoring what is usually taken to be the *only* reason for importing capital equipment – expected operating profits.[2]

The amount of financial profit (in rupees) from an over-invoiced capital goods import is, simply, what the industrialist earns by selling his Swiss bank deposit on the black market, less what he paid for it. So

$$\pi^r = E_b \left(C_i{}^\$ - C_a{}^\$ \right) - (1 + t) E_o \left(C_i{}^\$ -{}^c C_a{}^\$ \right) \qquad (1)$$

where the first term is proceeds (the amount earned by selling the overinvoiced dollars $(C_i{}^\$ - C_a{}^\$)$ at the black market exchange rate (E_b) and the second term is costs (the amount paid to buy the $(C_i{}^\$ - C_a{}^\$)$ of dollars at the official exchange rate E_o, given that he has to pay the tariff t, on the fictitious part of the import too). The invoiced value of the import is $C_i{}^\$$ while

---

[1] 'Equipment' is used to emphasise that the analysis deals with real capital investments. But it applies equally to non-tangible imports of services that go into an investment budget—consultant and engineering services being the most obvious.

[2] A more general analysis of allocational distortions of over-invoicing would have to recognize, in addition to financial profits and operating profits, the trading profits possible from reselling license-restricted imports at a domestic price higher than landed costs plus tariff [8, 10]. If trading profits were sufficiently large and licenses were issued for a limited value of imports, there would be an incentive to *under*invoice the imports and *buy* black market foreign exchange to pay the excess of actual over invoiced value [1]. The reason for ignoring this possibility here is simply that a small part of industrial investment in Pakistan can be resold, hence trading profits do not figure prominently in investment allocation decisions.

the amount actually paid to the supplier is $C_a t^\$$, so the difference is the amount accumulated through overinvoicing. Superscripts indicate dollars ($) or rupees (r). If the amount of over-invoicing is expressed as a fraction of the invoice value, we can deal with

$$\phi = \frac{C_i^\$ - C_a^\$}{C_i^\$} \qquad (2)$$

and in these terms, financial profits can be expressed simply as

$$\pi^r = \phi \, C_i^\$ \, [E_b - (1 + t) \, E_o]$$

or in rupees,

$$\pi^r = \phi \, C_i^r \, [E_b/E_o - (1 + t)]. \qquad (3)$$

This is a most useful result. The industrialist's profit depends (quite sensibly) on the fraction of the invoice that is fictitious; on the size of the equipment order; on tariffs; and on the spread between black market and official rates of exchange. Notice that if the government did not maintain an artificial exchange rate, overinvoicing profits would be eliminated – an official exchange rate within $(1 + t)$ of the black market rate (so $E_b = (1 + t) \, E_o$) would make equation (3) equal zero.

Profits affect behaviour. It is unimportant to the analysis of overinvoicing whether industrialists in an underdeveloped country 'maximise' profits in some purists' sense. What is important is that the promise of higher profits creates incentives – pressures – to which some industrialists may well respond all the time and all industrialists will respond some of the time. We can understand important, perhaps dominant pressures on industrialists' investment behaviour and therefore something about the structure of industry if we understand what influences profits. So at each step we will look carefully at the pressure of profit incentives. Among the determinants of profits we shall discuss, some apply to areas within the firm's discretion, some apply to industry as a whole, while some work only through government policy and thus provide an incentive to the industrialist to influence that policy.

Incentives

On the simplified level represented by equation (3), the drive for profits through overinvoicing creates among industrialists incentives for the following behaviour:

Industrialist will try to

1. Make the amount of sanctioned investment (C_i^r) as large as possible. This has two corollaries:

(*a*) Encourage inflows of foreign aid, discounting high social cost since these largely determine the amount of total industrial capital imports; and

(*b*) For any one individual or firm, increase his share of sanctioned investment.

2. Increase the fraction of overinvoicing (ϕ) on capital imports. Even if we assume at this stage that this fraction is determined by 'common business practices' and is constant between different kinds of capital imports (an assumption examined below), there is still an incentive to increase the overinvoiced proportion over time. And competition among suppliers will contribute to this.

3. Maintain or increase the disparity between the official and black market rates of exchange (E_b/E_o). This has two elements:

(*a*) devaluation should be resisted by whatever argument has political appeal (national pride [2], threat to industrial development, inflation); and

(*b*) the black market price should be maintained or increased by encouraging enforcement of foreign exchange controls on other suppliers of black market dollars.[1]

4. Discourage tariffs on capital imports since they directly reduce financial profits by increasing the cost of getting dollars through overinvoicing. The most persuasive argument within the compass of the industrialists would be that there is a severe limit on the ability to create projects that will use available foreign exchange – an 'absorbtive capacity limit' – so that higher tariffs will radically reduce industrial development.

---

[1] How this works depends on the interaction between official and black markets—whether the total supply of dollars is fixed or whether the black market itself is price-elastic [1]. If the supply of available foreign exchange is increased by increased black market activity, then 'too much' black market activity will lower the profit of overinvoicing. There is always an 'optimum degree of enforcement' for the law-breaking firm [12].

Estimated Profits

Just how strong these pressures are likely to be on the typical Pakistani industrialist depends on how much these variables affect actual profits. Quantities have to be substituted for the symbols of equation (3). We can estimate two figures: the rate of profit that business overinvoicing practices created in Pakistan four years ago (1966); and the rate of profit that business practices now generate (1970).

The typical magnitude of overinvoicing (ϕ) that prevailed in 1966 was ten per cent of the invoice price; the black market rate of exchange (E_b) was about ten rupees to the dollar for these highly liquid funds;[1] and the official exchange rate (E_o) was Rs. 4·75. The average tariff rate on capital equipment imports was 34 per cent [7]. Substituting these values into (3), the rate of purely financial profit on a capital import[2] in 1966 was 5·8 per cent. This is solely profit from overinvoicing and foreign exchange market manipulation. On the import of an invoiced Rs. 1,000,000 of foreign capital equipment, the financial profit earned by an industrialist taking advantage of overinvoicing was Rs. 76,514. An investment of Rs. 1,340,000 (including tariffs) would be recorded officially, but it would represent an actual import of only Rs. 900,000 of equipment.

By 1970, both the typical level of overinvoicing and the black market rate for highly liquid dollars had increased significantly. Estimates of 20 per cent overinvoicing (ϕ) and a free market exchange rate of 15 rupees to the dollar (E_b) are not extreme. The official exchange rate (E_o) still stood at Rs. 4·75. Average tariffs on capital imports had risen to about

---

[1] Which sell in large amounts, are untraceable, and are not subject to any national capital flow restrictions. So they are more valuable than London or New York dollars.

[2] It is not clear what the denominator of a profit rate from overinvoicing should be. The absolute amount of profit is as stated in (3), but should this be measured against the actual value of the capital $(C_g{}^r)$, against the invoiced value $(C_i{}^r)$, or against the total resources the industrialist has to commit to the transaction including invoice payment and tariffs on it all $[(1 + t)\ C_i{}^r]$? The estimates in the text are conservative; they are based on the largest of these defensible denominators (the last), so the reader who would choose a different base for calculating profit rates will increase the estimates (significantly).

40 per cent.[1] Substituting these values into (3), the rate of financial profit from overinvoicing becomes a remarkable 25·1 per cent. Now importing Rs. 1,000,000 of invoiced capital goods earns a financial profit of Rs. 351,540. The investment worth Rs. 1,400,000 in the official record represents capital goods with an actual pre-tariff value of Rs. 800,000.

Despite reservations about their accuracy, these estimates of profits from overinvoicing suggest that opportunities from overinvoicing capital goods may be terribly important in underdeveloped countries in creating conflicts of interest, political pressures and incentives that lower the price of industrial capital, systematically affecting its allocation and encouraging its waste. We shall explore this further below.

II. THE EFFECTIVE EXCHANGE RATE FOR CAPITAL IMPORTS

An alternative way to describe the distorting effect of over-invoicing is through the implicit exchange rate that applies to imports of capital goods when overinvoicing profits reduce the real rupee costs of capital. Tariffs increase the implicit exchange rate; overinvoicing profits reduce it. The real rupee cost of imported capital is

$$C_f^r = (1 + t) \, E_o C_a^\$ - [E_b \, (C_i^\$ - C_a^\$) - (1 + t) \quad (4)$$
$$E_o \, (C_i^\$ - C_a^\$)]$$

The first term describes the gross costs of the real transaction (buying the equipment) while the second, bracketed term describes the (offsetting) financial profits. Simplifying this expression gives

$$C_f^r = \frac{C_a^\$ \, [(1 + t) \, E_o - \phi \, E_b]}{(1 - \phi)} \quad (5)$$

as the real rupee cost of capital to the industrialist.

[1] There have been no careful estimates of the average tariff on capital goods since those for 1966. The rate on most capital goods has risen since then from a nominal 40 per cent to a nominal 50 per cent at the same time that the number of exceptions for which a 30 per cent rate applies (to spread regional distribution of investment) has increased. The net effect of these contradictory movements is estimated as 6 per cent, raising average tariffs on capital goods imports to about 40 per cent.

The implicit exchange rate for capital imports is derived simply by dividing the real rupee cost by the actual dollar cost of the same equipment. So

$$C_f{}'/C_a{}^\$ = \frac{(1 + t)\, E_\bullet - \phi\, E_b}{(1 - \phi)} \qquad (6)$$

is the effective exchange rate for capital imports that should be compared to other exchange rates in the economy (those applying to consumption goods and raw materials) and to other prices (labour, domestic materials) to judge the relative price of foreign capital. Notice again that in the absence of an artificial exchange rate, $(1 + t)\, E_o = E_b$ and the right hand side of (6) reduces to $(1 + t)\, E_o$, making the implicit exchange rate the same as the official exchange rate plus tariff. The overinvoicing distortion (and incentive) vanishes.

Estimated Effective Exchange Rate for Capital Imports
As with financial profits, two sets of estimates of the effective exchange rate are possible, one for 1966 and another for 1970.

Using the figures that describe 1966 business practices, equation (6) gives an effective exchange rate of Rs. 5·96 per dollar. So the industrialist taking advantage of overinvoicing in 1966 paid for imported capital at an exchange rate lower than the one derived from tariffs alone – Rs. 6·37 was used by Lewis [7]. But using figures describing 1970 practices, the effective exchange rate for capital goods falls to Rs. 4·56 per dollar and this, of course, includes the 40 per cent average tariff rate. So despite tariffs, the effective exchange rate for capital goods imports in Pakistan appears to be below the official rate. The subsidy effect of overinvoicing is larger than the tariff; the net 'tariff' is −4 per cent.

Because devaluation is an obvious way to eliminate over-invoicing profits (directly or through generalising the bonus scheme), it is interesting to ask what amount of devaluation is implied by these estimates. Mechanically applying the conditions of 1970 to equation (3), a devaluation to Rs. 10·71 would completely eliminate the profits from capital over-invoicing. But this is certainly a slight over-estimate of the required devaluation for two reasons:

(1) the existing black market rate is probably higher, given restrictions of exchange transactions, than an 'equilibrium rate' would be; and

(2) there are administrative costs of overinvoicing that we have (properly) ignored. So it seems reasonable to suggest that a devaluation to somewhat less than Rs. 10·71 might well eliminate capital overinvoicing.

These estimates of Sections I and II are summarised in Table 6.1 for Rs. 1,000,000 of invoiced imports.

TABLE 6.1

THE IMPACT OF OVERINVOICING ON THE COST OF CAPITAL GOODS IMPORTS

	1966	1970
1. Invoiced value $(C_i{}^r)$	1,000,000	1,000,000
2. Nominal cost $[(1+t)C_i{}^r]$	1,340,000	1,400,000
3. Financial profit from Overinvoicing (π^r)	76,514	351,540
4. Payment to supplier (rupees)$(C_a{}^r)$	900,000	800,000
5. Payment to supplier (dollars)$(C_a{}^\$)$	189,474	168,421
6. Real rupee cost $(C_f{}^r)$	1,129,265	768,000
7. Effective exchange rate $(C_f{}^r/C_a{}^\$)$	5·96	4·56
8. Tariff (+) or Subsidy (−) re Official Exchange Rate	+25·5%	−4·00%

III. THE CHOICE BETWEEN IMPORTED AND DOMESTIC CAPITAL GOODS

Not all capital is imported, of course, and the industrialist always has some choice in the import content of his investments, either through choosing the way a product is made or simply in the choice of which products to make.[1] So the proportion of imported capital is variable and can be increased by choosing to invest in the most import-intensive techniques to make a given product or by choosing the most import-intensive industries or sectors of production.

Using the subscript d to indicate domestically supplied capital, the total nominal cost of an investment project (or a

---

[1] The assertion that there is no choice of import coefficients in industrial development is indefensible unless all industries have fixed coefficients, all are identical, *and* all operate at the same level of utilisation [6, 15].

group of investments making up an investment budget) with both foreign and domestic components is

$$C^r = C_d^r + (1 + t) \ C_i^r \tag{7}$$

If we describe the choice between imported and domestic capital goods by the relative size of the imported component of investment,

$$f = C_i^r / C_d^r \tag{8}$$

then

$$C^r = C_i^r \left[(1 + t) + \frac{1}{f} \right]. \tag{9}$$

Earlier we showed profits as a function of the nominal value of foreign capital, C_i^r, (among other things) so we can solve that earlier equation (3) for C_i^r and substitute the result into (9) to get a total investment cost of

$$C^r = \frac{\pi^r \left[(1 + t) + 1 \right]}{\phi \left[E_b/E_o - (1 + t) \right]} \tag{10}$$

This, in turn, can be solved for π^r so that total financial profit from overinvoicing becomes

$$\pi^r = \frac{C^r \ \phi \ [E_b/E_o - (1 + t)]}{(1 + t) + \dfrac{1}{f}} \tag{11}$$

It is clear that total profit depends, as before, on the size of the investment budget, on tariffs, on the amount of over-invoicing and on the black market rate of exchange relative to the official market rate. What is added by equation (11) is that profit depends, too, on the amount of imported capital. For any given investment budget, the industrialist's profit is higher the larger is the proportion of imported capital that can be used – i.e. the less is the use of domestically produced capital goods.

Incentives
In addition to the profit incentives described in Section I, industrialists will try to

5. Increase their use of imported capital equipment. This can be done both (*a*) by selecting foreign capital intensive tech-

niques of production, and (*b*) by investing in those industries that use much foreign capital at the expense of those that use little.

Estimates

For the Second Plan period (1960–5), Naqvi has collected data on total sanctioned private investment and the amount consisting of foreign capital [9]. So from these, *f* can be computed for equation (11) and the effect on profits of changes in *f* can be illustrated. It should be remembered that the same rupee profits that were earlier expressed as a percentage of the cost of foreign capital alone (see p. 174 n. 2) are now expressed as a percentage of total capital cost, so the percentage on this larger base must necessarily be smaller.

Using the values for 1970, the rate of overinvoicing profit on total investment is 16·4 per cent for West Pakistan and 15·4 per cent in the East. The sensitivity of these profit rates to changes in the proportion of capital is illustrated if we assume a change from half imported capital/half domestic (*f* = 1) to two-thirds imported/one-third domestic (*f* = 2).[1] Such an increase in imported capital would cause the rate of financial profit on total investment to rise from 14·65 per cent to 18·51 per cent. Hence in this range, doubling the proportion of imported capital increases the financial profit rate by 3·9 percentage points. Profits are 26 per cent higher.[2]

IV. THE CHOICE BETWEEN EXPANDING CAPITAL OR UTILISING EXISTING CAPITAL

The last steps in the analysis recognise that the amount of overinvoicing depends on what kinds of capital equipment the industrialist imports. Earlier we accepted the fact that this

---

[1] These bracket the values of *f* from Naqvi's figures which are 1·35 for the West and 1·13 for the East.

[2] Since the elasticity of the profit rate with respect to *f* is $\dfrac{1}{(1 + t)f + 1}$, the sensitivity of profits to *f* declines as tariffs rise and as the proportion of foreign capital increases. 'Early' increases in the import coefficient of investment, therefore, are more powerful than the same proportional increases from a larger base.

fraction (ϕ) changes over time; now we consider different
fractions of overinvoicing among different classes of equipment
at one point in time. The fictitious portion of an invoice will
vary because of difference in bargaining power between
buyer and seller for different goods and because of differences in
the effectiveness of surveillance by the foreign exchange control
authorities between different capital goods. The first of these
is treated here; the second in Section V.

Capital equipment can be bought either to build new plants
or, alternatively, to maintain and balance existing plants
increasing the level of their utilisation. For any industrialist
(beyond the neophyte with his first investment) there is a
choice to be made in dividing an investment budget (C^r)
between expansion (C_e^r) and utilisation (C_u^r)

$$C^r = C_e^r + C_u^r. \tag{12}$$

The result of the investment allocation can be described by the
size of investment spending on utilisation relative to spending for
expansion

$$u = C_u^r/C_e^r \tag{13}$$

so that

$$C^r = C_e^r (1 + u) = C_u^r (1 + 1/u). \tag{14}$$

These two types of capital goods should be treated differently
as regards overinvoicing profits because of the very different
competitive position of the industrialist, *vis-à-vis* the equipment
seller, in the two purchases. A new investment is typically self-
contained, technically independent of existing capital except
through product flows. If these are similar for different brands
and configurations of equipment, the industrialist is free to
choose among suppliers and this freedom will lead to competition among suppliers appearing in part in the amount of
overinvoicing. In contrast, the industrialist seeking balancing
equipment has less freedom to choose his supplier since the
equipment must fit into an existing plant, maintenance organisation and parts inventory and this relative absence of competitive flexibility will show up in lower overinvoicing. So the
overinvoicing that can be had on new capital is likely to be

greater than that which can be had on capital to increase utilisation of existing plant; or formally

$$\phi_e \geqslant \phi_u. \tag{15}$$

An industrialist's financial profits from overinvoicing will thus be a weighted average of the profits from each kind of investment spending, the weights depending on the relative rates of overinvoicing on expansion capital (ϕ_e) and maintenance-balancing capital (ϕ_u) and on the distribution of investment between these two (u). Substituting from (14) into (11) for each type of capital investment separately and adding them together gives overinvoicing profits of

$$\pi^r = \left[\frac{1}{1+u} \phi_e + \frac{u}{1+u} \phi_u \right] \frac{C^r \left[E_b/E_o - (1+t) \right]}{\left[(1+t) + \frac{1}{f} \right]} \tag{16}$$

Despite the cumbersome appearance of (16), it is clear that if the rate of overinvoicing is higher for new, expansion investment, profits are increased by decreasing the allocation of investment for *using* the existing capital stock.

Incentives
Industrialists will try to

6. Devote as much investment as possible to new equipment to expand the capital stock and, as a concomitant, as little as possible to maintenance and balancing equipment to increase the utilisation of existing capital.

Estimates
If we assume, arbitrarily, that new capital can be overinvoiced by 20 per cent while maintenance and balancing capital is overinvoiced at 10 per cent, under the conditions assumed for 1970, the rate of profit would be 25·11 per cent for the imported new investment and 12·6 per cent for maintenance and balancing investment. If all other factors were comparable, an industrialist who spent nothing out of Rs. 1,000,000 of imports on maintenance and balancing ($u = o$) would earn Rs. 251,100

on overinvoicing profits while another who spent half his investment budget on increasing utilisation of existing capital ($u = 1$) would earn only Rs. 188,250. These are suggestive of the price incentives that induce firms to expand industrial capacity rather than increase its utilisation.

Such price incentives – along with the general cheapness of capital we have described – may go far to explain why, in capital-scarce West Pakistan, existing industrial capital is used 14 per cent of the time while in the capital-rich U.S., it is used 22 per cent of the time.[1] Where capital is scarce, it is wasted; where it is abundant, it is conserved. This is a paradox of no small significance for a poor developing country.

V. CAPITAL COMPLEXITY, INDUSTRIAL EMPLOYMENT AND OUTPUT GROWTH

Overinvoicing operates despite surveillance by the foreign exchange authorities. In Pakistan, engineering-price committees serve in the major agencies involved in capital import transactions[2] in order to scrutinise capital invoices and challenge the validity of those considered suspicious. If surveillance fell with an absolutely even hand on all capital imports, it would concern us only as part of the optimum enforcement of exchange control laws. But it cannot. These agencies have limited resources and must concentrate their efforts where they are most effective. This means that surveillance is heaviest where overinvoicing is most likely to be discovered and this inevitably is on imports of standardised kinds of capital equipment for which there is a well established world market. Surveillance is least effective on highly complex, modern plants that are tailored to a specific installation and user. For these, the task of accurately validating capital prices is beyond the competence of even the best intentioned price surveillance

---

[1] Based on Foss' estimates of U.S. capital use [5], adjusted for comparability with my estimates for Pakistan [14]. The details of comparison are included in a forthcoming paper.

[2] Which are Customs, Pakistan Industrial Credit and Investment Corporation (P.I.C.I.C.) and the Industrial Development Bank of Pakistan (I.D.B.P.).

group.[1] What gives this economic significance is that the complexity of equipment that makes surveillance of capital imports more difficult involves a high proportion of capital relative to labour and relative to output and, in all likelihood, a bias toward large scale installations. So the overinvoicing attainable on new equipment imports (ϕ_e) increases as the capital-labour ratio, the capital-output ratio and project size increase.

Incentives
Industrialists will tend to

7. Select investment projects and sectors that are as complex as possible though this typically involves more capital per labourer and per unit of output. Overinvoicing profit incentives thereby reduce employment creation and output growth in industry.

VI. THE IMPLICATIONS FOR INDUSTRIAL DEVELOPMENT

Of the many ramifications of overinvoicing for economic development, three sorts seem of central importance for underdeveloped countries.

A. The structure and growth of industry is affected seriously by the lowered general price of scarce capital equipment and by the distortions of relative prices among types and uses of capital.[2]

The problems created by generally low capital prices in poor, capital-scarce countries have worried some economists for a long time and these problems are compounded by overinvoicing. They all rest on the fact that capital with too low a

[1] And scholars. Engineering complexity of capital imports combines with illegality to make it impossible to verify or deny the parameters of overinvoicing reported off the record by industrialists, bankers, foreign exchange authorities, aid officials and others. Bhagwati's experience in investigating faked invoices in Turkey and India was much the same as mine, though his concern with balance of payments aspects of faking allowed him one rough measure of total magnitudes [1, p. 66].

[2] There is a third, statistical distortion in the overstatement of industrial investment that overinvoicing produces. This is significant when overinvoicing practices change as in Pakistan between 1966 and 1970.

price relative to its actual scarcity is wasted: it is used in place of abundant factors (notably labour) and it is left idle too much of the time. Moreover, a low price of capital makes the wrong products appear profitable. Our analysis of overinvoicing provides a good indication of just how low capital prices really are. The analysis also indicates how tariffs can effectively be circumvented by changing the practices of overinvoicing – as in the estimate that overinvoicing in Pakistan more than offsets the existing tariffs on capital imports thereby providing a 4 per cent subsidy to foreign capital at the official exchange rate. Capital appears to be even cheaper to the industrialist than we had originally thought.

The distortions *among* capital prices that are created by overinvoicing are more interesting both because they have not previously been identified and because they appear to explain (at least in part) patterns of industrial growth that are increasingly disturbing. Among capital goods, overinvoicing tends to raise the relative price and discourage the use of domestically produced capital, of capital that increases the utilisation of existing plant and equipment, and of capital that creates employment.

To the extent that the profit incentives of overinvoicing influence investment decisions, they will create or accentuate a set of familiar problems in economic development:

1. by discouraging the growth of a domestic capital goods industry which must compete with an effectively subsidised import. In Pakistan, domestic producers must compete with foreign capital goods at Rs. 4·56 to the dollar but with foreign consumption goods at rates as high as Rs. 22·00 to the dollar [13]. This clearly increases the bias of cascaded protection under import substitution policies [3, 11];

2. by creating industry that is unnecessarily foreign-capital-intensive in its techniques and sectors of production and by perpetuating that pattern so that growth is heavily dependent on foreign capital;

3. by discouraging the *use* of existing plant and equipment in favour of adding new capital, with a consequent reduction in both the level and growth of consumption and employment [14]; and

4. by discouraging industrial employment both through reduced capital utilisation and through selection of complex, labour-saving and capital-using techniques and products.

B. The distribution of income is affected by overinvoicing at both ends of the income scale. Investment in employment-denying techniques and sectors reduces potential earnings of the unemployed and underemployed at the same time that profits accruing to the already privileged industrialists are increased.

C. The wider effects of overinvoicing on the growth of the economy may be among its most costly consequences. The civil servants in the investment sanctioning agencies have something very valuable to give away and it is hardly surprising that they are not always able to resist the pressures and temptations they confront. Indeed it is natural that they should wish to share in the profits. Thus there is a tendency for some of the profits from overinvoicing to be redistributed to the bureaucracy, spreading corruption and raising 'the cost of doing business'. And whatever economic criteria these agencies may have applied to investment decisions[1] will tend to get lost under mutual political and financial payoffs that have nothing to do with economic development objectives. In a sort of Greshams Law of Honesty, bad intentions drive out good as the rising cost of doing business forces corruption on even the reluctant businessman. The increase in overinvoicing in Pakistan over the past four years tends to be cumulative and it becomes in-

---

[1] Quite apart from individual temptations to ignore overinvoicing, note that the agencies mainly responsible for the surveillance of overinvoicing are semi-private investment loan organisations and as such they have an inherent conflict between their interest in honesty-and-economic-development on the one hand and their interest as a bank in the volume of loans and the financial solidity of their borrowers on the other. Overinvoicing gives foreign exchange market profits to their borrowers, increasing their financial resources (if profits are kept within the company) and the loans made by the agency thereby become more secure. Even without this added protection to already well secured loans, a policy of tolerance increases loans outstanding and therefore profits to the lending agency. Ethics and economic development aside, there is a clear motive for these agencies to nod at overinvoicing of capital goods imports. Even if they do not succumb to this temptation, it can certainly be doubted whether they should have the major role in policing overinvoicing.

creasingly difficult for a businessman to choose not to over-invoice.

Finally, corruption increases the demands on industrialists' energies at the same time that it restricts the number of persons who can be trusted to share management's (often illegal) decisions. Industrial corruption diverts limited entrepreneurial talents towards illicit financial intricacies and away from concern with production, innovation, marketing and employment. Furthermore, its illegality also restricts – often to family members – the number who can be trusted to know of a firm's methods of operation.

REFERENCES

[1] Bhagwati, Jagdish, 'Fiscal Policies, the Faking of Foreign Trade Declarations, and the Balance of Payments', *Bulletin of the Oxford University Institute of Economics and Statistics*, vol. 29 no. 1, Feb. 1967.

[2] Bhagwati, Jagdish, *The Theory and Practice of Commercial Policy* (Princeton University, 1968).

[3] Bruton, Henry J., 'The Import-Substitution Strategy of Economic Development: A Survey', *Pakistan Development Review*, x, 2, summer 1970.

[4] Despres, E., and Kindleberger, C. P., 'The Mechanism of Adjustment in International Payments: The Lessons of Post-War Experience', *American Economic Review*, XLII, May 1952.

[5] Foss, Murray, F., 'The Utilization of Capital Equipment: Postwar Compared with Prewar', *Survey of Current Business*, June 1963.

[6] Khan, Azizur Rahman, 'Capital-Intensity and the Efficiency of Factor Use – A Comparative Study of the Observed Capital-Labour Ratios of Pakistani Industries', *Pakistan Development Review*, x, 2, summer 1970.

[7] Lewis, Stephen R., Jr., *Pakistan: Industrialisation and Trade Policies* (London: Oxford University Press, for the Organisation for Economic Development and Co-operation, 1970).

[8] Lewis, Stephen R., Jr., and Guisinger, S. E., 'Measuring Protection in a Developing Country: The Case of Pakistan', *Journal of Political Economy*, Nov./Dec. 1968.

[9] Naqvi, S. N. H., 'Investment Licensing in Pakistan' (Karachi, forthcoming).

[10] Pal, Mati Lal, 'The Determinants of Domestic Prices of Imports', in Islam, Nurul (ed.), *Studies on Commercial Policy and Economic Growth* (Karachi: Pakistan Institute of Development Economics, 1970).

[11] Power, John, 'Import Substitution as an Industrialisation Strategy,' mimeographed, Quezon City, 1966.

[12] Shelling, Thomas C., 'Economic Analysis of Organised Crime', in The President's Commission on Law Enforcement and Administration of Justice, *Task Force Report: Organised Crime* (Washingon, 1967).

[13] Thomas, Philip S., 'Effective Exchange Rates in Pakistan', mimeographed, 1967.

[14] Winston, Gordon C., 'Capital Utilisation in Economic Development', *Economic Journal*, March 1971.

[15] Winston, Gordon C., 'On Factor Prices, Factor Proportions and Capital Utilisation', mimeographed (Karachi, 1970).

7 A Note on the Degree of Dependence on Foreign Assistance

KEITH GRIFFIN
and AZIZUR RAHMAN KHAN

AN ANALYSIS of Pakistan's growth would be incomplete without some discussion of the role of foreign capital. Pakistan has been the recipient of a large amount of foreign assistance and it has often been asserted that this was the most significant cause of the rapid growth achieved during the last decade. Professor Mason, for example, claims that the increased inflow of foreign aid per capita from Rs. 10·8 in 1960/1 to Rs. 25·8 in 1964/5 is responsible for much of Pakistan's success in the 1960s.[1] Indeed, the flow of foreign aid has been large by most standards and has increased over time. While capital inflow was 31 per cent of domestic investment in 1959/60, the proportion rose to the level indicated by the following figures in more recent years:[2]

Year	Foreign Assistance (Rs. million)	Domestic Investment (Rs. million)	Foreign Assistance (as % of investment)
1964/5	3,163	8,066	39
1965/6	2,778	7,078	39
1966/7	3,242	8,517	38
1967/8	3,491	9,935	35
1964/5–67/8	12,674	33,596	38

[1] E. S. Mason, *Economic Development in India and Pakistan* (Cambridge, Mass.: Center for International Affairs, Harvard University, 1966).

[2] Sources of these data are: foreign assistance figures from the *Fourth Five-Year Plan* and investment figures from *Memorandum on Aid to Pakistan Consortium 1968/69*, both by the Planning Commission, Government of Pakistan.

In spite of official pronouncements on the virtue of self-reliance, there has been too little concern in practice about the degree of dependence on foreign assistance. In fact one is struck by the frivolity with which the Perspective Plan, as reported in the *Third Five-Year Plan*, deals with the objective of becoming independent of foreign aid by 1985. As Anisur Rahman demonstrates, the whole twenty-year planning exercise was conducted without making provision for debt servicing![1]

Both the donors and the recipients were enthusiastic about the policy of relying on a massive capital inflow. The donors hoped to use the experience of Pakistan as a case study of rapid growth which combined an efficient absorption of foreign aid with liberal economic policies and a high domestic marginal saving rate. The government was happy to be a major recipient and confident that the debt would repay itself, since capital was highly productive both in terms of additions to output and foreign exchange. If the expectations of donors and recipients alike are to be fulfilled, foreign aid must not become a substitute for domestic saving but rather be a complement to savings; the effect of aid must be to eliminate the foreign exchange gap that would otherwise prevent *ex-ante* savings from being transformed into investment. In addition, debt-servicing must not be allowed to pre-empt a substantial proportion of foreign exchange earnings. As a matter of fact, the planners anticipated that exports would grow rapidly, and thus debt-servicing as a proportion of foreign exchange earnings would rise only moderately. In other words, disposable foreign exchange earnings, defined as total foreign exchange earnings less debt-servicing, were expected to grow rapidly, and this would more than cover import requirements. Moreover, in order to achieve independence of foreign aid at some future date, it was assumed that the domestic structure of production would be altered in such a way that the import propensity would increase at a lower rate than the export propensity.

By the end of the 1960s, after more than a decade and a half

---

[1] See Anisur Rahman's comments in 'The Pakistan Perspective Plan and the Objective of Elimination of Dependence on Foreign Assistance', *Pakistan Development Review*, autumn 1967,

of large capital inflows, the country found itself in a somewhat different situation than was envisaged. Debt-servicing increased from 3·6 per cent of export earnings in 1960/1 to 9·9 per cent in 1964/5 and to an alarming 19·2 per cent in 1969/70.[1] Disposable foreign exchange from exports declined as a proportion of national product over the last decade while import requirements as a proportion of national product have gone up rather sharply. In view of the increasing share of loans in the total inflow of capital (from less than 50 per cent in the late 1950s to 93 per cent in the late 1960s)[2] and the increasing rates of interest and stricter repayment terms, even an extrapolation of the current unfavourable trend would paint an excessively optimistic picture of the future. In the spring of 1971 Pakistan joined the queue of nations applying to their creditors for a moratorium on the interest and repayment on outstanding debt. This present state of affairs is far removed from the earlier assumptions of foreign debt repaying itself through rapid growth of output and exports.

Some observers may still argue that the difficulties Pakistan has encountered are due not to the volume and composition of the foreign capital inflow, but to government policies and political circumstances which affected the way aid was used. Those who hold this opinion, however, ignore the fact that aid is not neutral with respect to policies and their political consequences. In several instances donors have used aid to influence the government on behalf of certain measures. Even if this did not occur, however, aid would still be heavily implicated in government policy. This is because an inflow of foreign resources inevitably strengthens established governments and enables them to carry out their policies more easily. If these policies lead to disaster, whether the donors like it or not, they are involved and are partly responsible. Donors cannot claim part of the credit when things appear to be going well and then dissociate themselves when events turn out badly.

Several economists have discovered a negative association between the domestic savings rate and the rate of capital inflow, and this has led them to argue that the flow of a large

[1] Government of Pakistan, *Economic Survey of Pakistan*, 1969/70.
[2] Ibid.

quantity of aid could easily raise the level of consumption.[1] The experience of Pakistan supports this hypothesis and sheds considerable light on the relationship between foreign aid and domestic savings.

Unfortunately, there is not enough information available to enable one to study the distribution of benefits of foreign aid among various economic groups. Nor are there any estimates of the true social cost of foreign borrowing. It is obvious, however, that the largest recipients of foreign aid have been the private capitalists, traders and high-income consumers who have benefited from the low official price of foreign exchange and the import licensing system. The cost of foreign capital to society as a whole has been much higher than is implied by the prices of foreign exchange and capital that private capitalists have paid on their borrowings and purchases. There is no doubt that the social cost of foreign capital has been much higher than the concessional rate of 6 per cent interest which is currently charged on most loans. Empirical evidence for Pakistan suggests that procurement tying alone can raise this above 10 per cent, depending on the degree of overpricing, the length of the repayment period and the initial grace period.[2] To this must be added the cost imposed upon the society by the fact that the technology in the donor country, to which aid is tied, is less appropriate to the factor endowments of the recipient country than the technology available elsewhere. Thus the society has in many cases been borrowing from abroad at a 10 to 15 per cent real rate of interest. At the same time, private industrialists have obtained credit from the banking system at much lower rates of interest. Indeed the government-imposed ceiling on bank lending rates was 7 or 8 per cent. In addition, industrialists were allowed to import capital equipment at a significantly overvalued exchange rate.

[1] See Anisur Rahman, 'Foreign Capital and Domestic Savings: A Test of Haavelmo's Hypothesis with Cross Country Data', *Review of Economics and Statistics*, 1968; Keith Griffin, 'Foreign Capital, Domestic Savings and Economic Development', *Bulletin* of the Oxford University Institute of Economics and Statistics, May 1970; and the discussion in the same journal, May 1971.

[2] See Mahbub-ul-Haq, 'Tied Credits—A Quantitative Analysis', in John Adler (ed.), *Capital Movements and Economic Development* (New York, 1967).

In other words, private businesses were acquiring resources at less than half their real cost. It is no wonder that these powerful groups maintained their pressure for more and more foreign aid, for it was aid which enabled the government to continue to underprice these resources.

In the previous table we reproduced the official estimates of the degree of dependence on foreign assistance. For the period between 1964/5 and 1967/8, nearly 38 per cent of investment was financed by foreign capital and the remaining 62 per cent by domestic saving. This is a very high degree of dependence on foreign resources by any standard. It is important to note, however, that the accountant, no less than the decision-maker, has suffered from an illusion created by the overvalued official rate of exchange. By substituting the scarcity price for the official price of foreign exchange, it can be shown that the dependence on foreign assistance has been far greater (and the contribution of domestic savings much smaller) than is implied by the official statistics. Such an exercise also highlights the remarkable regional differences in savings ratios and aid dependence between East and West Pakistan.

As in a great many underdeveloped countries, domestic savings in Pakistan are estimated as a residual, i.e. the difference between an independent estimate of total investment and net capital imports. This conventional definition overestimates true domestic savings if the exchange rate is overvalued. The reason for this is that the local currency value of net capital imports (A) will be understated if the official exchange rate is used. If the overvaluation is x per cent, the relation between the true domestic currency value of capital imports (A^*) and its conventional estimate will be $A^* = (1 + x)A$.

To the extent that estimates of investment are obtained from a survey of the investing firms (as has been the case in Pakistan, where investment surveys are carried out by the C.S.O.) and that the firms obtain their foreign capital goods directly under licensing at the overvalued exchange rate, an unrecorded scarcity premium would be appropriated by the firms. Total investment, then, would also be underestimated because the import component of physical capital formation would be incorrectly evaluated at the official exchange rate. Assuming that a proportion λ of investment (I) consists of imported capital goods, the true value of investment would then be $I^* = (1 + \lambda x)I$; and the true value of domestic savings would be $S^* = I^* - A^* = (1 + \lambda x) I - (1 + x)A.$[1]

From an examination of input-output tables, it appears that a reasonable value of λ for Pakistan is about 0·2. The coefficient is low because at least two-thirds and perhaps as much as three-fourths of total investment consists of the product of the construction sector, which is non-traded. Using 0·2 as the value of λ and a modest 0·6 as the value of x, we get the following estimates for Pakistan during the period 1964/5 to 1967/8:

$A^*/I^* = 53 \cdot 9$ per cent, as compared to $A/I = 37 \cdot 7$ per cent;
$S^*/I^* = 46 \cdot 1$ per cent, as compared to $S/I = 62 \cdot 3$ per cent.

Thus the true dependence on foreign assistance has been much greater than the official estimates suggest. Correspondingly, the contribution of domestic saving has been far smaller than is conventionally supposed.

The results are even more striking when the ratios are calculated separately for East and West Pakistan. The regional estimates we shall provide are somewhat illustrative because of the great difficulty in obtaining regional measurements of these sensitive variables. During the four years under review, the capital inflow into East Pakistan was only Rs. 2,011 million, according to the best estimates available of the trade deficit.

---

[1] Note the effect of this adjustment on the results obtained in the studies reported in p. 191 n. 1. These studies claim that capital imports result in higher consumption (lower savings) as well as in higher investment, and some investigators have attempted to test this hypothesis by regressing ΔS on ΔA. In countries with overvalued exchange rates such regressions could produce very misleading results. Imagine, for instance, that a country receives additional capital imports (correctly valued) equal to $\Delta A(1+x)$ and that this raises investment by the full amount $\Delta I = \Delta A(1+x)$. Conventional accounting methods would report a rise in domestic savings equivalent to $\Delta A(x - \lambda x)$. That is, there would be a positive correlation between ΔS and ΔA, although there is, in fact, a zero correlation between ΔS^* and ΔA^*. Indeed, provided the rise in investment ΔI^* is less than $\Delta A(1+x)$, one may have an illusion of rising S when in fact S^* is falling. In summary, the savings rate is likely to be overestimated in countries which have an overvalued exchange rate, and the extent of overestimation will vary positively with the difference between the true and official rate of exchange, the degree of dependence on foreign finance and the size of the domestic capital goods industry.

Much of the inflow, however, was in the form of an import surplus with West Pakistan (Rs. 1,928 million); there was only a small import surplus with the rest of the world (Rs. 83 million). The West appears to have had a total capital inflow of Rs. 10,663 million, of which Rs. 12,591 million was in the form of an import surplus with the rest of the world and Rs. 1,928 million in the form of an export surplus with East Pakistan. Capital flows which are a result of regional trade surpluses or deficits are not subject to underestimation arising from the overvaluation of the rate of exchange.[1] Hence we have

$$A^*_e = (1 + x) A_e^r + A_e^w$$
$$A^*_w = (1 + x) A_w^r + A^e_w = (1 + x) A_w^r - A_e^w$$

where for East Pakistan

A^*_e = true value for capital inflow,
A^r_e = nominal import surplus with rest of the world,
A^w_e = import surplus with West Pakistan, and similarly

for subscripts w, which refer to West Pakistan.

East Pakistan's investment during the period has been officially estimated to have been around 35 per cent of national investment. Using this and a value of 0·2 for λ in both regions, we obtain the following estimates:

	East Pakistan %	West Pakistan %
Ratio of true capital inflow to true investment	15·7	74·5
Ratio of nominal capital inflow to nominal investment	17·1	48·8

It is not possible to obtain regional estimates of domestic product in current prices. We can construct a pretty good estimate, however, by applying the regional shares of domestic

[1] Strictly speaking, this is not correct. Ideally, we should estimate the overvaluation for each commodity that is traded and not assume uniform overvaluation for each traded item. This would allow for possible differences in the degree of overvaluation in exports sent from one region to the other. Casual observation suggests that our failure to follow such a procedure understates the differences in regional behaviour.

product in constant prices to the current price data of domestic product for the nation as a whole. Following this procedure, we obtain the following estimates of regional saving rates for the four-year period 1964/5 through 1967/8:

	East Pakistan %	West Pakistan %
True saving rate	11·4	5·1
Nominal saving rate	10·2	9·4

where true saving rate is defined as S^*/Y^* and $Y^* = Y + I^* - I$.

Note the asymmetry between the regions. In East Pakistan, the true rate of saving is higher, and the true rate of capital inflow is lower, than the nominal rates, whereas in West Pakistan the nominal rate overstates true savings and understates aid dependence. These results arise from the fact that the capital inflow in East Pakistan, which consists largely of an import surplus from the West, is understated to a smaller extent than is investment, while the reverse is true in West Pakistan. During the period as a whole, the true regional savings rate in East Pakistan was double that of West Pakistan, while the proportion of total investment financed by foreign capital was nearly five times higher in the West than in the East.

PART FOUR

Wages, Income
Distribution and Savings

Wages, Income
Distribution and Savings

Commentary

The conscious promotion of inequality is a distinctive feature of the development strategy pursued in Pakistan. Unlike many countries which have followed a similar strategy, Pakistan has been relatively candid; the government itself has claimed on many occasions that concentration of income is a necessity if the nation is to achieve a high rate of domestic savings and economic growth. The concentration of income and wealth in the hands of the rich has been a key ingredient in a development strategy which uses the manipulation of the market mechanism to redistribute resources from agriculture to industry and from East to West Pakistan. Even on its own terms, however, the strategy has not generated a high savings rate in Pakistan over the last two decades. While the savings rate increased between 1955 and 1965 from about 7 per cent to about 12 per cent, it declined to about 9 per cent by 1969–70. The average savings rate was about 9 per cent in the Third Plan period (1965–1970) as compared to about 8 per cent during 1955–60.

It could be argued, of course, that the purpose of inequality is not only to generate a high rate of savings but also to provide incentives to a scarce factor of production, entrepreneurship. A perusal of official literature, however, does not suggest that this latter consideration played an important part in government thinking. Statements by policy makers have stressed savings rather than incentives. Even so, it is true that entrepreneurship has been a scarce factor in the industrial field in Pakistan. The industrial entrepreneur has been the beneficiary of exceptional profits – sometimes the result of controls and fiscal policy, which have been manipulated in his favour, and sometimes the unintended result of domestic industrial protection and exchange rate policy. The relevant question however is whether such exceptional rewards were necessary. Could not a lower rate of profits have induced the same degree of entrepreneurial activity?

The promotion, or at least tolerance, of inequality has been advocated, even if reluctantly, by many prominent economists who have concerned themselves with problems of economic development.[1] This position is exemplified by Harry Johnson, who argues that

> ... the remedies for the main fault which can be found with the use of the market mechanism, its undesirable social effects, are luxuries which underdeveloped countries cannot afford to indulge in if they are really serious about attaining a high rate of development. In particular, there is likely to be a conflict between rapid growth and an equitable distribution of income; and a poor country anxious to develop would probably be well advised not to worry too much about the distribution of income.[2]

G. F. Papanek, in his well-known book on the economy of Pakistan, has made similar statements referring specifically to that country. For example, Papanek asserts that 'great inequality of incomes is conducive to increased savings' in Pakistan, at least in the 1950s, and that despite the problems they create, 'the inequalities in income contribute to the growth of the economy'.[3] He too believes that 'a conflict exists here between the aims of growth and equality'.[4]

---

[1] See, for example, the books of Arthur Lewis: *The Theory of Economic Growth* and *Development Planning*.

[2] H. G. Johnson, 'Planning and the Market in Economic Development', in *Money Trade and Economic Growth*, 1962, p. 153; originally published in *Pakistan Economic Journal*, June 1958. Taken at its face value this is a highly controversial statement. Prof. Johnson claims that elimination of social justice is a luxury and that there is a conflict between the rate of increase of output and its equitable distribution. The first claim is a value judgement which many would not share and the second is a statement of fact for which no facts are given.

[3] G. F. Papanek, *Pakistan's Development: Social Goals and Private Incentives*, 1967, pp. 199, 242.

[4] Ibid, p. 178.

The theme is repeated by official economists and the Planning Commission in its successive five-year plans. A Pakistani planner writes that 'savings are a function not only of the level of income but also its distribution'.[1] From this it seems to follow almost automatically that "the underdeveloped countries must consciously accept a philosophy of growth and shelve for the distant future all ideas of equitable distribution and welfare state. It should be recognised that these are luxuries which only developed countries can afford'.[2] The policy conclusion is obvious: 'additional output should be distributed in favour of the saving sectors'.[3]

The weight of professional economic opinion, combined with the interests of groups which had considerable political influence in the government, was reflected in the Planning Commission and the government's strategy of planning. The Third Five Year Plan states that 'it is clear that the distribution of national product in the third plan should be such as to favour the saving sectors'.[4]

It is remarkable to note that economic theory does not provide an unambiguous guide as to the relationship between savings and inequality of incomes. There are various hypotheses concerning the relationship between income distribution and saving, some of which cast doubt on any positive relationship between the two. If one assumes, following Duesenberry, that consumption preferences are interdependent, 'a decrease in inequality might *increase* the propensity to save'.[5] Harry Johnson also shows, in a very rigorous and complex piece of analysis, that it is possible that a redistribution of income from rich to poor would lead to an increase in savings, if interdependence of preferences are taken into account.[6] Friedman's permanent income hypothesis implies that the

[1] Mahbub-ul-Haq, *The Strategy of Economic Planning*, 1963, p. 20.

[2] Mahbub-ul-Haq, *The Strategy of Economic Planning*, 1963, p. 30.

[3] Ibid, p. 25.

[4] Government of Pakistan, Planning Commission, *The Third Five-Year Plan (1965–1970)*, May 1965, p. 33.

[5] J. S. Duesenberry, *Income Saving and the Theory of Consumer Behaviour*, 1952, p. 44 (emphasis in the original).

[6] H. G. Johnson, 'The Effects of Income-Redistribution on Aggregate Consumption with Interdependence of Consumers' Preferences', *Economica*, May 1952.

average propensity to consume is independent of the level of permanent income. In other words, the rich do not save a higher proportion of their permanent income than the poor.[1] If, at any particular moment in time, actual savings out of actual income are relatively high among the upper income groups while negative savings are found in the low income groups, this may be because the former are receiving transitory income and capitalising it, while the latter have experienced a temporary decline in income and have liquidated previously accumulated assets in order to maintain their level of consumption.

Rural savings rates
It is widely believed, in Pakistan and elsewhere, that poor farmers cannot and do not save. This view was stated quite explicitly by Ragnar Nurkse in his famous book on *Problems of Capital Formation in Underdeveloped Countries* and has since become accepted doctrine. Evidence is accumulating, however, that when peasants are provided with incentives and investment opportunities they can achieve a surprisingly high rate of savings. Propertyless workers, be they the industrial proletariat or landless rural labourers, have few productive outlets for savings and hence tend to save very little. Landowning peasants and secure tenants, on the other hand, may have numerous investment opportunities which yield high returns, and hence may save a significant fraction of their income – despite the fact that their income is very low. Thus it is investment opportunities rather than income that may be a more important determinant of household savings in low-income countries. An agrarian reform which converts landless labourers into owner-cultivators may well result both in reduced inequality and higher savings.

Bergan's study of Pakistan, part of which is reprinted as Chapter 8, shows that income inequality is less in rural than in urban areas and less in East than in West Pakistan. Despite less inequality and a lower per capita income, Bergan's data indicate that the East saves proportionately more than West Pakistan: gross personal savings in 1963/4 were 11·8 per cent of gross personal income in the East and 8·8 per cent in the

[1] See M. Friedman, *A Theory of the Consumption Function*, 1957.

West. Moreover, the East wing saved more than the West in the First Plan period as well. Mahbub-ul-Haq reports that during the period 1955–60 gross domestic savings were 6·5 per cent of regional G.D.P. in East Pakistan and only 5·3 per cent in West Pakistan.[1] There are two factors which are worth noting in this context. First, the commodity composition of income of the rural areas of the East may encourage saving, since jute, being a commercial crop which is entirely marketed, may not facilitate as much consumption as would production of a food crop. Secondly, a large part of East Pakistan's high

RURAL SAVINGS RATES IN ASIA

Study	*Average propensity to save*	*Author*
1. Jute farmers of eastern India, 1949–55	0·13	Pilhofer
2. Rural families of Hyderabad State, 1949–51	0·08	Iyengar
3. Rural families, India, 1950–51		Panikar
All families	0·12[a]	
Cultivating families	0·13	
Non-cultivating families	< 0·04	
4. Farmers of Jogjakarta region, Indonesia, 1959	0·11[b]	Kelley and Williamson
5. Rural areas, Pakistan, 1963–4		Bergan
Personal savings, all Pakistan rural areas	0·11	
Personal savings, East Pakistan rural areas	0·12	
Personal savings, West Pakistan rural areas	0·09	

Sources: Studies (1)-(3): P. G. K. Panikar, 'Rural Savings in India', *Economic Development and Cultural Change*, Oct. 1961. Study (4): A. C. Kelley and J. G. Williamson, 'Household Saving Behaviour in the Developing Economies: The Indonesian Case', *Economic Development and Cultural Change*, Apr. 1968. Study (5): A. Bergan, 'Personal Income Distribution and Personal Savings in Pakistan, 1963/64', *Pakistan Development Review*, summer 1967. Also see Chapter 8 below.

[a] Panikar estimates that total savings would rise to 20 per cent if direct investment by farmers in their land were included.

[b] Marginal propensity to save, i.e. β in the function

$$\frac{S}{N} = \alpha + \beta \frac{Y}{N}$$

where S is savings, Y income and N the number of persons per family.

---

[1] Op. cit., Table 16, pp. 98–9. Mr Haq did not notice an inconsistency between his facts and his advocacy of inequality.

saving rate may be due to the large trade surplus which was extracted through export licensing and exchange rate policy; these savings clearly were involuntary.

Bergan estimates that the personal savings rate in rural East Pakistan, the poorest region of the country, was 12 per cent, compared with only 6·7 per cent in the prosperous urban areas of West Pakistan. Furthermore, the high rural savings rates that he reports are quite consistent with empirical findings from other Asian countries, as the table above indicates. All of the studies cited in the table can be criticised, but the basic point that peasants can and do save is no longer subject to doubt. Furthermore, although the evidence is fragmentary, of poor quality and inconclusive, it does not appear to lend much support to the hypothesis that there is a necessary conflict between equality and growth, given appropriate institutions and policy.

GROWING POVERTY

Pakistan is not unique in following a development strategy which accentuates inequality. It is unusual, however, in that this policy has been carried to such an extreme that the standard of living of the majority of the population has declined, despite the fact that national income per capita has grown.

It was first suggested in 1965, rather tentatively, that the standard of living of the mass of the population was lower than when the country achieved its independence in 1947.[1] Research in the last five years has confirmed this original judgement and shows that the process still continues. In Chapter 9 we have reprinted A. R. Khan's study of industrial wages. Dr Khan shows that real wages in industry declined over the period from 1954 to 1963/4.

The findings of Khan's study, though quite revealing, were still less than conclusive to some who argued that his data, covering the mid-fifties and early sixties, did not extend to the most rapid period of growth and industrialisation during the middle and late sixties. It was during these years, the sceptics argued, that it would be natural to expect that the standard of

[1] See Chapter 1 above.

living of the workers would begin to improve. Since the publication of the original study, data from similar sources have become available for the late sixties. Following the same methodology as in the original study and utilising the cost of living index to deflate money wage rates, the following real wage indices are obtained for the most recent years for which data are available:

East Pakistan for the year 1967–8 (using 1954 as the base)
All industries	101·1
Jute textiles	94·6
Cotton textiles	81·7

West Pakistan for the year 1966–7 (using 1954 as the base)
All industries	88·8
Cotton textiles	76·9

Thus the real wages *continued to decline* during this period of most rapid industrialisation and growth. The decline is rather remarkable for the various textile groups which account for about half of total industrial employment and are relatively unaffected by factors such as a change in the composition of skills. The nominal rise in the index for all industries in East Pakistan is almost certainly due to a change in the composition of employment in favour of high skill and high wage sectors.

It should be noted that the cost of living index used to derive the above real wage indices certainly understates the true increase in the workers' cost of living. This has been shown in considerable detail in Khan's paper, which also contains alternative estimates based on different assumptions of the true rise in prices. Given a more accurate cost of living index, the decline in real wages would appear to be far more serious. The conclusion thus seems inescapable that over the decade and a half ending around 1967, real wages in industry must have declined by at least 25 per cent.

Of course, the majority of the working class in Pakistan still lives in rural areas, and it is the movement of real incomes in these areas that determines whether poverty is increasing or diminishing. Changes in real incomes in the rural areas of East Pakistan are especially important, since the poorest people in the country are concentrated there in vast numbers. Swadesh Bose, in an outstanding piece of research, has studied the trend in income of 'the poorest of the poor', the landless labourers of East Bengal. His study is reprinted as Chapter 10.

Per capita income in Pakistan as a whole was stagnant in the 1950s and rose rapidly thereafter. Per capita income declined in East Pakistan in the 1950s, and the decline in the per capita income in agriculture was particularly noticeable. Bose demonstrates that the real income of the poorest section of the rural population in East Pakistan declined in the 1950s and did not rise significantly in the 1960s. This was associated with a falling ratio of land per man and an increasing proportion of landless labourers. The real wages of these labourers fell substantially until 1957 and then rose; only in 1961, however, did they regain the level of 1949. By 1966 real wages were lower again than in 1949, after reaching a peak in 1964.

There is other evidence which suggests that the standard of living of the mass of the population has continued to decline in recent years, particularly in East Pakistan. We know, for example, that the per capita availability of several essential commodities, including foodgrains, declined during the Third Plan period. This is found by comparing the results of the various rounds of the National Sample Survey (called the 'Quarterly Survey of Current Economic Conditions', published annually since 1963–4). The statistical quality of these surveys is much more reliable than many of the estimates of production which enter the national income accounts. Thus, ironically, precisely in a period when consumption as a proportion of G.N.P. was rising, consumption of commodities of greatest importance to the masses was falling.

Who, then, were the beneficiaries of rapid growth and the redistribution of income? Essentially there were three groups: (i) a small number of wealthy industrialists who obtained enormous profits from the policy of import-substituting industrialisation; (ii) the larger farmers of West Pakistan, those with 25 acres or more, who have prospered as a result of investments in tubewells, fertilisers, improved wheat varieties and now subsidised tractors; and (iii) to some extent the middle class – the civil service, army, and white-collar workers – who benefited from what social programmes there were. The great majority of the population has experienced continued poverty. They are the ones who pay high prices for manufactured goods;

they are the ones who bear the burden of the regressive tax system; and they are the ones who do not benefit proportionately from the small programme of public expenditure on health, education and housing, which is mainly concentrated in urban areas.

8 Personal Income Distribution and Personal Savings in Pakistan

ASBJORN BERGAN*

SCOPE AND LIMITATIONS

ONE of the objectives of Pakistan's Third Five-Year Plan is 'to make substantial progress towards achieving certain specific social objectives such as diminishing inequalities in the distribution of income . . .' [4, p. 39]. The main purpose of the present study is to measure these inequalities. As the basic source we have used provides data on private consumption as well as on personal income, some rough calculations on personal savings (as residuals) have been included in this paper.

Income distribution and savings in Pakistan have been studied by others in the past. A few papers have appeared in the *Pakistan Development Review* and elsewhere [3; 6 and 10].

However, owing to the limitations of data, all of them have been confined to the coverage of particular geographical areas, population groups or industrial sectors; whereas the present paper, in principle, deals with all personal income and savings in the country.

The data for this study were mainly obtained from the 'Quarterly Surveys of Current Economic Conditions' conducted by the Central Statistical Office (C.S.O.) during the fiscal year 1963/4. Since similar information was not available for other years, the scope of the present study had to be limited to the one year, 1963/4. This severe limitation must be fully kept in

* An extended version of this paper was originally published in the *Pakistan Development Review*, summer 1967. The author is deeply indebted to Dr Taufiq M. Khan, who devoted much of his time and made a substantial contribution to the study. He is also grateful to Mr Ikhtiar-ul-Mulk, Director of the Central Statistical Office, and Syed Aftab Ahmed, Survey Officer I, for their readiness to make the basic data available.

mind when conclusions are drawn on the basis of our findings. While the results may be valid for 1963/4, their generalisation over time would depend on the degree of stability of the various functional and structural relationships involved. For example, aggregate personal savings rates are probably very unstable, particularly in the rural areas of Pakistan and hence in the country as a whole. As pointed out by Lewis and Khan: 'there are not likely to be any stable aggregate relations between saving and income in a developing country . . . a variable (saving) so strongly affected by world markets and by agricultural output' [10, p. 23]. Savings rates by income groups (by size of income) should, however, be less affected by year-to-year fluctuations in prices and physical output. Similarly, the relative income distribution by size might be fairly stable over a number of years, even if aggregate income is subject to substantial fluctuations. The functional distribution of personal income (wages, self-employment, etc., as relative shares of the total) may be somewhat, but perhaps not significantly, affected by short-term fluctuations in total income. Again, this effect, if any, relates more to the rural than to the urban areas. Finally, the East-West and even more the rural-urban relative shares of total personal income are influenced by changes in agricultural factor income.

The degree of instability in the various relations which the present paper deals with will remain uncertain until basic data become available for a number of years. In spite of these uncertainties, estimates based on actual observations for one year may be useful supplements to mere guesses based on subjective considerations only.

Apart from the instability problem, the reliability of some of the findings for the year 1963/4 can, of course, also be questioned.

Income data from the income tax returns have, to a minor extent, been used as supplementary material. The CSO's national income estimates, the government budgets, and a few other sources have provided the basis for an attempt to check the estimated aggregate personal income.

The income distribution results might be a little more reliable than the savings figures, because the latter are extremely sensitive to even relatively small errors in the observations of income and household expenditures. The main emphasis should, therefore, be put on the income distribution aspect of the study . . .

REGIONAL DISTRIBUTION OF PERSONAL INCOME

Aggregate personal income for each of four areas and their relative shares of the national total are shown in Table 1. The distribution of this total by province appears in the bottom row, and that between rural and urban areas in the last column.

TABLE 8.1
TOTAL PERSONAL INCOME 1963/4

	East Pakistan	West Pakistan (Rs. crores)	All Pakistan
Rural areas	1730 (44·3%)	1456 (37·2%)	3186 (81·4%)
Urban areas	158 (4·0%)	568 (14·5%)	726 (18·6%)
Combined (rural and urban)	1888 (48·3%)	2024 (51·7%)	3912 (100%)

These figures are obtained by blowing up each of the four samples, on the basis of the population figures used for the per capita G.N.P. estimates by province in 1963/4 [8, pp. 200–2], the rural-urban population ratios of each province according to the 1961 census of population [9] and the average number of persons per household in the respective areas as estimated in the survey.

TABLE 8.2
AVERAGE PERSONAL INCOME PER CAPITA 1963/4*

	East Pakistan	West Pakistan (Rs. per year)	All Pakistan
Rural	305	373	333
Urban	509	515	513
Combined	316	406	357

* Differences between the areas with regard to persons per household are taken care of in the computations. On the average a household stands for 5·5 persons in the rural areas of both provinces, and for 5·7 in East urban and 5·9 in West urban.

Urban personal income counts for less than one-fifth of the national total. In East Pakistan, the urban share comes to one-twelfth only, compared to one-third on West Pakistan.

In terms of per household and per capita income the urban areas are far ahead of the rual. East Pakistan lags substantially behind West, except in the urban areas.

The relative East-West disparity in per capita personal income turns out to be as follows:

	Rural areas	Urban areas	Combined rural & urban	G.N.P. per capita 1963/4*
East Pakistan as percentage of West Pakistan	82%	99%	78%	78%

*At 1959/60 factor cost.

It may be noticed that the overall disparity between the provincial per capita income is much higher than any of the partial disparities shown in our figures. There is almost no disparity between urban East and urban West, and for the rural areas separately the per capita income in East is 18 per cent below that of West, but when we combine the rural and the urban areas the overall disparity rises to 22 per cent. The higher overall disparity is a result of the rural areas' much larger share of the provincial income in East than in West Pakistan and the much higher per capita income in the urban than in the rural areas in both provinces.

The rural–urban disparity in personal income per capita, according to the estimates, works out as below:

	East Pakistan	West Pakistan	All Pakistan
Rural per capita income as % of urban	60%	72%	65%

The rural–urban disparity in factor income per capita would be higher, because gross profit of corporations, which is included in G.N.P. but not in personal income except for dividends, accrues primarily to the urban areas. Interest on national debt, which is included in private income (personal and corporate), but not in G.N.P., may have some offsetting effect.

Keith B. Griffin has in his article [5, pp. 606–8 and 628] related gross value added in agriculture to the total rural population and called it rural income per capita, which then came to only 16 per cent of urban per capita income. He thus assumes that either no income accrues to the rural population for their activities in non-agricultural sectors or that the rural population does not take any part in those activities.[1] This is incorrect. In fact, non-agricultural sectors, e.g. transport, trade, small scale industry and others, contribute substantially to the income of the rural population.

PERSONAL INCOME DISTRIBUTION BY SIZE OF INCOME

Ranking the households according to the size of their monthly income and cumulating from the bottom the household frequencies of each income group, we get a relative distribution of households as shown in Table 8.3.

An area-to-area comparison of the frequency distribution columns should be subject to a few qualifications. In terms of welfare (however defined), a given household income does not mean exactly the same in each of the four areas, because of the differences in family size, regional prices and consumption patterns. Disregarding all these considerations for the moment, if we assume that a household income of Rs. 100 a month represents the lower limit for subsistence, the figures tell that more than one-third of all households lie below the subsistence level. The ratio is two-fifths in East and one-fourth in West Pakistan. It is substantially lower in the urban areas than in the rural, but the number of urban households is so small compared to the rural, particularly in East Pakistan, that the ratios for combined rural-urban come close to those for the rural areas.

If we raise the limit to Rs. 150 per household per month, almost two-thirds of all the households living in East Pakistan and one-half of those in West Pakistan, adding up to almost 60 per cent of the households in the country, lie below the limit. At the top income brackets we find only 0·6 per cent of the

[1] Griffin has mentioned cottage industry as the only sector that has been omitted.

TABLE 8.3
DISTRIBUTION OF HOUSEHOLDS BY INCOME GROUP

Cumulated percentage of total number of households 1963/4

Monthly income per household	East Pakistan			West Pakistan			All Pakistan		
	Rural	Urban	Combined	Rural	Urban	Combined	Rural	Urban	Combined
Rs.									
up to 50	9·0	5·0	8·8	5·4	1·7	4·6	7·2	2·5	6·9
up to 100	42·8	28·3	41·5	28·5	15·7	25·7	35·6	18·6	34·3
up to 150	66·7	52·6	66·0	54·0	38·4	50·5	60·6	41·7	59·0
up to 200	82·2	65·3	81·3	71·8	57·4	68·5	77·1	59·2	75·5
up to 250	90·0	73·7	89·1	82·3	69·7	79·4	86·2	70·6	84·7
up to 300	94·2	80·8	93·5	89·3	78·4	86·5	91·8	78·9	90·3
up to 400	97·2	85·7	96·6	95·2	87·0	93·6	96·2	86·6	95·3
up to 500	98·6	90·2	98·2	97·1	91·7	96·0	97·5	91·3	97·2
up to 700	99·5	94·7	99·2	99·1	95·5	98·4	99·3	95·3	98·9
up to 900	99·8	96·7	99·6	99·6	97·3	99·1	99·7	97·2	99·4
up to inf.	100	100·0	100·0	100·0	100·0	100·0	100·0	100·0	100·0

TABLE 8.4

INCOME SHARES OF ORDINAL GROUP

Cumulated percentage of total personal income 1963/64

Cumulated percentage of households	East Pakistan			West Pakistan			All Pakistan		
	Rural	Urban	Combined	Rural	Urban	Combined	Rural	Urban	Combined
Lowest 5% get	1·0	0·7	1·2	0·8	1·0	0·8	1·1	0·9	1·0
Lowest 10% get	3·5	1·5	2·7	2·3	2·5	2·3	2·5	2·2	2·5
Lowest 20% get	8·0	5·0	7·0	6·8	6·0	6·5	6·5	6·0	6·5
Lowest 30% get	13·0	9·0	12·0	12·0	11·0	11·5	12·0	10·0	11·5
Lowest 40% get	18·5	13·5	18·0	18·0	16·0	17·5	18·5	15·5	17·5
Lowest 50% get	26·0	19·0	24·5	26·0	21·5	24·5	26·0	21·0	24·5
Lowest 60% get	35·0	25·5	33·5	34·5	29·0	33·0	34·0	28·0	33·0
Lowest 70% get	45·0	33·0	43·5	44·5	38·5	43·0	44·5	37·0	42·5
Lowest 80% get	57·0	43·0	55·5	57·0	49·0	54·5	57·5	48·0	55·0
Lowest 90% get	73·0	59·5	71·5	72·0	63·5	69·5	72·5	63·0	70·0
Lowest 95% get	82·5	70·5	81·5	83·0	74·0	80·0	82·0	74·0	80·0
Lowest 100% get	100·0	100·0	100·0	100·0	100·0	100·0	100·0	100·0	100·0

households above Rs. 900 a month – 0·4 per cent in East and 0·9 in West Pakistan. We must go down to Rs. 400 (or even slightly below that) in order to cover 5 per cent of all the households (3·4 per cent only in East and 6·4 per cent in West), and down to Rs. 300 to get 10 per cent.

Table 8.4 shows how much of the total personal income goes to the lowest 5 per cent of the households (lowest in terms of income per household), how much to the lowest 10 per cent, 20 per cent and so forth.

The last column in the table shows that the lower half of the households in the country get about one-fourth of the total personal income. In other words, on the average their income

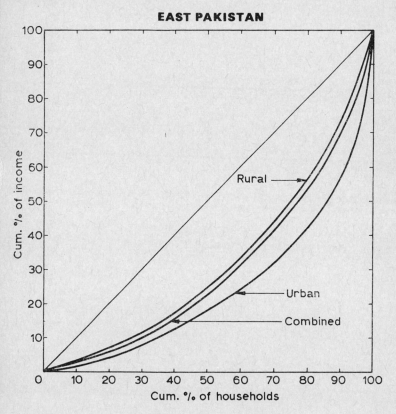

Figure 8.1. Personal Income Distribution

per household is only one-third of the average income of the other half of the households. The top 5 per cent of the households get 20 per cent of the income, which means that they on the average are about five times as well off as the rest of the population.

The table also shows that a much higher degree of inequality exists in the urban areas than in the combined rural and urban areas. The inequality is higher in urban East than in urban West Pakistan. Out of the total urban personal income in the country only one-fifth goes to the lowest half of the households, whereas the top 5 per cent get more than one-fourth.

When making comparisons of this kind between urban and

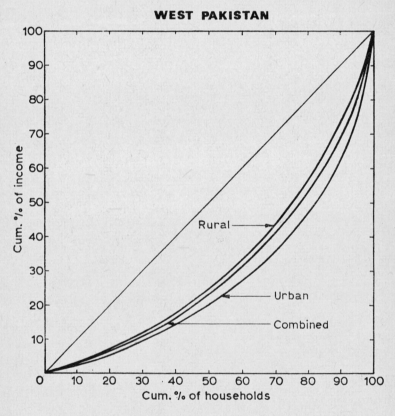

Figure 8.2. Personal Income Distribution

ALL PAKISTAN

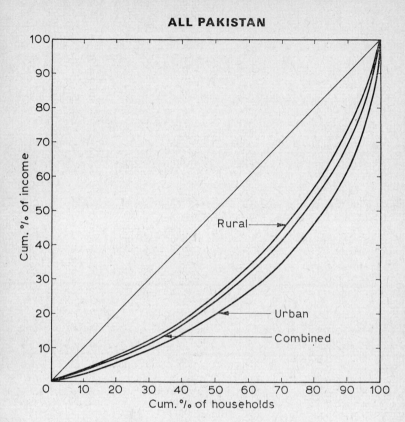

Figure 8.3. Personal Income Distribution

rural areas, or between the two provinces, one should keep in mind the regional differences in average income per household. Thus, even though the bottom half of the urban households get only 21 per cent of the urban personal income, whereas the bottom half of the rural households get 26 per cent of the rural income, the former are on the average better off than the latter. Similarly, with the same relative share of the provincial total the bottom half is on a lower level in East than in West Pakistan.

One implication of regional differentials in average income is that when combining two (or all the four) areas, the income distribution in the combined area may be more unequal or less unequal than the distribution within any of the two (or four) areas.

Figs. 8.1, 2 and 3 are graphical illustrations, in terms of Lorenz curves, of the income distribution shown in Table 8.4. The cumulated household frequencies are measured along the X-axis and the corresponding cumulated income shares along the Y-axis.

By definition we have got perfect equality if every income receiving unit gets the same income. In this extreme case, the Lorenz curve will be a straight line coinciding with the diagonal. If there is any inequality, then the curve must, at least from a certain point, lie below the diagonal. Parts of the curve may still be straight lines, which would illustrate equal distribution within the corresponding ranges.

Our notion of inequality can be rationalised in a simple way by defining the degree of inequality as the area between the curve and the diagonal divided by the whole area below the diagonal, the so-called concentration ratio or Gini coefficient. This ratio is to be regarded as an index of inequality shown in the curve and in the relevant columns of Table 8.4.

The concentration ratios corresponding to Table 8.4 and Figs. 8.1, 2 and 3 are shown in Table 8.5 below:

TABLE 8.5
CONCENTRATION RATIO,
1963/4

East Pakistan, rural areas	0·346
East Pakistan, urban areas	0·491
East Pakistan, combined	0·368
West Pakistan, rural areas	0·357
West Pakistan, urban areas	0·430
West Pakistan, combined	0·381
All Pakistan, rural areas	0·356
All Pakistan, urban areas	0·445
All Pakistan, combined	0·381

For the interpretation of the income distribution figures (and curves) it must be noticed that the equality concept is automatically linked with the definition of the income receiving unit, which in this case is the household. Had the receiving unit been an individual, an income earner, a person in the labour force, a taxpayer or something else, then the income distribution would have been different. Any comparison of income distribution between countries or regions might be misleading unless the distribution figures refer to the same income receiving unit, e.g. household. In case the base units are different, a comparison must at least be duly qualified.

The Quarterly Survey schedules, which form the basic source of information for the present study, also contain information on the number of persons and number of earners in each household. There is a high correlation between these two characteristics and even more so between the household size and income. For the country as a whole the average size of household was 5·5 persons but it ranged from 2·4 in the very low to around 10 in the high income groups. The average number of earners per household came to 1·5, ranging from 1·1 to 2·3 . . .

SAVINGS

Personal saving is by definition disposable (i.e. post-tax) personal income less consumption expenditures. The gross personal income figure in the present paper is not disposable income, but personal income before taxes. The household expenditures as they appear in the Quarterly Surveys schedules include direct taxes (they are included in miscellaneous expenditures). So, if we deduct from our personal income estimates the household expenditures, and add 'gifts and assistance' which were excluded from income, we should get gross personal savings.[1]

Expressed in savings rates the amount of savings should be related to disposable income and not to personal pre-tax income. Since the information available does not allow that, the savings rates we have worked out relate to income before taxes.[3] If related to disposable income, the rates would have been a little higher.

As pointed out in the first Section of this paper, the savings estimates that can be calculated on the basis of the survey

---

[1] Net of taxes, but gross of depreciation, if any.
[3] Including gifts and assistance.

income and expenditure data are very sensitive to relatively small errors in the income and/or the expenditure figures. In the survey data there might be substantial errors on both sides. For these reasons, the aggregate personal savings rates, which are presented in Table 8.6. below, are very doubtful.

TABLE 8.6

GROSS PERSONAL SAVINGS, 1963/4

	Gross personal savings	
	Per year (Rs. crore)	% gross personal income (before taxes)
East Pakistan, rural areas	207·6	12·0%
East Pakistan, urban areas	15·6	9·9%
East Pakistan, combined	223·2	11·8%
West Pakistan, rural areas	139·5	9·2%
West Pakistan, urban areas	38·1	6·7%
West Pakistan, combined	177·8	8·8%
All Pakistan, rural areas	347·1	10·9%
All Pakistan, urban areas	53·7	7·4%
All Pakistan, combined	400·8	10·2%

For that part of urban personal income in the highest income group which was based on income tax data, there was no information available about savings. We have applied an average savings rate of 35 per cent for these incomes, which may be an underestimation. The savings rate for the survey incomes about Rs. 900 a month was around 30 per cent in both of the urban areas, and these incomes were on the average much lower than the incomes incorporated on the basis of the tax data.

Personal saving is not the same as private saving, which also includes private corporate saving. If we assume that all the corporations are located in the urban areas and that private corporate saving amounted to Rs. 52 crores, the gross private saving in the All Pakistan urban areas would come to Rs. 105·7 crores. This private saving amount, related to gross private income (personal income plus corporate retained earnings and direct corporate taxes), gives a rate of private urban saving of 12·8 per cent.

The picture we get of private saving would then be as follows:

TABLE 8.7

GROSS PRIVATE SAVINGS, 1963/4

| | Gross private savings | |
	Per year (Rs. crore)	% of gross private income
Pakistan, rural areas	347·1	10·9%
Pakistan, urban areas	105·7	12·8%
Pakistan, combined	452·8	11·3%

The major part of corporate profit accrues to West Pakistan. On the assumption that corporate retained earnings are divided between East and West in about the same ratio as the urban population of the country, we would get the following results.

TABLE 8.8

GROSS PRIVATE SAVINGS, 1963/4

| | Gross private savings | |
	per year (Rs. crore)	% of gross private income
East Pakistan, rural areas	207·6	12·0%
East Pakistan, urban areas	24·4	13·9%
East Pakistan, combined	232·0	12·2%
West Pakistan, rural areas	139·5	9·2%
West Pakistan, urban areas	81·3	12·5%
West Pakistan, combined	220·8	10·5%
All Pakistan, rural areas	347·1	10·9%
All Pakistan, urban areas	105·7	12·8%
All Pakistan, combined	452·8	11·3%

To repeat once more, we think that the corporate gross profit figures are on the low side and also that the personal income and savings figures for West Pakistan urban areas in the high income groups are too low. If that is true, our urban savings figures for West Pakistan, and hence the West combined and the All Pakistan urban and combined are too low.

However, even if urban savings have been grossly understated in our calculations, the rural areas would still appear to have contributed at least three-fourths of the total private savings in the country. East Pakistan with its much lower total income has, according to these figures, saved at least as much as West Pakistan in absolute amount and more than West in terms of savings rates.

The most striking feature, which calls for further examination, is the high savings rate in the poorest of all the four areas, namely rural East Pakistan. One possible explanation is that 1962/3 was a bad crop-year and also a year of natural disaster, whereas 1963/4 was a very good crop-year, which enabled the farmers to build up again inventories, livestocks, wells, implements, etc.[1] In other words, their savings may have been extraordinarily high in 1963/4 in order to meet reinvestments which were badly needed for their future subsistence. This possible explanation underlines the warning that the results for one year cannot be applied to other years.

A proper study of private savings should, of course, include an analysis of savings rate by income groups, and other important details. The Quarterly Survey's data could have been arranged in such a way that savings could be estimated separately for each income group, but it would have required time and resources beyond the limit we had to set for the present study.

By adding government savings to gross private savings in the country we get total gross domestic savings. This total related to G.N.P. at market price would show the overall gross domestic savings rate for the country . . . An examination of government savings and thus also of total savings is beyond the scope of the present paper.[2] If, for illustration, we adopt the Planning Commission's estimate of government savings for 1964/5, 1·7 per cent of G.N.P. at market price, and also the ratio of G.N.P. at market price to G.N.P. at factor cost for 1964/5 implicit in the Planning Commission's figures [4, pp. 62 and 64], and apply these ratios to 1963/4, our estimate of the overall gross domestic savings rate would be 12·5 per cent of G.N.P. at market price, compared to the Planning Commission's estimate of 10·3 per cent.

Perhaps the main conclusion to be drawn from this paper

[1] This point was made by Dr T. M. Khan.

[2] Government saving in Pakistan is not an unambiguous concept, because the definition depends on the distinction between current (non-investment) and investment development expenditures.

is that the present basis for studies of income distribution and savings in Pakistan is too weak. Considering the economic planners' need for better information in these fields it is important to improve the statistical basis for studies of savings.

REFERENCES

[1] Ahmed, Syed Aftab, 'Some Methodological Problems in Consumer Expenditure Surveys', mimeographed paper read at the CENTO Symposium on Household Surveys in Dacca, 25 Apr–2 May 1966.

[2] Pakistan, Central Statistical Office, *Monthly Statistical Bulletin*, Sep. 1966.

[3] Farooq, G. M., *The People of Karachi: Economic Characteristics*, monographs in the Economics of Development no. 15 (Karachi: Pakistan Institute of Development Economics, July 1966).

[4] Pakistan, Planning Commission, *The Third Five-Year Plan (1965–70)* (Karachi: Manager of Publications, June 1965).

[5] Griffin, Keith B., 'Financing Development Plans in Pakistan', *Pakistan Development Review*, v, 4, winter 1965. Also see chap. 1 of this volume.

[6] Haq, Khadija, 'A Measurement of Inequality in Urban Personal Income Distribution in Pakistan', *Pakistan Development Review*, iv, 4, winter 1964.

[7] Khan, Taufiq M., 'Capital Formation in Pakistan', in Khan, Taufiq M. (ed.), *Middle Eastern Studies in Income and Wealth* (London: Bowes & Bowes, 1965).

[8] Khan, Taufiq M. and Asbjorn Bergan, 'Measurement of Structural Change in the Pakistan Economy: A Review of the National Income Estimates 1949/50 to 1963/64', *Pakistan Development Review*, vi, 2, summer 1966.

[9] Pakistan, Ministry of Home and Kashmir Affairs, Home Affairs Division, *Census of Pakistan Population 1961*, vol. i (Karachi: Manager of Publications).

[10] Lewis, Stephen R., Jr., and Khan, M. I., 'Estimates of Noncorporate Private Savings in Pakistan: 1949–1962', *Pakistan Development Review*, iv, 1, spring 1964.

9 What Has been Happening to Real Wages in Pakistan?

AZIZUR RAHMAN KHAN[*]

I. INTRODUCTION

IT seems unnecessary to prepare an elaborate case emphasising the need for some knowledge about the movement of real wages. Such knowledge would help confirm our ideas about the supply of labour and its abundance or scarcity, shed light on the mechanism of transfer of labour from the traditional sector to the modern sector by highlighting the incentive differential between wages in these two sectors and its change over time, and provide insight into the question of the distribution of incremental income.

In view of the obvious importance of the subject, it seems unfortunate that practically no enthusiasm has been shown by researchers in estimating the course of this variable in Pakistan. Certainly part of the explanation lies in the inadequacy of statistical information. Over the vast agricultural sector, wage labour is not the dominant mode of production. Whatever wage-labour relations exist there and in the services sectors are not systematically reported by the data collecting machinery in the country. Inevitably one is therefore limited to the examination of the movement of wages in the manufacturing industries only.

In this essay we do not aim at a comprehensive analysis of

* This chapter first appeared in the *Pakistan Development Review*, autumn 1967. The author expresses his deep sense of gratitude to Arthur MacEwan, who suggested many improvements in the argument. Some of the ideas are his although all errors and inadequacies belong strictly to the author. Marvin Rozen read through earlier drafts and suggested many corrections and improvements. Among others who helped are: Professor Nurul Islam, Swadesh Bose, Stephen Lewis Jr., Gordon Winston, Abdul Ghafur and Carl Stevens.

the movement in real wages. Our aim is the more modest one of (a) deriving indices of real wages in manufacturing industries in each of the two regions of Pakistan after a reasonably careful examination of the different sources of data, and (b) obtaining certain related measurements such as the regional difference in wage rates, the relative position of the wage-earners in the scale of income distribution and labour's factor share in the value of output.

II. WHAT DO WE WANT REAL WAGES TO MEASURE?

One can distinguish several interesting measures of real wages in the industrial sector or in any single industry. The first of them is the usual index of the average standard of living of the workers and is obtained by deflating the index of money wage rates by the index of workers' cost of living:

$$U_{1t} = \frac{W_t}{W_o} \div \frac{P_t}{P_o}$$
$$= \bar{W}_t/\bar{P}_t \tag{1}$$

Where U_1 = index of workers' standard of living,
W = money wage rate,
P = cost of living, i.e. cost of the consumption bundle of an average worker,
$\bar{W}$ = index of money wage rate, and
$\bar{P}$ = index of cost of living.

Subscripts refer to time periods: t to any current period and o to base period.

Variations in this index indicate the direction and extent of changes in the standard of living of an important social class, the workers. The most important hypothesis about the movement of this index over the long period in a surplus labour economy is that it remains unchanged at some subsistence level which is determined by the average standard of living of the workers in the subsistence (i.e. traditional agricultural) sector plus some mark-up [9].

One can devise a second index of real wages to measure what may be called 'the real cost of labour' from the employers' point of view. This is obtained by deflating the index of money wage rates by the index of the price of the product turned out by the enterprise or the industry employing the workers:

$$U_{2t} = \frac{W_t}{W_o} \div \frac{P_t^m}{P_o^m}$$

$$= \bar{W}_t / \bar{P}_t^m \qquad (2)$$

Where U_2 = index of 'the real cost of labour' from the employers' point of view,

P^m = price of the product turned out by the workers, and

$\bar{P}^m$ = price index of the product turned out by the workers.

Other things being equal, variations in this index would indicate changes in the capitalists' share of output and hence capacity to reinvest.

That the two indices may easily be different can be demonstrated with the help of the traditional two-sector model of the dual economy. Let us have a traditional sector which produces food and a modern sector which produces manufactured goods. Cost of living for industrial workers would be determined by the prices of the products of both the sectors:

$$\bar{P}_t = a\bar{P}_t^f + (1-a)\ \bar{P}_t^m$$

where $\bar{P}^f$ = price index for food and a and $(1-a)$ are respectively the weights of food and manufactured goods in the total consumption of the workers. We therefore have:

$$U_{2t} = U_{1t}\ (\bar{P}_t/\bar{P}_t^m)$$

$$= U_{1t}\ \left[\frac{a\bar{P}_t^f + (1-a)\ \bar{P}_t^m}{\bar{P}_t^m}\right]$$

$$= U_{1t} + a\left(\frac{\bar{P}_t^f}{\bar{P}_t^m} - 1\right) U_{1t} \qquad (3)$$

What it shows is that if food prices rise faster than manufactured prices (i.e. if $(\bar{P}_t^f/\bar{P}^m) > 1$); the real cost of labour from the capitalists' point of view would rise even if the workers' standard of living remains unchanged.[1] This would mean, other things remaining unchanged, a fall in the share of profits in manufacturing. This is the famous exception to the theory of growth with unlimited supplies of labour to which Arthur Lewis refers: even if labour supply is infinitely elastic at some subsistence real wage, share of profits in total product will decline and act as a brake on the growth of the economy if 'the increase in the size of the capitalist sector relatively to the subsistence sector ... turn the terms of trade against the capitalist sector ... and so force the capitalists to pay workers a higher percentage of their product, in order to keep their real income constant' [9].

To mention the exceptions to the exception, labour's factor share would still not rise if the increase in 'the real cost of labour' is offset by (*a*) a rise in the gross value of output per worker, and/or (*b*) a rise in the share of value added in the gross value of output. (In this essay we subsume the effects (*a*) and (*b*) under the name of 'a rise in labour productivity'.)[2]

The index of labour's factor share (which we call U_3) in period t is given by:

$$U_{3t} = \frac{W_t N_t}{(1-v_t)P_t^m Q_t} \div \frac{W_o N_o}{(1-v_o)P_o^m Q_o}$$

Where N = total employment of labour,

v = ratio of total raw materials and other current inputs to the gross value of output,

Q = quantity of output.

We have:

$$U_{3t} = \left(\frac{W_t}{W_o} \div \frac{P_t^m}{P_o^m}\right) \div \left(\frac{(1-v_t)Q_t}{N_t} \div \frac{(1-v_o)Q_o}{N_o}\right)$$

$$= U_{2t}/Z_t \tag{4}$$

[1] If $a = 0\cdot6$ (which seems to be the right order of magnitude for a country like Pakistan) a 10 per cent relative use in the food price index would mean that U_2 is 6 per cent higher than U_1.

[2] Note that this is not entirely legitimate. Change in the value added coefficient may not have anything to do with labour efficiency, e.g. if this is caused simply by a change in the relative price of an important input.

Where Z_t = index of labour productivity according to our
        definition (i.e. index of real value added per
        worker) in period t.

The labour's factor share would remain unchanged (even
decline) if labour productivity exactly (more than) offsets the
rise in the real cost of labour. Thus, we have a third measure of
real wage, that of labour's factor share or what may be called
the real cost of labour in efficiency units.

A decline in the workers' standard of living (U^1) would be
undesirable from the standpoint of the desirable pattern of
incremental income distribution. An increase in labour's factor
share or what we call the real cost of labour in efficiency units
(U_3) may be undesirable from the standpoint of maximising
growth.[1] Depending on what is happening to relative prices
and labour productivity, it is, however, possible for both the
standard of living of workers to go up and labour's factor share
to go down.

In this essay the basic wage index we derive refers to the
index of workers' standard of living. In most of the following
sections, we concern ourselves with the problem of estimating
this index and analysing the movement of this index. Only
towards the end do we consider the other two measures of real
wages. The term real wage in the rest of this essay means
workers' standard of living while the other two measures are
respectively called the real cost of labour and the real cost of
labour in efficiency units (or labour's factor share).

III. DATA

Real wage rate is defined to be the rate of wage at some constant purchasing power. In other words, it is the money wage
rate deflated by the index of the cost of living for wage earners.
Thus the estimation of the real wage index requires the estimation of the rate of money wages and the index of workers' cost

---

[1] We are assuming no particular economic system. The argument would
hold if the economy were completely socialized. What we now call capitalists'
share would then be renamed the share of the state or society. Note we are
assuming that the supply of savings is the main constraint to growth and
that workers save at a lower rate than do the capitalists or the state.

of living. We therefore turn our attention to the available data on these two indicators.

3.1 *Sources of wage data*

There are at least two possible sources of data on wage rates:

(*a*) Under the Payment of Wages Act, the Ministry of Health, Labour and Social Welfare (H.L.S.) collects information on employment and earnings of workers in manufacturing industries [6]. This series includes the non-production workers and clerks earning up to Rs. 2,400 per year (see [2, p. 45]) which is on the average about two and a half times the earnings of a production worker in recent years. These data refer primarily to the 2(j) factories (i.e. those employing 20 or more persons and using power) although for some years at least it seems that some 5(1) factories (employing 10 or more workers) and railwaymen have been included [7]. The H.L.S. publishes two separate series: one for the perennial factories (which we call the H.L.S. perennial series) and the other for all factories, both perennial and seasonal (which we call the H.L.S. overall series).

(*b*) The Census of Manufacturing Industries (C.M.I.) provides information about wages and total number of production workers for each of the census years. By now such information is available for about a decade (from 1954 to 1962/3 in East Pakistan and to 1963/4 in West Pakistan) with a few intermediate years missing. Before 1962/3 the C.M.I.s were confined to 2(j) factories while since 1962/3 5(1) factories have also been covered.

3.2 *A comparison of the two sources*

After a careful analysis of the two sources, it seems to us that the C.M.I. series is superior to the two H.L.S. series. First, the C.M.I. series refers to production workers whereas the H.L.S. data include clerical and supervisory workers as well. Thus, the C.M.I. data refer to a more homogenous group of the labour force – the one in which our interest primarily lies.

Secondly, the C.M.I. provides enough background information to enable us to check the consistency of the data reported. For each region a four-digit industrial classification is provided so that it is possible to get some rough idea about the effect of the change in the composition of industries on wage rates. It is also possible to estimate wage rates separately for the major industries.

The H.L.S. data for the two regions, on the other hand, give money wages at the aggregate level only. Although the H.L.S. perennial series for Pakistan as a whole provides some sector classification, regional data are for the aggregate manufacturing sector only. Moreover only the money wage rate is shown without any information about the wage bill and employment. The H.L.S. overall series provides no sector classification either, but it does show total employment and the wage bill. The aggregate nature of the H.L.S. data makes it impossible to check doubtful entries. And there are rather too many doubtful entries. To give some examples: (*a*) in 1959 it is reported that employment in Karachi declined by 34 per cent from the preceding year while the wage bill rose by 8 per cent;[1] (*b*) in 1959 employment in West Pakistan (excluding Karachi) declined by 13 per cent while the wage bill rose by 48 per cent;[1] (*c*) in 1962 the wage bill in Karachi rose by 57 per cent while employment declined by over 2 per cent.[4] In all these cases money wage rates change by 60 per cent or more. It does not seem likely that wage rates actually changed so erratically, and, therefore, quixotic changes in coverage are probably the cause. Coverage in East Pakistan dropped from 100 per cent of factories in 1960 to only 51 per cent in 1961 (see [6] January-March 1964). Coverage in terms of employment in West Pakistan excluding Karachi in 1955 was only about 11 per cent of that in 1954 (see [2, p. 74]). Such erratic changes in coverage can do anything to the overall wage rate simply by concentrating the under-coverage in a particular year in certain low or high wage industries. From the available H.L.S. sources it is impossible to determine how the changes in coverage were distributed in each year.

In comparison the C.M.I. has generally steadily improved its coverage and for any two consecutive C.M.I.s the change in coverage at the aggregate level is far less than can be called erratic. For individual industries, however, there have been certain erratic changes, most of them in the year 1955. One

[1] See [2, p. 74, Table 28].

advantage of the C.M.I. is that it provides enough information to make judgements on the plausibility of such sudden changes. To emphasise the limitation of the data, we make the following observations:

(*a*) In both regions the major textile industries show no erratic change in wage rates, wage bill or employment. In view of the fact that textiles employ more than half the industrial labour force in each region, this is reassuring. Movement of real wages in textiles can serve as the major basis in testing our hypotheses and deriving our conclusions.

(*b*) Certain non-textile industries in East Pakistan (notably printing and publishing, transport equipment, 'miscellaneous industries', chemicals and metal products) in 1955 showed a rather sharp decline in wages from the preceding year. Some of the declines can at least partly be explained by the change in intra-industry product composition, but quite a few of these changes cannot be explained satisfactorily. This phenomenon exists, although to a much smaller extent, in West Pakistan as well. As a result, real wages in non-textile industries declined in 1955 over 1954. This decline is particularly sharp in East Pakistan – nearly 25 per cent. One inevitably becomes sceptical about such a big and sudden change and the scepticism is justified by our inability to explain some of the sharp wage declines in that year.

(*c*) Wages in food manufacturing in East Pakistan have shown severe fluctuations in other years as well. These fluctuations seem to be correlated with fluctuations in the coverage of rice milling, a low wage industry. In both regions we have a few more unexplained sudden changes, all in the non-textile sectors. Below we estimate for each region two indices of real wages, namely for (*a*) all industries and (*b*) textiles on the basis of the C.M.I. data. In view of what has been said above, our faith in the index for the aggregate industries is somewhat less than for textiles.

3.3 *Adjustments made in the C.M.I. data*

In view of the above, it appears to us that the C.M.I. data, in spite of obvious limitations, are superior to the other source so that it seems reasonable to use the C.M.I. as our basic source of data and base our conclusions on them, with appropriate qualifications. We, of course, compare the findings based on the C.M.I. series with those derived from the H.L.S. data.

In this study, the term wages means wages, dearness allowance, and cash benefits.[1] While the C.M.I.s for 1957, 1959/60, 1962/3 and 1963/4 show these separately, the 1954 and 1955 C.M.I.s show wages and benefits (presumably including non-cash benefits) together while the 1958 C.M.I. shows only wages and dearness allowance. To render them comparable, we make the following adjustments. We estimate the proportion of non-cash benefits in total wages and benefits on the basis of the 1957 and 1962/3 C.M.I.s (which provide such information separately) and make a downward adjustment in wages and benefits shown in the 1954 and 1955 C.M.I.s. Similarly on the basis of the 1959/60 C.M.I. we ascertain the proportion of cash benefits in total wages and use it to make an upward adjustment in the 1958 wages shown in the C.M.I. It is reassuring that all such adjustments are very small.

For 1962/3 for East Pakistan we use the information for 2(j) factories only. For West Pakistan our information for 1962/3 and 1963/4 is based on unpublished C.M.I.s and they refer to both 2(j) and 5(1) factories. We use these figures for want of separate information about 2(j) factories and make appropriate qualificctions in the interpretation of the results.

3.4 *Cost of living index for industrial workers*

C.S.O'.s General Consumer Price Index for Industrial Workers for the relevant period was originally based on a commodity list and weights derived from a 1943/4 survey of working-class family expenditures. The new C.S.O. Consumer Price Index for Industrial Workers is based on weights derived from a more recent (1955/6) family expenditure survey, but cannot be applied to the period before 1961 for want of past price series for the new commodities introduced. However, the C.S.O. claims that 'the old series have been spliced into the new series' [4]. This means that the new *relative* weights for the commodities in the old index have been used to recalculate the old index, thus reducing the difference between the two indices to the

---

[1] This definition is partly dictated by the convenience of obtaining data, but seems good enough for our purpose.

fact that within each broad group the new index incorporates many new commodities each quantitatively unimportant.

An important limitation of the index is that it uses fixed weights while we should like to allow for changes in consumption patterns caused both by income and price changes. The fixed-weight wage-deflator is given by:

$$P = \sum_i (P_t^i / P_o^i) \ (P_o^i \ Q_o^i / \sum_i P_o^i \ Q_o^i)$$

Where P^i = price of i, Q^i = quantity purchased of i and subscript t and o refer to time periods. The price relative for the i-th commodity is weighted by the base-year proportion of total expenditure on i. If the price increase is concentrated in the commodities with inelastic demand then such a deflator would understate the increase in price because the actual expenditure on the commodities having high price relatives would be higher than the base-year proportion. In Pakistan food prices have risen considerably more than the prices of other commodities in the index over the relevant period [4] and demand for foodgrains is highly inelastic. It seems very likely that an average wage-earner spends a higher percentage of income on food today than when the weights were derived. And this precisely is the condition which is sufficient to show that the present index understates the rise in the cost of living (unless of course counterbalancing forces are in operation).

The C.S.O. points out [4] that the prices are collected from the retailers and not from the consumers so that they may have been underquoted to some extent. More importantly, it may have led to the underquotation of the increase in prices. This will be the case, for example, if a shortage appears in the supply of a product for which a price norm is suggested either by the producer or by the government.

Finally, for house rent the same price relative is reported each year for want of information. This has almost certainly caused some downward bias in the index.

In the above we have tried to point out a few factors which may have caused a downward bias in the C.S.O. cost of living index. It is possible, though not so obvious, that there are factors which counterbalance the above forces. In the absence of any other estimate of the index of cost of living, we are forced

to use the C.S.O. index as our wage-deflator, but the results
have to be interpreted with the weakness of the cost of living
index in mind.

By far the most important cause of our scepticism about the
C.S.O. index is due to the fact that the food price index used by
it shows a much lower increase, particularly in East Pakistan,
than do the alternative sources of price information.[1]

IV. MOVEMENT OF REAL WAGES

Table 9.1 shows real wages and real wage indices obtained by
deflating the adjusted C.M.I. money wage rate by the C.S.O.
General Consumer Price Index for Industrial Workers. For
each region we have shown real wages (*a*) for all industries,
and (*b*) for textiles separately. The reason we show the index
separately for textiles has already been mentioned: it employs
more than half the labour force in manufacturing in each
region, the composition of the labour force in this sector has
probably remained reasonably stable (certainly more so than for
aggregate manufacturing) with respect to product, skill, etc.,
and finally, we have argued above that the data for textiles are
more reliable than for the rest as a whole.

In East Pakistan real wages for aggregage industries have
remained lower in all years as compared to the base year
(1954). They declined sharply in 1955 (see our comments in
Section 3.2) and then remained fairly stable until 1962/3 when
the recovery is more pronounced. For textiles in East Pakistan
there was a small rise in 1955 over the base year and then a
fairly sharp decline in 1957. Recovery starts from 1958 and
continued up to 1962/3 when the base-year value was slightly
exceeded. It should, however, be pointed out that an upward
bias in East Pakistan textile wages is created throughout the
period due to the continuous rise in the share of jute textiles,
wages in jute textiles being on the average about 20 per cent
higher than wages in cotton textiles. If the real wage rates for
jute and cotton textiles are estimated separately, we still have
very considerably lower real wage in each of them by 1962/3
as compared to the base year.

---

[1] See Section VIII below and Appendix B in the ori ginal article.

TABLE 9.1

REAL WAGES (WAGES DEFLATED BY 1954-BASED COST OF LIVING INDEX) BASED ON C.M.I. DATA

(rupees per year per worker)

Year	East Pakistan				West Pakistan			
	All industries		Textiles		All industries		Textiles	
	Real wage	Index	Real wage	Index	Real wage	Index	Real wage	Index
1954	794·5	100·0	759·4	100·0	966·2	100·0	963·7	100·0
1955	702·3	88·4	783·8	103·2	911·5	94·3	960·5	99·7
1957	726·5	91·4	644·4	84·9	909·4	94·1	892·7	92·6
1958	743·3	93·6	672·4	88·5	933·6	96·6	887·3	92·1
1959/60	737·5	92·8	718·3	94·6	936·7	96·9	894·4	92·8
1962/3	766·2	96·4	773·0	101·8	854·4	88·4	859·4	89·2
	(727·8)	(91·6)	(727·7)	(95·8)				
1963/4	...	...	...	...	870·6	90·1	...	...

Notes: 1. See the original article, Appendix Tables A-1, A-2, and A-3 and notes following them, for the background information and the method of estimation.

2. East's 1962/3 figures in parentheses refer to combined 2(j) and 5(l) factories.

3. ... means not available.

4. It may appear that the change of base to 1955 would show steady (though slow) rise in aggregate manufacturing real wages in East Paskistan from that year onwards. But note our argument in Section 3.2 that the 1955 real wage in East Pakistan for aggregate industries is understated.

In West Pakistan the result is more striking. Real wage rate for aggregate industries dropped in 1955 over the base-year level and remained fairly stable until 1962/3 when it dropped sharply again. For textiles we again have a decline in real wages in stages, fairly sharply up to 1957 after which it remained stable for about half a decade. It again declined a few percentage points in 1962/3.

We must add that the West Pakistan real wage rates for 1962/3 and 1963/4 are estimated for workers employed both in 2(j) and 5(1) factories while all previous years' wage rates are based on 2(j) factories only. On the basis of the information obtained from the 1962/3 C.M.I. for East Pakistan, it seems that wages are lower in 5(1) factories (which are on a smaller scale than 2(j) factories). But the share of 5(1) factories is small in both the regions' C.M.I.s and in the East the real wage indices for 1962/3 go up only by about 5 percentage points if 5(1) factories are left out. If West Pakistan real wage indices for 1962/3 and 1963/4 are adjusted upward by 5 percentage points, the above conclusions remain unaffected: at the aggregate industry level real wage rates in the last two years would still be lower than in 1959/60 and way below the level in the base year. For textiles, real wages in 1962/3 after this adjustment would only be slightly higher than in 1959/60 but still considerably lower than in the base year.

To summarise: the real wage rates estimated on the basis of the adjusted C.M.I. data show the following pattern during the decade beginning 1954: In East Pakistan not much of a trend can be found; there was a decline early in the decade, followed by a period of steady real wages until at the end of the period near recovery to the base-year level was attained. In West Pakistan, real wages declined early in the decade and remained steady without showing any sign of recovery right up to the end of the period.

How do the H.L.S. data compare with the above findings? Table 9.2 shows the real wages for East Pakistan, Karachi and the rest of West Pakistan estimated on the basis of the H.L.S. perennial series. For East Pakistan the above finding is confirmed somewhat strongly: the real wage rate declined from 1955 to 1959 fairly rapidly and then recovers a good deal but even in 1963 it is lower than in the base period. In Karachi by the end of the period there is a slight rise over the earlier periods but in the rest of West Pakistan a considerable drop takes place.

TABLE 9.2

REAL WAGES (i.e. WAGES DEFLATED BY THE 1954-BASED COST OF LIVING INDEX) BASED ON THE H.L.S. PERENNIAL SERIES

(Rs. per worker per year)

Year	East Pakistan	West Pakistan*	Karachi
1955	845·2	993·2	1084·4
1956	750·3	1136·2	1048·3
1957	709·9	893·0	1058·2
1958	722·5	972·5	1015·5
1959	704·8	979·9	931·7
1960	768·0	907·1	1140·8
1961	765·6	793·4	1117·0
1962	832·4	. . .	. . .
1963	826·9	——1051·3——	

*Excluding Karachi.

The H.L.S. overall series (Table 9.3), however, leads to different conclusions. According to this series, real wages in all three areas have shown increases in recent years. Presumably the only difference between the two H.L.S. series is that the perennial series is obtained by subtracting seasonal factories from the overall series. Thus the increase must be concentrated in the seasonal factories. One explanation would be that the seasonal factories operate at the time of peak demand for labour and hence they are better placed for wage bargains. But this does not seem plausible in view of the lower wages in seasonal factories than in perennial factories.[1] What seems more likely (barring of course the possibility of straightforward arithmetic errors) is that the extremely erratic changes in coverage have led to serious changes in the proportion of seasonal factories covered. In other words, the overall wage rate is a weighted average of two rates, one considerably higher than the other. If the relative weights change erratically from year to year, the overall rate may show erratic changes in spite of the fact that the two constituent rates are fairly stable.

[1] Overall money wage rate is lower than that for perennial factories according to H.L.S. data for Pakistan as a whole [2].

TABLE 9.3

REAL WAGES (i.e. WAGES DE-
FLATED BY THE 1954-BASED COST
OF LIVING INDEX) BASED ON THE
H.L.S. OVERALL SERIES
(Rs. per worker per year)

Year	East Pakistan	West Pakistan
1954	682·2	842·7
1955	767·1	1095·2
1956	690·8	1106·7
1957	675·3	970·1
1958	676·4	1004·3
1959	543·1	944·6
1960	724·1	1030·3
1961	719·1	937·2
1962	793·3	1270·3
1963	787·3	1032·3

V. SOME QUALIFICATIONS

In so far as our concern is with the average welfare of the
working class as a whole, we should compare the standard of
living of an average worker today with that of an average
worker in some base period (while allowing the average worker
to change between the period with respect to skill, age, sex,
etc.) and not the standard of living of a worker of given skill,
age, sex, etc., today as compared to that in some base period.
For the purpose of measuring the change in the average well-
being of the workers, it is just as important to know how workers
have been moving between jobs of varying rates of skill and
income as to know how specific rates have been changing. To
illustrate, if nothing happens to the specific rates while all
workers move to better paid jobs due to increase in their skills,
then it is right to say that the workers' standard of living has
increased.

If the above statement is correct then the only adjustment we
have to make in our estimates is for changes in the number of
hours worked per labourer. If, however, we are interested in
measuring the well-being of a worker of given skill, age, sex,
etc., then our estimates have also to be adjusted for changes in
skill, age, sex, etc., composition of the labour force.

We may actually go one step further and argue that in a country like Pakistan it is the average earnings per worker (irrespective of the number of hours worked per labourer) which is the relevant indicator of workers' welfare. In other words it is our measure which is the ideal indicator of workers' standard of living. This claim is based on the reasoning that the marginal utility of leisure at the relevant level of employment and income is probably negligible so that the workers would still be better off (worse off) if wage per hour declines (increases) but wage per worker increases (declines) due to an increase (decrease) in the number of hours worked per labourer.

In the following we comment on the possible effects of the disturbing factors while maintaining that if our argument above is broadly right, our index need not be adjusted for any of these factors to measure workers' 'welfare' or real standard of living.

(*a*) Skill Composition of the Labour Force: With all the specific wage rates unchanged, the overall rate would change if the skill composition of the labour force changes. There are broadly two types of such change: first, change in the share of more skill-requiring industries in total employment and second, change in the proportion of skill-requiring jobs within individual industries.

Although our overall index is subject to the influence of the first kind of factor, the textile wages are not. The same is true at least to a large extent about many of the individual industries we have examined. A comparison of the money wage rates in these industries and the relevant cost of living indices shows that real wage rates in most of the major industries have followed the pattern of the overall real wage index.

It also seems unlikely that the skill composition within an industry like textiles would vary significantly over time. If at all, workers on the average are likely to have become generally more 'learned' over time. Thus, this factor is unlikely to have 'distorted' the change in real wages in a downward direction.

(*b*) Sex and Age Ratios: This factor could not have played any significant role in view of the fact that women and non-adults have been an extremely small proportion of the total manufacturing labour force (less than 2 per cent and 1 per cent respectively in East Pakistan and less than 1½ per cent and 1 per cent respectively in West Pakistan in as recent a year as 1959/60 [3], the only year for which we have the information).

(c) Number of Hours Worked: If working hours per labourer have been getting longer (shorter) then our figures would overstate (understate) the increase in hourly real wage rates. The only information we have is limited to the change in East Pakistan over the period between 1959/60 and 1962/3 which shows that in the latter year an average production worker worked about 30 per cent longer hours than in the former year. According to these figures the hourly real wage rate in East Pakistan declined very sharply (more than 25 per cent) between the years 1959/60 and 1962/3.

Some increase in working hours may have been made possible by the greater rate of capacity utilisation in more recent years which facilitated the provision of more overtime work. In view of the well-known hypothesis that the rate of capacity utilisation over the same period went up in West Pakistan also, the same may have happened there. But such a sharp reduction in the hourly wage rates as implied by the information in Table 9.4 seems at best unlikely. Our scepticism about the working hours shown in the 1962/3 C.M.I. arises out of the fact that the same document shows that during the year less than 300 shifts were worked per factory. Thus unless the large factories were working many more shifts than the small ones the two figures are inconsistent.

TABLE 9.4

AVERAGE NUMBER OF HOURS
WORKED PER PRODUCTION
WORKER PER WEEK IN EAST
PAKISTAN IN 2(j) FACTORIES

Year	All industries	Textiles
1959/60	45·3 (100)	46·5 (100)
1962/3	58·4 (129)	60·9 (131)

Note: Figures in parentheses are indices with bases 1959/60.
Source [3]

We end this section with a word on a final factor in which a change does affect the real wage index an an indicator of workers' welfare. In Section VII we measure per capita income of an average working class family on the basis of information on family size and earners per family for a particular year in the mid-fifties. We do not know how the number of earners per family (the number of dependents per employed worker) has been changing. If this has been going up (down) fast, the workers' average standard of living may also have been going up in spite of the reduction in real wages that we observe. We have no empirical evidence whatsoever on the movement of the number of dependents per worker and *a priori* it is difficult to argue that it has been changing in any particular direction.[1]

VI. COMPARISON OF REGIONAL REAL WAGES

It is estimated by the Planning Commission that the regional per capita income in West Pakistan is 31 per cent higher than in East Pakistan for the year 1962/3 (see [10, chpater IX]). Such comparisons are made on the basis of regional outputs at constant prices of a particular year (1959/60 is the latest C.S.O. base) without any correction for the regional difference in the purchasing power of income.

How do regional real wages compare? Again without any adjustment for the regional difference in purchasing power, real wages at the aggregate level have on the average been about 25 per cent higher in the West than in the East.[2] To

---

[1] Over the period under review, industrial employment expanded a good deal. If one takes into account the workers' extended families (including those left behind in the village) then it is plausible to argue that the number of dependents per worker has declined. This is because some members of extended families have probably found employment and hence need not be supported any more.

[2] If adjusted for the difference in the purchasing power of wages in the two regions, the disparity would be greater. This claim is based on a forthcoming study by Mr Abdul Ghafur of this Institute. He compares the relative prices of wage goods of the two regions by using the workers' consumption bundle in the two regions as weights separately. Prices of wage goods on the average are about 10 to 15 per cent higher in East for the years for which he undertakes the study.

It should be noted that a similar correction would also give a greater disparity in regional incomes per head than is shown by the simple comparison of regional incomes. It has been claimed that such a correction factor is much greater than 15 per cent. See [5, p. 93].

TABLE 9.5

WEST'S REAL WAGE AS MULTIPLE
OF EAST'S REAL WAGE
(based on C.M.I. data)

Year	All industries	Cotton textiles
1954	1·22	1·38
1955	1·30	1·46
1957	1·25	1·46
1958	1·26	1·47
1959/60	1·27	1·48
1962/63	1·17	1·42

Note: Figures for 1962/3 refer to both 2(j) and
5(l) factories while for other years they refer to
only 2(j) factories.

overcome the possible distortion due to the difference in the
regional composition of industries, one could refer to the regional
disparity in cotton textile workers' wages: it is considerably
greater than the disparity for the aggregate manufacturing
sector (about 45 per cent higher in West than in East Pakistan
on the average).[1]

VII. WHERE DO THE INDUSTRIAL WAGE-EARNERS STAND IN THE INCOME DISTRIBUTION SCALE?

In 1962/3 in East Pakistan the wage rate at current prices was
Rs. 1004·4 per worker per year (in all 2(j) and 5(l) factories
together). In 1959/60 purchasing power this turns out to be
Rs. 936·9. The number of dependants per earner in working-

---

[1] Cotton textile wages in East are lower than the average industrial
wage while wages in West Pakistan cotton textiles are just about equal to
the average industrial wage. If the disparity between the cotton textile
wages of the two regions approximately represents the difference between
skill-specific wages of the two, then production workers in manufacturing
industries have a higher level of average skill in East so that the overall
wage disparity is less than the disparity in cotton textile wages. It should
also be noted that the regional disparity in cotton textile wages is greater
than the regional disparity in per capita income as measured by the
Planning Commission while the regional disparity in overall manufacturing
wages is less than the regional disparity in per capita income.

class families in East Pakistan average 4·6.[1] Thus per capita income of an average wage-earner's family turns out to be Rs. 203·7 or about 73 per cent of regional per capita income (see [10, chapter IX]) at 1959/60 prices.

West Pakistan's average wage rate per year in 1962/3 was Rs. 1035·5 at current prices or Rs. 976·9 at 1959/60 purchasing power of the workers. Average number of dependants per wage earner being 4·7,[1] per capita income turns out to be Rs. 207·9 or 54 per cent of regional per capita income.

It is interesting to note that a very large majority of the rural population in each region is better off than an average industrial worker. Approximately less than 40 per cent of the East's rural population has a lower income than the average urban wage earner (compare data shown in [1] with our wages). A comparison of our findings with those of [1] also reveals that urban wages are way below average income in rural areas (not average rural 'workers' income).[2]

We have already noted that over the period under review real wages have failed to rise and almost certainly have declined somewhat. During this period per capita income has increased, particularly in the urban areas and quite impressively in West Pakistan. Thus income distribution over the decade under review must have changed unfavourably for the working class and in particular the urban income distribution must have become more unequal. This effect must have been more pronounced in West Pakistan than in East Pakistan.

VIII. REAL LABOUR COST FROM EMPLOYERS' POINT OF VIEW AND LABOUR'S FACTOR SHARE

The above discussion is exclusively concerned with one of the three indices of real wages to which we referred in Section II, that of workers' standard of living (U_1). In this section we

[1] Average for Dacca, Chittagong, Narayanganj and Khulna in East Pakistan and averaged for Karachi, Lahore, Peshawar, Hyderabad, Multan and Quetta in West Pakistan. Source [2].

[2] The comparison between urban wages and rural incomes must be qualified by the statement that it depends a good deal on the relative coverage given to the components of income by [1] for rural areas and by the C.M.I. for urban wage earners.

discuss what little we can about the behaviour of the other two indices, those of the real cost of labour from the employers' point of view (U_2) and labour's factor share (U_3).

We cannot estimate U_2 for the aggregate industrial sector for want of an index of producers' price for the products of the entire sector. We, however, estimate it for jute and cotton textiles in East and for textiles in West Pakistan, products for which we have some price information of the necessary type.

In a recent study, Stephen Lewis Jr. and S. Mushtaq Hussain find that the relative prices of agricultural goods have risen very considerably faster than the price of manufactured goods over the relevant period in both the regions of Pakistan [8]. Since our estimates show that U_1 has gone down only very slightly in East Pakistan and not very much in West Pakistan over the whole period, can we conclude from this, according to our equation (3) in Section II, that U_2 has risen rapidly over the period under review for the manufacturing sector as a whole? Our answer is in the negative because of the following: In the C.S.O. cost of living index (which is our wage-deflator in obtaining U_1 from money wage rates) food prices have over 60 per cent of total weight [4]. The food price index that is included in our wage-deflator shows a much smaller increase than the food price index used by Lewis and Hussain to reach their conclusions (Table 9.6). If we had substituted the Lewis–Hussain food price index in our wage-deflator we would undoubtedly get a very great decline in real wages (i.e. in U_1, the index of workers' standard of living) and particularly so in

TABLE 9.6

COMPARISON OF FOOD PRICE INDICES

Year	East Pakistan		West Pakistan	
	Lewis–Hussain	C.S.O.: Cost of Living Index	Lewis–Hussain	C.S.O.: Cost of Living Index
1954	100·0	100·0	100·0	100·0
1959/60	192·8	133·0	131·0	122·8
1962/3	199·1	141·1	135·5	127·2
1963/4	—	—	146·3	132·9

Note: Lewis–Hussain index is the one that uses the marketed quantities as weights. Source [8]. Source for the C.S.O. index is [2]. In both cases the 1954 index is the average of the 1953/54 and 1954/55 indices.

East Pakistan. To what extent the adverse terms of trade for manufacturing as shown by Lewis and Hussain would be powerful enough to outweigh the decline in U_1 can only be ascertained after empirical analysis of each case.

The main explanation of the discrepancy between the two sets of food prices lies in the C.S.O.'s use of controlled prices for a large part of the major foodgrains. For example, between a half and three-quarters of the rice in East Pakistan is assumed to have been bought at ration shops. This procedure makes the food price index lower than it would be if free market prices were used because (a) controlled prices have shown a smaller increase than free market prices and (b) the C.S.O. has been varying the share of rice/wheat bought at controlled prices from year to year, the correlation between these shares and free market prices being on the whole positive.

The objections against the C.S.O.'s procedure are powerful. The C.S.O.'s assumption of the share of purchase at ration shops is not based on any statistical information about actual purchases. They are pure guesses. In most years statutory rationing did not extend beyond municipal areas while the factories and workers' homes are located outside these areas. The changes in the shares of rice/wheat sold at controlled prices are also based on pure guesses and not on the facts about actual sales.[1]

If our argument about C.S.O.'s procedure is correct then real wages (i.e. U_1, workers' standard of living) have actually declined more than our estimates show.[2]

Our estimates of the real labour cost from the capitalists' point of view (U_2) for cotton and jute textiles in East Pakistan and for cotton textiles in West Pakistan are shown in Table 9.7. These are estimated directly by dividing money wages by the indices of respective wholesale prices of textiles.

---

[1] Note that neither [4] nor [2] give even a hint that controlled prices are used.

[2] Lewis and Hussain have prepared an index of wholesale prices of manufactured goods. We do not use it to obtain U_2 directly from U_1 because: (a) their index does not refer to the same commodity bundle as our industrial sector produces; (b) they use 1959/60 fixed weights while we want weights to vary according to outputs; and (c) their prices are not necessarily for the domestically produced goods.

TABLE 9.7

INDEX OF REAL LABOUR COST FROM THE
MANUFACTURERS' POINT OF VIEW

| Year | East Pakistan | | West Pakistan |
	Cotton textile	Jute textile	Cotton textile
1954	100·0	100·0	100·0
1955	111·8	92·8	118·0
1957	105·2	79·5	97·2
1958	95·4	92·9	104·2
1959/60	95·7	90·6	98·6
1962/3	98·7	101·8	103·9

Not much of a trend can be found for real labour cost in any of the three cases. If anything, for cotton textiles in East Pakistan there seems to be a downward trend after an initial rise. For jute textiles we observe a gradual decline up to 1957 and then, followed by a period of stability, recovery just above the base-year level by the end of the decade. For cotton textiles in West Pakistan there is quite a bit of fluctuation, but no definite trend. One should note, however, that the index of workers' standard of living for all three industries shows some decline over the period, markedly so for cotton textiles in both the regions. Thus in general U_2 has a higher value relative to U_1 in all three cases.

Table 9.8 shows labour's factor share (U_3) in the three industries listed below and also in the aggregate manufacturing sector of the two regions. For West Pakistan we observe quite a sharp rise very early in the period and gradual decline since. For East Pakistan it declines for aggregate industries and goes up a bit for cotton textiles. For jute textiles there is quite a bit of fluctuation, an increase until the late fifties and then a decline.

The fact that labour's factor share shows a somewhat higher increase by the end of the period over the base period than real labour cost in cotton textiles in both regions indicates that labour productivity according to our definition declined somewhat in both cases (equation (4) of Section 2). A closer examination reveals that this is due primarily to the declining share of value added in gross value of product. Similarly, the rather sharp reduction in recent years in labour's factor share in East's jute textiles in the face of rising real labour cost indicates

TABLE 9.8

LABOUR'S FACTOR SHARE

Year	All industries	Cotton textiles	Jute textiles
A. East Pakistan			
1954	·463	·356	·454
1955	·378	·371	·381
1957	·370	·422	·551
1958	·394	·451	·510
1959/60	·376	·370	·423
1962/3	·260 (·288)	·438	·295 (·411)
B. West Pakistan			
1954	·303	·305	
1955	·367	·399	
1957	·380	·392	
1958	·329	·384	
1959/60	·341	·384	
1962/3	·338	·361	

Note: Factor share is defined as total employment cost (production and non-production workers) divided by gross value added. Since 1962/3 is the first year in which C.M.I. includes indirect taxes in value of output and value added, we have subtracted them to make the value added comparable with other years. We are still left with a sudden fall in labour's factor share in jute textiles and all industries in East. The low share in jute textiles in that year is due to the high share of value added which is caused by the serious underestimate of raw jute input, as a comparison with previous C.M.I.s reveals. If we revise 1962/3 raw jute input by using the 1959/60 ratio of raw jute to jute manufactures in physical weight, we get a lower value added coefficient and a higher coefficient of labour's factor share, which is shown in parentheses.

a dramatic increase in 'labour productivity', again largely caused by the rising share of value added in gross value of product (which again is largely due to the reduction in the price of a major input).

IX. CONCLUSIONS

None of the findings about the course of real wages is startling. In a surplus-labour economy, one expects real wages to stabilise around some subsistence level. Fluctuations would still occur in so far as the cost of living changes and it takes time for wages to adjust, and wage adjustment can rarely be exactly equal to the change in the cost of living because of forecasting and estimating difficulties.

Again in a situation of general surplus labour, one does not expect industrial wages to be disproportionately greater than the average 'wage' in the traditional (i.e. agricultural) sector. Some differential probably has to be maintained to compensate for the urban-rural differences in cost of living (such costs being broadly defined). But the industrial wage cannot remain disproportionately in excess of the average agricultural 'wage'; competition in the labour market would lower the gap to near the minimum level dictated by the incentive-differential requirement. The cost of rudimentary training provided to the unskilled or semi-skilled workers, the presence of the trade unions, and government actions in regulating minimum wages are not strong enough to create a large gap.

The experience of West Pakistan in recent years shows that the industrial employers have been able to draw labour from rural areas at a rapid rate with a steady real wage and a fairly low incentive differential. Only about a quarter of the rural population had a lower income than the average income of a wage-earning family. But labourers (presumably from the poorest income groups) nevertheless moved from villages to urban areas. During the period 1951 to 1961 the urban labour force grew at nearly 4 per cent per year while the rural labour force grew at only 1 per cent per year (population censuses quoted in [2]).

It is also interesting to note that the urban-rural wage differential is considerably greater in the East than in the West. This may have something to do with the tenancy system in the traditional sector of the two regions. In West Pakistan agriculture pure wage-labour relations are more dominant while in East Pakistan there are fewer landless wage-earning labourers. Thus the choice before a rural labourer in the East is frequently not one between a job in a rural area and a job in an urban area. It often involves giving up the status of a farmer partly owning his land and this has to be adequately compensated.

REFERENCES

[1] Bergan, Asbjorn, *Personal Income Distribution and Personal Saving in Pakistan, 1963/64,* mimeographed (Karachi: Pakistan Institute of Development Economics, 1966). See chap. 8 in this volume.

[2] Pakistan, Central Statistical Office, *Statistical Yearbook, 1964* (Karachi: Central Statistical Office, 1965).

[3] Pakistan, Central Statistical Office, *Census of Manufacturing Industries,* relevant numbers (Karachi: Central Statistical Office).

[4] Pakistan, Central Statistical Office, *Consumer Price Index Numbers for Industrial Workers (1961 = 100)* (Karachi: Central Statistical Office, 1964).

[5] Haq, Mahbubul, *Strategy of Economic Planning* (Karachi: Oxford University Press, 1963).

[6] Pakistan, Ministry of Health, Labour and Social Welfare, *Pakistan Labour Gazette* (quarterly), relevant issues.

[7] Pakistan, Ministry of Health, Labour and Social Welfare, *Working of the Payment of Wages Act,* relevant issues.

[8] Lewis, Stephen R., Jr., and Mushtaq Hussain, S., *Relative Price Changes and Industrialisation in Pakistan, 1951–64* (Karachi: Pakistan Institute of Development Economics, 1967).

[9] Lewis, W. Arthur, 'Economic Development with Unlimited Supplies of Labour', *Manchester School of Economic and Social Studies,* May 1954.

[10] Pakistan, Planning Commission, *The Third Five-Year Plan* (Karachi: Manager of Publications, June 1965).

[11] P.I.D.E., Monetary and Fiscal Section, *A Measure of Inflation in Pakistan, 1951–60* (Karachi: Pakistan Institute of Development Economics, Mar. 1961).

10 Trend of Real Income of the Rural Poor in East Pakistan

SWADESH R. BOSE*

I. SCOPE OF THE STUDY

PAKISTAN's gross national product has been rising over time. While G.N.P. per capita remained practically unchanged during the 1950s, it increased appreciably in the 1960s. The trend of per capita income does not, however, indicate whether and to what extent economic development had 'trickle down' effects and improved the lot of the relatively poorer sections of society. Studies of intertemporal changes in inequality of income distribution and in levels of income (consumption) could show what changes actually took place in the absolute and relative income position of the poor.

'Diminishing inequalities in the distribution of income' is one of the professed objectives of Pakistan's Third Five-Year Plan [21, p. 40]. This objective implies both an absolute and a relative improvement in the income level of the poorer sections of the population. The two studies which are known to have been made on income distribution in Pakistan do not cover enough ground to indicate whether this was achieved in the past: the study by Mrs Haq [10] is limited to personal income distribution in the high-income brackets (income tax payers) in urban areas for the period 1948/9 to 1960/1, and that by Bergan [1], although comprehensive, refers to a single year, 1963/4.

* This chapter first appeared in the *Pakistan Development Review*, autumn 1968. The author is grateful to Professor Mosharaff Hussain, Department of Economics, Rajshahi University, for kindly giving him access to some unpublished data collected through a survey conducted under the auspices of the university. He is indebted to Dr Nuruddin Chowdhury and Dr A. R. Khan for making helpful comments on an earlier draft. He is, however, solely responsible for any errors remaining in this paper.

It is, however, generally held that Pakistan's pattern of development has generated increasing income inequalities among classes (and also between the two Wings). The development strategy has placed major reliance on private enterprise and sought to generate a higher saving rate through redistributing income in favour of those groups whose saving rates are considered to be relatively high. This has meant an increasing concentration of income in the hands of a small group of wealthy industrialists. Apparently some non-industrial groups in trade, the professions and services also experienced large increases in their incomes. One cannot even exclude the possibility that the process of economic development redistributed income in such a way and to such an extent that the bottom group (say, the quartile) in the income scale has become absolutely poorer while per capita income of the population as a whole increased.

About two years ago Griffin [8] suggested, on the basis of some important although inadequate data, that the real income of Pakistan's rural population declined from 1949/50 onwards till the early 1960s, whenceforward it gradually rose to the 1949/50 level in 1964/5. Griffin's provocative remarks have not been followed up by any research into the changes over time in the level of real income (consumption) of the poorest sections of society in rural areas.[1]

The present writer's efforts to make such an enquiry have been hindered by non-availability of necessary information. This paper, much more restricted in scope than was originally intended, presents the preliminary findings of an attempt to indicate in an indirect way the changes in the level of real income of the bulk of the poorest people in rural East Pakistan from 1949 to 1966. It does not represent a comprehensive study of the intertemporal changes in the inequality of income (consumption) distribution and the levels of living of the various sections of the rural population of East Pakistan. Such a

---

[1] Griffin has been rightly criticised by Bergan [1, p. 172] for assuming that agricultural income is the only income that accrues to the rural population. It is, however, very doubtful if the inclusion of income accruing to rural population for their activities in non-agricultural sectors (if such income could be estimated) would show a rising trend of per capita income in rural areas.

study does not appear to be feasible for lack of necessary historical data.[1]

The Central Statistical Office's multipurpose sampling enquiry (National Sample Survey) which collected data on consumption and income of rural households began as late as 1959, and only three rounds (1959, 1960 and 1961) are available. The same enquiry restarted in 1963/4[2] and so far only the 1963/4 survey is available. Because of the short period of time covered by these surveys and the admittedly poor quality of the 1959 survey, one cannot use them for the purpose of studying long-term changes in the income-consumption level of the poorest among the rural population. They may, however, be used as evidence of such changes in the early 1960s.[3]

Main Assumptions and Findings

Since these limitations of available data preclude any direct estimation of long-term changes in real income of the rural poor, some indirect and somewhat crude methods are used in this study. The main assumptions which underlie the statistical computations and their interpretations are the following:

An increase in income of the poorest section of the rural

---

[1] Given expenditure distributions (i.e. distributions of persons by monthly or yearly per capita consumption expenditure, at current prices) relating to different periods, and given the appropriate consumer price indices with which to bring the distributions to some common set of prices, one could attempt an estimate of the intertemporal changes in inequality or level of living. The appropriate consumer price index is unlikely to be the same for all levels of living (income-consumption groups). Hence, if the index varies with the level of income or consumption, it would be necessary to work out a set of price deflators, one deflator for each income-consumption group, for comparing intertemporal changes in levels of living and inequality of expenditure (income) distributions. About the need for a set of deflators, see Iyengar and Bhattacharya [12].

[2] It has been re-named Quarterly Survey of Current Economic Conditions and covers both urban and rural areas.

[3] It has, however, been pointed out by Mahalanobis [16] that frequency distributions in which the class ranges are fixed in terms of money value of per capita expenditure (or income) have limitations for purposes of intertemporal comparisons of levels of living. Even when price changes are corrected by use of the price deflator(s) a fixed range frequency class (income or expenditure) would represent different fractile groups in two or more periods and would not be comparable in any important sense.

population would not take place in the absence of an increase in average incomes of the agricultural population and rural population.

An increase in per capita income in agriculture would show up in rising crop yield and higher monetary returns from land per head of agricultural population.

Those who are agricultural labourers by chief occupation constitute the bulk of the poorest among rural people and any increase in their real income must show up in the movement of real wages which are the major source of their income.

It is assumed that the dependency ratio per labourer has remained unchanged since 1949.

On these assumptions, the estimated movement of per capita rural income, per capita income in agriculture, crop yield, and real wages, shown in Sections II and III, suggest a decline in the real-income level of the poorest stratum of rural population of East Pakistan in the 1950s and no significant rise in the 1960s.

II. EVIDENCE OF MOVEMENT OF PER CAPITA FACTOR INCOMES OF AGRICULTURAL AND RURAL POPULATIONS

We begin with the observation of estimated changes in real incomes of rural, and agricultural populations of East Pakistan, and urban-rural disparity in per capita income. A clear distinction is made between rural and agricultural population, and between rural factor income and factor income in agriculture. Rural population is larger than agricultural population, because rural areas contain almost all people engaged in agriculture, and also a large proportion of non-agricultural population. Similarly, total rural factor income is larger than factor income (gross value added) in agriculture.

Table 10.1 presents some estimates of per capita factor incomes of total, agricultural, rural and urban populations of East Pakistan from 1949/50 to 1963/4. The series could not be made up-to-date because 'province-wise breakdown of Pakistan' national income data has not been published, or made available to the author, for any year after 1963/4.

Table 10.2 shows some historical data on cropped area per head of agricultural population, cropping intensity and yield.

Agricultural stagnation, slow industrial development and rapid population growth characterised the economy of East Pakistan in the 1950s. This resulted in a lower per capita income in the late 1950s than in the early 1950s. Only in the 1960s

TABLE 10.1

PER CAPITA FACTOR INCOMES OF TOTAL, AGRICUL-
TURAL, RURAL AND URBAN POPULATIONS OF EAST
PAKISTAN

(in rupees at 1959/60 prices; the last column is in per cent)

Year	Gross provincial product per capita	Agricultural value added per head of agricultural population	Per capita rural income	Per capita urban income	Per capita rural income as % of urban
	(1)	(2)	(3)	(4)	(5)
1949/50	285 ⎫	228 ⎫	271 ⎫	609	44
1950/1	289 ⎪	229 ⎪	274 ⎪	619	44
1951/2	290 ⎬(290)	225 ⎬(228)	274 ⎬(275)	634	43
1952/3	292 ⎪	228 ⎪	277 ⎪	619	45
1953/4	295 ⎭	230 ⎭	280 ⎭	615	46
1954/5	282 ⎫	216 ⎫	265 ⎫	617	43
1955/6	263 ⎪	194 ⎪	247 ⎪	597	41
1956/7	281 ⎬(271)	212 ⎬(201)	261 ⎬(253)	666	39
1957/8	270 ⎪	199 ⎪	253 ⎪	607	42
1958/9	257 ⎭	184 ⎭	238 ⎭	616	39
1959/60	271 ⎫	196 ⎫	252 ⎫	618	41
1960/1	279 ⎪	203 ⎪	259 ⎪	644	40
1961/2	289 ⎬(285)	207 ⎬(202)	267 ⎬(268)	671	40
1962/3	281 ⎪	195 ⎪	258 ⎪	696	37
1963/4	305 ⎭	208 ⎭	279 ⎭	755	37

Note: Figures in parentheses are five-year averages.

does a slight reversal in the movement of per capita income appear to have begun. As Table 10.1 shows, the average per capita income during 1949/50 to 1953/4 was 290 rupees, during 1954/5 to 1958/9 271 rupees, and during 1959/60 to 1963/4 285 rupees. During the four-year period, 1959/60 to 1962/3, it was only 280 rupees.

TABLE 10.2

CROPPED LAND PER HEAD, CROPPING INTENSITY AND YIELD

Period (July–June)	Cropped area (in acres) per head of Agricultural population		Male agricultural labour force Net (B)	Cropping intensity (per cent) (C)	Rice yield per acre (maunds) (D)	Rice output per head of agricultural population (maunds) (E)	Total agricultural value added per acre of net cropped land (1959/60: Rs.) (F)
	Gross (A)	Net (B)					
1948/9	n.a.	n.a.	n.a.	131·0	10·8	n.a.	n.a.
1949/50	0·73	0·57	n.a.	127·7	10·3	5·9	402
1950/1	0·72	0·56	2·07	127·8	10·0	5·6	406
1954/5	0·68	0·52	n.a.	131·4	9·7	5·0	415
1955/6	0·62	0·49	n.a.	127·0	8·9	4·4	393
1959/60	0·58	0·45	n.a.	129·6	10·9	4·9	439
1960/1	0·58	0·44	1·74	131·6	11·8	5·2	460
1961/2	0·56	0·43	n.a.	130·8	12·3	5·3	478
1962/3	0·56	0·42	n.a.	132·5	11·1	4·7	463
1963/4	0·56	0·41	n.a.	133·7	12·8	5·2	503
1964/5	n.a.	n.a.	n.a.	n.a.	12·3	n.a.	n.a.
1965/6	n.a.	n.a.	n.a.	n.a.	12·2	n.a.	n.a.
1966/7	n.a.	n.a.	n.a.	n.a.	12·9	n.a.	n.a.

Notes: $C = \dfrac{A}{B} \times 100$ $E = B \times D$ 'n.a.' means not available.

Decline in Per Capita Income in Agriculture

The decline in per capita income of the agricultural population was even more pronounced. As Table 10.1 shows, from about 228 rupees in the early 1950s it went down to 201 rupees in the late 1950s and to 202 rupees in the early 1960s. But if 1963/4 is excluded the average for the period 1959/60 to 1962/3 becomes only 200 rupees. There is little doubt that the fall in per capita income of the agricultural population during the 1950s has not been made good by the slight reversal observed in 1963/4.

Agricultural income data used in this paper are based on the C.S.O. estimates and include value added in fishing and forestry as well as crop production. However, output of crops accounts for 80 per cent of total agricultural income. One can, therefore, go a step further and see whether the combined effect of changes in land per head and yield per acre appear to support the observed decline in per capita income in agriculture. It is clear from Table 10.2 that both net and gross cropped area per head of agricultural population has declined significantly since 1949/50. The increase in cropping intensity has been too insignificant to offset the decline in net cropped area per head resulting from virtually given land and rapidly growing population. The yield of rice, which accounts for over 50 per cent of gross value added in agriculture, decreased in the middle-1950s but showed some increase in the 1960s. However, the per cent increase in yield has been smaller than the per cent decrease in cropped acreage per head, so that output of rice per head of agricultural population was lower in the middle-1950s and the early 1960s than in the early 1950s.

A recent study [15] has shown that the agricultural sector consumes about 80 per cent of rice output and sells about 20 per cent to the non-agricultural sector, and that the wholesale price of rice declined both absolutely and relative to the price of cotton textiles (and other consumer manufacturers) from 1951/2 to 1955/6 but registered some increase from 1956/7 to 1963/4. This indicates that the real returns from the marketed portion of rice output per head of agricultural population clearly declined in the earlier period but may have improved somewhat in the later period.

The decline in gross value added in agriculture per head of agricultural population as shown in Table 10.1 is at constant agricultural prices of 1959/60. We have implicitly assumed so far that this decline measures the decline in per capita real income of the agricultural population. There may, however, be objections to this on two grounds. One is the movement of the terms of trade of the agricultural sector, and the other is income earned by the agricultural population from subsidiary occupations.

Since the agricultural sector sold a part of its output to other sectors in exchange for certain products, a decline in the prices of these products relatively to agricultural prices could partly or fully offset the decline in per capita income in the sector measured in the way stated above. There was, however, no such offsetting influence. For one, the proportion of agricultural output sold outside the sector was likely to be considerably less than 50 per cent. Secondly, as Lewis and Hussain [15] have shown, the terms of trade were actually moving against agriculture till the late 1950s, and only since then has there begun a reversal of this trend.

It is agricultural output which essentially determines the income level of the agricultural population. Inclusion of income earned by agricultural population from subsidiary occupations would only slightly raise the absolute level of per capita income in all years, but would not alter the observed trend over time. Moreover, income from subsidiary occupations is included in our estimate of per capita rural income, and this also moved roughly in the same direction as per capita income in agriculture, as we shall presently see.

One would expect that a decline in per capita factor income within the agricultural sector would be accompanied by a similar decline in income of the poorer people in the sector, unless the relative income of these people was sufficiently raised by a change in the distribution of income within the sector. But there appears to be no reason why such a redistribution should have taken place over time in favour of poorer agriculturists and agricultural wage labourers. On the contrary, it is reasonable to maintain, as was observed by Papanek [23], that whatever increase in agricultural production occurred in the 1960s has accrued mainly to large farmers who could obtain subsidised fertilisers and some benefits from the government's agricultural development programme.

Fall in Per Capita Rural Income and Increase in Rural-Urban Disparity

As can be seen from Table 10.1, per capita rural income declined from 1949/50 to 1958/9. Although a reversal began from 1959/60, the income level was still lower in 1962/3 than in 1949/50; only in 1963/4 did it rise slightly above the 1949/50 level. From an average of 275 rupees during 1949/50 to 1953/4, it fell to 253 rupees during 1954/5 to 1958/9 and moved to 268 rupees during 1959/60 to 1963/4. If 1963/4 is excluded the average for 1959/60 to 1962/3 comes down to 259 rupees only.

Per capita urban income increased steadily, although slowly, during the entire period. It rose from just over 600 rupees in the early 1950s to about 700 rupees in the early 1960s. As a result, the rural-urban disparity in factor income per capita has increased. The ratio of per capita rural income to urban has gone down from 44 per cent in 1949/50 to 37 per cent in 1963/4. This differs from Bergan's [1, p. 172] estimate of 60 per cent for 1963/4, based on the C.S.O.'s quarterly survey [19]. Total population and its rural-urban distribution used in our estimates are practically the same as in Bergan's. These two estimates are not, however, strictly comparable, because Bergan's measure relates to disparity in personal income per capita, while our estimate is based on factor income.

There is also some transfer of income between rural households and urban households. Those urban households which receive income remittances from rural areas are usually rich (mainly landlords and businessmen) and those rural households which receive remittances from urban areas are usually poor. If these transfers are taken into account the average per capita factor income accruing to rural population may not be changed very much. But what is likely is that the income enjoyed by the poorer rural people could be found to be higher when these transfers are taken into consideration. We do not know how much higher, but it is unlikely to be very much. This is because urban employment did not increase fast enough to make such remittances significantly large.

The decline in agricultural value added per head of agricultural population and in per capita rural income indicates, if anything, that the real income of the poorest stratum of rural population declined over time, perhaps quite appreciably. This decline is very likely to show up in the movement of real income of agricultural labourers who constitute a large segment, and are among the poorest, of the rural population in East Pakistan. This is considered in the following section.

III. EVIDENCE OF DAILY WAGE RATES AND WAGE EARNINGS OF AGRICULTURAL LABOURERS – THE POOREST OF THE RURAL POOR

Size of Landless Agricultural Labour Force and Sources of its Income

In rural areas income is derived chiefly from agriculture, and therefore, landlessness and extreme poverty go together. Although self-employment far outweighs wage-employment in agriculture, and cultivators (owners and tenants) outnumber landless agricultural labourers, the latter constitute a large proportion of the agricultural labour force in East Pakistan. This proportion has been rising over time. During the period 1951–61, its relative importance in the agricultural labour force rose from 14 per cent to 17 per cent (Table 10.3). Census data show that in this period, while the agricultural labour force increased by 33·8 per cent the number of landless labourers increased by 63·6 per cent.

It should be noted, however, that the increase in the total agricultural labour force as shown by the census (Table 10.3, column (E)) is to a considerable extent illusory, while the increase in landless agricultural labourers (column (D)) is not. This is because there is apparently a distinct under-enumeration of the female agricultural labour force in the 1951 census. Out of a total increase of 3·62 million in the agricultural labour force (column (E)), 1·52 million is attributed to the female labour force, which is shown to have increased from 0·82 million in 1951 to 2·34 million in 1961, i.e. an increase of 184 per cent in ten years. There is no evidence of any great social change which can explain this enormous increase in female participation. It seems, however, that there is no such under-enumeration of female landless labourers (column (D)) in the 1951 census. Out of the total increase of 0·96 million in the landless agricultural labour force only 0·03 is attributed to females. Also the increase in the number of owners and tenants who also work for hire (column (C)) is almost entirely attributed to males.

TABLE 10.3

COMPOSITION OF AGRICULTURAL LABOUR FORCE
BY LAND TENURE AND SEX: EAST PAKISTAN, 1951
AND 1961, PERSONS OF AGE 12 YEARS AND ABOVE
* The figures in brackets refer to the number of products.

(in millions, except the percentage)

Year	Sex	Owning all land tilled or fully tenant (A)	Part-owner, part-tenant (B)	Owner, tenant or full tenant who also works for hire (C)	Landless agricultural labourers (D)	Total agricultural labour force including others (E)	Landless agricultural labour as % of total (F)
1951	Both sexes	3·74	4·96	0·41	1·51	10·72	14·09
	Males	3·38	4·67	0·39	1·40	9·90	14·14
	Females	0·36	0·29	0·02	0·11	0·82	13·41
1961	Both sexes	5·01	5·60	1·01	2·47	14·34	17·22
	Males	4·74	3·75	0·98	2·33	12·00	19·42
	Females	0·27	1·85	0·03	0·14	2·34	5·98
Per cent change							
1951–61	Both sexes	34·0	12·9	146	63·6	33·8	
	Males	40·2	−19·7	150	66·4	21·2	
	Females	−25·0	537·9	50	27·3	185·4	

Sources: [20, 1951, vol. I, Table 14; 1961, vol. II, Table 51].

Since the decline in land holding per head has driven an increasing number of small owners and tenants into the employment market for at least a part of the year (column (C)), the effective supply of man-days seeking employment in agriculture is even greater than is indicated by the increasing number of landless agricultural labourers. It does not follow, however, that wage employment in agriculture (or in rural areas in general) increased in the same proportion.

The main sources of current income of families of agricultural labourers are presumably (a) cultivation of land, if any land is held, (b) agricultural labour, (c) non-agricultural labour, and (d) other non-farming activities such as handicrafts. No historical series of income of such households is available. But wage earnings, particularly those in agriculture, are likely to be the most important component of their income, and we shall mainly consider this component.

For families of agricultural labourers without any land, wages constitute almost the total income. For all such families with or without land, sampling enquiries made in India indicate that agricultural wages accounted for 64 per cent and 73 per cent of income in 1950/1 and 1956/7 respectively, and non-agricultural wage earnings were respectively 12 and 8 per cent of income in those years [27]. A survey [26] conducted by the Rajshahi University (hereinafter called the Survey) in East Pakistan for 1965/6 indicates that 53 per cent of income of families of agricultural labourers were derived from wage earnings. But in view of the high proportion of landless labourers in the agricultural labour force as shown by the census, this estimate for East Pakistan appears to be low.

Sources of Wage Data

Except for the excellent *Report* by Darling [2], the conditions of agricultural labourers and their wages in Pakistan have remained practically an untouched field. Available statistics are also very scanty and poor in quality. No importance is attached to collection of such statistics. At the same time the large number of small employers and the conditions obtaining in agriculture and rural life in general make the task very difficult. For studying the movement over time of wage earnings of agricultural labourers we had to make do with the little bits of available data.

The only source of historical data on agricultural wages in East Pakistan is the Directorate of Agriculture, East Pakistan. It prepares a Weather and Crop Report [5] either for every week or for every month, which is published in the supplement to the *Dacca Gazette*. It reports daily money wages for every week or every month in each district of East Pakistan. The series is available from 1948 onwards. The reported wage rate for each district is based on an unweighted average of the rate obtaining in the subdivisions of the district. The wage rate in each subdivision is reported on the basis of 'random' queries by agricultural officers to a few local farmers, and is not weighted by man-days employed during the week or the month.

Limitations of Wage Data, and Adjustments Made in the Data

Because of this lack of information on employment one cannot directly estimate monthly or yearly wage earnings per labourer. Another problem arises due to the prevalence of wage payment in cash-cum-kind.

Consider first the method of wage payment in agriculture. Payment of wages in money is not universal in East Pakistan's agriculture. As both Darling and Habibullah [2; 9] have found, although wage payment in money is much more prevalent, in some cases wages are paid partly in money and partly in kind; e.g. one or two meals a day plus some money. As the rural economy becomes increasingly monetised one would expect money wages to replace wage payments in kind. This would imply that the recorded rise in money wages is partly a replacement of wage payment in kind. Therefore, if the reporting of money wages by the Directorate includes cases where payment in kind has been replaced over years by payment in cash, the rise in wages would be overstated. However, in the absence of exact information we may assume that the Directorate reports are based on cases where only cash wages have been paid during all years. Further, employers and labourers may be considered to be sufficiently aware of the costs and prices of payment in kind so that in any small area the purely cash wage rate would be approximately equal to the cash-cum-kind wage rate expressed in money. This agricultural wage rate is also likely to approximate the prevailing wage rate for the general run of rural unskilled labourers.

Inter-district wage differences introduce real difficulties, even if a district is considered fairly homogeneous. An estimated daily wage for East Pakistan during any week or month based on a simple average of daily wages in the constituent districts hardly gives a satisfactory description of reality. The adjustment one should make is to weight the wage rate in each district during any month by the number of man-days of agricultural wage labour employed in that district. But this information is not available. Nor do we know the number of landless agricultural labourers in each district for most of the years. We have, therefore, made a simple average of daily wage rates in districts to obtain the daily wage rate for East Pakistan for each month. This provincial daily wage rate for each month is then weighted by the corresponding monthly wage-employment per labourer. An estimate of the number of days an agricultural labourer in East Pakistan gets wage-employment in each calendar month of the year has been obtained from a sub-sample of the Survey. These data on monthly employment have been used for all years to estimate the average labourer's adjusted daily wage rate, and total annual wage-earnings.

Nominal Wage Rates and Wage Earnings
With these adjustments, the average annual wage-earnings per labourer and the daily wage rates for the years 1948–66 are presented in Table 10.4 which also shows the unadjusted daily wage rates reported by the Directorate of Agriculture.

The estimated yearly wage earnings over time are based on the implicit assumptions that the seasonal pattern and total days of wage-employment per year did not change over time in the relevant period. So far as the adjusted daily wage rate for each year is concerned the implicit assumption is only that the seasonal pattern of wage-employment did not change over time.

It is reasonable to assume that the seasonal pattern of wage-employment has not changed in any significant way in the last twenty years It is, however, possible and even likely that there has been a decline over time in the quantum of yearly employment per agricultural labourer, chiefly because agriculture remained practically stagnant while the rural population grew fast. It has been noted earlier (Table 10.2) that net cropped area per head declined, and cropping intensity did not increase at all significantly. There is also little doubt that the cropping pattern remained virtually unchanged, and non-agricultural employment opportunities did not expand as fast as population. Therefore, the assumption of unchanged annual wage-employment per labourer perhaps gives an overestimate of annual wage-earnings per labourer in the later years as compared with those in the earlier years.

Both the adjusted and the unadjusted series shown in Table 10.4 indicate that money wage rates were lower in the early 1950s than in 1949 (or 1948) and began to rise after the middle 1950s, but were above the 1949 level only in the 1960s.

It should be mentioned here that nominal wage rates

reported by the Directorate of Agriculture for the early 1950s are corroborated by the evidence of Darling [2], who obtained some first-hand information on daily wages in various parts of the province. However, the officially reported wage rates for the 1960s are considerably higher than the rates reported to the present author by quite a number of people who are supposed to have first-hand knowledge of the situation in rural areas. Moreover, the subsample of the Survey shows that the daily wage rate during 1965/6 was about 1·75 rupees, which is much lower than that reported by the Directorate. On the other hand, it has been reported by both PARD and Rahman [22; 24] that the average daily wage rate during January–June of labourers employed in the Rural Works Programme was 1·50 rupees in 1962, 2·00 rupees in 1963 and 2·40 rupees in 1964, which are more in line with the agricultural wage rates reported by the Directorate. One may, however, still suspect that the wage rates during the 1960s, as reported by the Directorate, are probably overestimates.

Consumer Price Index

The real worth of money wages depends on the prices of goods purchased by labourers from the market. The use of an appropriate price deflator is obviously essential for estimating the real worth of nominal wage earnings. While indices of the cost of living of industrial workers are prepared and published by the C.S.O., no agency or individual has computed a series of the cost of living or a consumer price index relevant to agricultural labourers. Hence, we have to compute such an index, however crude and imperfect it may be.

The determination of consumption items and of their relative weights for the construction of this index is far from easy, because, unlike industrial workers, agricultural labourers consume some own-produced goods. For example, even the landless agricultural labourers do not purchase fuel, or pay house rent. They erect their huts on deserted spots or on the employer's land, and gather from the surroundings firewood and straw for use as fuel for cooking. They also catch some fish from public canals and rivers, and perhaps grow some vegetables around the hut. Because of this fringe income in kind total household income is greater than wage earnings.

TABLE 10.4

NOMINAL WAGE RATES PER DAY AND
ANNUAL WAGE EARNINGS OF AGRICUL-
TURAL LABOURERS IN EAST PAKISTAN
(rupees per worker)

Year	Nominal wage rates per day Unadjusted (a)	Adjusted (b)	Annual wage earnings (c)
1948	1·81	1·79	464
1949	1·92	1·92	497
1950	1·62	1·62	419
1951	1·56	1·55	402
1952	1·52	1·53	396
1953	1·38	1·38	357
1954	n.a.	n.a.	n.a.
1955	1·32	1·31	339
1956	n.a.	n.a.	n.a.
1957	1·70	1·70	441
1958	1·85	1·86	480
1959	1·85	1·85	478
1960	1·95	1·95	506
1961	2·18	2·18	564
1962	2·25	2·24	581
1963	2·41	2·41	624
1964	2·65	2·65	687
1965	2·34	2·34	606
1966	2·40	2·40	621

Sources and Methods:
Col. (*a*): Unadjusted daily wage rates as reported by the
Directorate of Agriculture.
Col. (*b*): Unadjusted wages during each month of the
year are weighted by days of employment of an average
labourer in each corresponding month.
Col. (*c*): Wage earnings during any year are estimated by
multiplying adjusted daily wage rate during the year by
number of days employed in each year (i.e. 259 days)

Agricultural labourers with some land derive some income
from cultivation as well, and most of this income is directly
consumed in kind, and only part of this is marketed for other
purchases. This general pattern of a mixture of market-pur-
chases and own-produced goods in the consumption bundle of
families of agricultural labourers has been observed in studies by

both Hussain and Rajshahi University [11; 26] covering both small localities and larger areas in East Pakistan.

However, so far as landless agricultural labourers are concerned, as a rough approximation one can assume that they have to purchase all consumption items other than fuel and housing. On this assumption we have estimated the relative weights of various consumption items from the budget data of a subsample of families of agricultural labourers from the Survey. We have excluded from total consumption the imputed value of fuel, and rent, and estimated from the rest the relative proportions of other consumption items at current prices. These weights have been applied to price relatives based on retail prices of individual items to obtain two series of a consumer price index, one taking 1966 price relatives as 100, and the other taking 1949 price relatives as 100. This is done to see if the two indices are significantly different.

The relative weights of various items, as obtaining in the twelve-month period August 1965 to July 1966, may be considered reasonably normal. The only important factor that might have distorted the relative weights was the abnormally high price of rice in that period. The implicit average retail price of rice, as estimated from the subsample, was about 31 rupees per maund. This was somewhat higher than the prices obtaining in the earlier three or four years. A higher price of rice – a basic need and the most important consumption item – would usually give a large weight to it and hence smaller weights to other items. But in this particular case there was an offsetting factor. This was the substitution of some wheat for rice. Increasing quantities of wheat at prices substantially lower than those of rice have been made available to East Pakistan, including its rural areas, since the early 1960s. There is little doubt that both the absolute quantity of wheat and the proportion of total expenditure spent on wheat by rural households were higher in the mid-1960s. Therefore, the estimated relative weight can be considered as reasonably normal. These weights are roughly in line with the findings of several other surveys, as shown in both Hussain and Rao [11; 27].

It should be emphasised that our consumer price index is almost certainly an underestimate. This is chiefly because of the constant price assumption for 17·5 per cent of household expenditure and because coarse saree prices are assumed to represent clothing as a whole. As a matter of fact other varieties of cloth such as shirting and long cloth registered greater increases in price than sarees.

Movement of Real-Wage Earnings

Nominal-wage earnings are deflated by each of these two consumer price indices, and these two indices and estimated real-wage earnings are shown in Table 10.5. The price index

TABLE 10.5

NOMINAL-WAGE EARNINGS, CONSUMER PRICE INDEX AND REAL-WAGE EARNINGS

Year	Nominal wage earnings (Rupees)	Consumer price index Based on 1949	Based on 1966	Real-wage earnings Nominal earnings deflated by index (A) based on 1949		Nominal earnings deflated by index (B) based on 1966	
		(A)	(B)	(Rs.)	(Index)	(Rs.)	(Index)
1949	497	100·0	71·3	497	100·0	697	112·1
1950	419	89·2	63·1	471	94·8	666	107·1
1951	402	104·8	73·3	386	77·7	549	88·4
1952	396	103·7	70·5	383	77·1	562	90·5
1953	357	95·5	69·6	363	72·9	513	82·5
1954	n.a.	77·6	n.a.	n.a.	n.a.	n.a.	n.a.
1955	339	73·6	53·7	461	92·8	635	102·3
1956	n.a.	105·5	71·5	n.a.	n.a.	n.a.	n.a.
1957	441	112·9	77·6	389	78·1	567	91·3
1958	480	110·7	75·9	435	87·5	632	101·7
1959	478	108·8	74·7	440	88·5	642	103·3
1960	506	115·4	79·5	438	88·0	635	102·1
1961	564	113·2	76·9	500	100·5	733	117·9
1962	581	121·9	82·4	477	96·0	704	113·4
1963	624	123·3	82·5	505	101·6	756	121·7
1964	687	115·7	80·5	593	119·3	852	137·1
1965	606	125·6	83·5	482	96·9	723	116·2
1966	621	152·2	100·0	409	82·3	621	100·0

Sources: Nominal-wage earnings reproduced from Table 10.4. Consumer price indices based on weights shown in Appendix Table B-1, column (6) and retail prices of items discussed in Appendix B of the original article. Real-wage earnings are obtained by deflating nominal-wage earnings by each price index.

based on 1949 along with indices of nominal and real-wage earnings are plotted in Fig. 10.1.

Estimates of real-wage earnings based on the two consumer price indices appear to indicate an essentially similar pattern of change over the relevant period. It appears from both series that real-wage earnings were lower in any year during the period 1951/60 than in 1949 or even 1950. The fall from the level of 1949 or 1950 was quite pronounced until the middle 1950s, whenceforward a reversal appears to have occurred. But it was only after the sharp rise in 1961 that real-wage earnings, for the first time, slightly exceeded the level of 1949. After a decline in 1962, they rose again to reach the peak in 1964 and then declined in the following two years, so that the level of real earnings in 1966 was again lower than that of 1949.

The estimate using the 1949-based consumer price index indicates that except for three years – 1961, 1963 and 1964 – real-wage earnings were always below the 1949 level; and only in 1964 were they substantially above those in 1949. The estimate using the 1966-based consumer price index indicates that real-wage earnings were above the 1949-level during all years of the period 1961/5, but only in 1964 were they substantially higher. Alternative interpretations of the estimated movement of wages are possible. But it is reasonable to conclude that real-wage earnings declined in the early 1950s and in spite of some reversal in the late 1950s remained below the 1949 level in this latter period, and did not show any significant rise in the 1960s.

Moreover, as suggested earlier, the consumer price indices very probably understate the rise in prices, and the reported money wage rates for the 1960s are probably overestimates. Hence, the estimated movement of real-wage earnings, particularly in the 1960s, may be considered to have an upward rather than a downward bias, so that some observed rise in the 1960s may be just illusory.

What Does the Movement of Real-Wage Earnings Indicate?

The estimated real-wage earnings do not measure the level of living of the families of even the landless agricultural labourers because (a) these are wage earnings per labourer and not per family and (b) these do not also include consumption of own-produced goods such as fuel or housing. But for reasons which

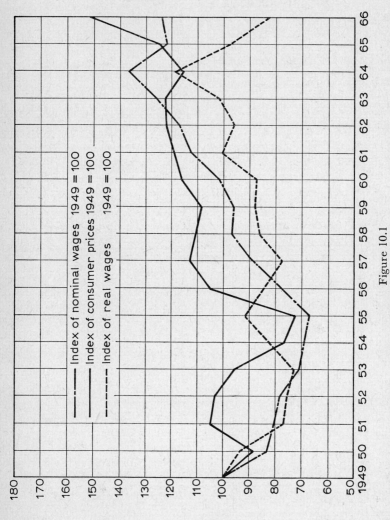

Figure 10.1

Note: Figures for 1954 and 1956 not available for index of nominal wages and real wages

we shall presently mention a proportionate change in real-wage earnings indicates the same proportionate change in the level of living of the population dependent on wage labour.

We do not have any direct evidence regarding family composition over the period covered in this study. But the census data show that the average size of rural *households* in East Pakistan has increased from 4·8 in 1951 to 5·3 in 1961 [20]. The census finding for 1961 seems to be corroborated by the C.S.O.'s surveys which found that the average *family* size in rural East Pakistan was 5·3 in 1960, 5·4 in 1961, and 5·5 in 1963/4 [19; 19a]. It may be assumed that the size of families of agricultural wage labourers has increased in much the same way as the average rural family size.

But we are not quite sure that the average number of wage earners per family has increased in the same proportion. It is true that the census data [20] indicate an increase in the labour force (age 12-and-above) participation ratio in rural East Pakistan from 30·4 per cent in 1951 to 33 per cent in 1961. But we have noted earlier in connection with Table 10.3 that there is apparently a clear underenumeration of the female agricultural labour force in the 1951 census. Hence, the increase in the labour-force participation ratio, as shown by the census, seems illusory.

Our contention is also supported by the observed changes in the age distribution of the census population. While a comparison of age distributions of rural populations of 1951 and 1961 is not possible because the necessary data are not available for 1951, it is clear from the age distributions of the total census population of East Pakistan that the proportion of working-age population decreased and that of young people increased during the period 1951/61. Population under 10 years of age rose from 29·5 per cent of the total in 1951 to 37 per cent in 1961. Population below 15 years rose from 42·1 per cent in 1951 to 46·1 per cent in 1961. Male population of age 15 years and above as a proportion of total population decreased from 30·4 per cent in 1951 to 28·1 per cent in 1951. Whether working-age is considered to begin from age 10 or 12, it is the *male* population of age 15 and above which supplies the greatest bulk of the labour force, particularly wage earners, in countries in which female participation is low.

It is reasonable to maintain, therefore, that the labour-force participation ratio has not increased over the period covered by this study, either for the population as a whole or for the population dependent on wage labour in agriculture. It may actually have declined as the population age profile widened at the lower age groups. Moreover, the proportion of wage labour force that could obtain regular employment has very probably declined to some extent since 1949, because, for reasons stated earlier, the demand for labour in agriculture or in rural areas has not grown as fast as the labour force. It is generally believed that disguised and open unemployment in rural areas has increased. In view of this we may assume that the number of dependants (infants, children or adults) per regular wage earner has probably increased over the period covered in this study. But since the ratio of infants and children to adults also increased it is not unreasonable to assume that dependants in terms of adult equivalents per wage earner remained very much the same. Hence, the per cent *changes* in real-wage earnings per labourer measure the per cent changes in real wage income per adult equivalent of the population dependent on wage labour.

Income in kind in the form of fuel and housing can hardly be a large proportion of total income, and therefore, cannot offset the effect of changes in wage earnings on total income. Moreover, it is likely that with decreasing land and known natural resources per head of rural population income in kind derived through gathering firewood, and materials for making dwelling houses and catching fish has tended to decline over time. Therefore, a fall in real-wage earnings must necessarily indicate a fall in the standard of living of such population, while a small increase in real-wage earnings may not necessarily indicate a rise in the level of living.

The same line of argument should be true for those agricultural labourers who have some land. We have seen earlier that the small increases in yield and cropping intensity have not been adequate to offset completely the effect on income of the decline in land per head, so that output (and income) per head of agricultural population has fallen over time. It is almost certain that this has also happened to income from land obtained by agricultural labourers having some land.

We may conclude, therefore, that the movement of estimated real-wage earnings indicate that the level of living of the population having some or no land and depending mainly on wage labour in agriculture was lower in the 1950s than in 1949 and did not appreciably rise in the 1960s.

A Tentative Explanation of the Observed Movement of Wages
In the early 1950s the decline in real wages was due largely to a fall in money wages. From the late 1950s money wages began to move upwards but they never caught up with or exceeded the rise in consumer prices, except in a few years of the 1960s.

The fall in money wages in the early 1950s might be due in large part to lower agricultural prices in that period, excepting the months of the Korean boom. From the late 1950s agricultural prices began to rise. This may partly explain the reversal of money wages observed in this period. In the 1960s, as have been noted by several observers, e.g. Papanek [23], reduction of duties on agricultural exports and abandonment of procurement of foodgrains at low prices, raised domestic agricultural prices. This together with larger public investment in agriculture began to have some favourable effects on agricultural growth.

The expenditure on the Rural Works Programme, which started in the fiscal year 1962/3 (July-June), introduced a new factor increasing demand for rural labour during the dry season, roughly January to June. The expenditures on Rural Works, as shown in East Pakistan Budgets [6], have been as follows:

Fiscal year	1962/3	1963/4	1964/5	1965/6	1966/7
Rupees (crores)	10	20	25	12	15

No comprehensive study of the employment effect of the programme is available. But Rahman [24, p. 79–80] has estimated for 1963/4 that at thana and union levels a total of 25·8 million labour man-days were employed, which was over two times the employment created in the previous year. If the average labourer worked for 100 days during the season, i.e. January to June, 258 thousand workers were employed in

1963/4. While this is not a high proportion of the rural or agricultural labour force, it probably had some appreciable effect on wages in 1964, the peak year in our series.

But since consumer prices increased faster than money wages during most of the period, except a few years in the 1960s, real wages remained below the 1949 level during the 1950s and rose above the 1949 level only in some years in the 1960s.

Wage-price adjustment is likely to be slower in agriculture than in industry. Most of the wage labourers in agriculture are casual labourers who are not in the permanent employment of any farmer. Their bargaining power is practically nil because of lack of any trade union organisation and the existence of a large labour surplus in rural areas. Agriculture is really a residual sector for the labour force. Under such circumstances, a rise in consumer prices is unlikely to be matched quickly by a rise in money wages.

A recent study by Khan [13] has shown that real wages of industrial workers in East Pakistan have fallen between 1954 and 1962/3. But the index has never been below 88 (1954 = 100). The period of observation and the coverage of the consumer price index of that study are different from those of ours. But it is worth noting that our estimates indicate that the real wage in agriculture has been much more flexible, and in some years the index was around 25 per cent below the 1949 level.

It is generally held that in a labour surplus, underdeveloped country, the real wage tends to stabilise around the subsistence level. Therefore, our estimates may be considered suspect, unless we explain the movement of real wages, particularly the large decline in some years below the 1949 level.

The explanation is based on the appropriate meaning of the subsistence level in traditional agriculture. If the subsistence level of income (consumption) is defined as the minimum requirement for physiological survival, than an estimated real wage below that level must be considered fictitious. If, for example, the 1949 real wage is assumed to have been at such a subsistence level, our estimates for any other year should not be appreciably lower than that for 1949. Thus, the notion of increased poverty of wage earners is completely ruled out. This, however, is unrealistic.

It is more appropriate to think that the subsistence level means the conventional minimum standard of living, and not the minimum calories and the minimum clothing required for survival. This conventional standard of living may be depressed at times by the pressure of circumstances. A simple example is the possible reduction in the consumption level as a result of two or three successive crop failures. Again it is possible that agriculture is squeezed in the process of industrial development, resulting in some reduction in the consumption level. Agricultural labourers and small farmers may be compelled to eke out a living with smaller quantities of rice, pulses, cloth and other consumption goods. They may reallocate consumption in favour of goods which are cheaper or of poorer quality and this may adversely affect their well-being. Thus, a temporary reduction in the level of consumption below the conventional minimum is possible.

Our estimates indicate some such reduction in the level of living of the very poor in rural areas after 1949 and 1950. In some years of the early 1950s the actual level appears to have been considerably below the conventional minimum. A reversal began in the late 1950s, and real wages seem to have fluctuated around the conventional minimum standard of living in the early 1960s.

REFERENCES

[1] Bergan, A., 'Personal Income Distribution and Personal Savings in Pakistan, 1963/4', *Pakistan Development Review*, VII, 2, summer 1967. See chap. 8 of this volume.
[2] Darling, M., *Report on Labour Conditions in Agriculture in Pakistan* (Karachi: Ministry of Labour, Government of Pakistan, 1955).
[3] East Pakistan, Bureau of Statistics, *Monthly Economic Statistics of East Pakistan* (relevant months).
[4] East Pakistan, Bureau of Statistics, *Statistical Digest of East Pakistan, 1965* (Dacca: Bureau of Statistics).
[5] East Pakistan, Directorate of Agriculture, *Weather and Crop Report* (weekly and monthly issues).

[6] East Pakistan, Finance Department, *Budget Documents*, 1965/6 and 1967/8 (speech of Finance Minister).

[7] East Pakistan (a group of experts), *Transportation Survey of East Pakistan*, 1967.

[8] Griffin, K. B., 'Financing Development Plans in Pakistan', *Pakistan Development Review*, v, 4, winter 1965. See chap. 2 of this volume.

[9] Habibullah, M., *The Pattern of Agricultural Unemployment: A Case Study of an East Pakistan Village* (Dacca: Bureau of Economic Research, Dacca University, 1962).

[10] Haq, K., 'A Measurement of Inequality in Urban Personal Income Distribution in Pakistan', *Pakistan Development Review*, IV, 4, winter 1964.

[11] Hussain, M., *The Pattern of a Peasant Economy: Puthia, A Case Study* (Rajshahi: Socio-Economic Research Board, Rajshahi University, 1963).

[12] Iyengar, N. S. and Bhattacharya, N., 'On the Effect of Differentials in Consumer Price Index on Measures of Inequality', *Sankhya*, series B, 27, Sept. 1965.

[13] Khan, A. R., 'What has been Happening to Real Wages in Pakistan?', *Pakistan Development Review*, VII, 3, autumn 1967. See chap. 9 of this volume.

[14] Khan, T. M. and Bergan, A., 'Measurement of Structural Change in the Pakistan Economy: A Review of National Income Estimates, 1949/50 – 1963/4', *Pakistan Development Review*, VI, 2, summer 1966.

[15] Lewis, S. R. and Hussain, S. M., *Relative Price Changes and Industrialisation in Pakistan, 1951–64* (Karachi: Pakistan Institute of Development Economics, 1967).

[16] Mahalanobis, P. C., 'A Method of Fractile Graphical Analysis', *Econometrica*, 28, 2, April 1960.

[17] Pakistan, Central Statistical Office, *Pakistan Statistical Year Book*, 1964 (Karachi: C.S.O.).

[18] Pakistan, C.S.O., *Statistical Bulletin* (monthly).

[19] Pakistan, C.S.O., *The Quarterly Survey of Current Economic Conditions*, 1963/4. (Karachi: C.S.O.).

[19a] Pakistan, C.S.O., *National Sample Survey, 1960 and 1961* (second and third rounds) (Karachi: C.S.O.).

[20] Pakistan, *Census of Pakistan*, 1951 and 1961 (Karachi: Manager of Publications).

[20a] Pakistan, Ministry of Finance, *Economic Survey*, 1966/7 (Rawalpindi: Office of the Economic Adviser, Ministry of Finance).

[21] Pakistan, Planning Commission, *Third Five-Year Plan* (*1965–70*) (Karachi: Manager of Publications, 1965).

[22] Pakistan Academy for Rural Development (PARD), *An Evaluation of the Rural Works Programme: East Pakistan, 1962/63* (Comilla: Pakistan Academy for Rural Development, 1963).

[23] Papanek, G. F., *Pakistan's Development – Social Goals and Private Incentives* (Cambridge, Mass., Harvard University Press, 1967).

[24] Rahman, A. T. R., *An Evaluation of the Rural Works Programme: East Pakistan, 1963/64* (Comilla: Pakistan Academy for Rural Development, 1966).

[25] Rahman, M. A., 'East-West Pakistan: A Problem in the Political Economy of Planning' in G. F. Papanek (ed.), *Government Policy and Private Enterprise in Pakistan* (forthcoming; tentative title).

[26] Rajshahi University, Committee for the Economic Evaluation of the Rural Works Programme in East Pakistan, 'Survey of Employment, Income and Expenditure of Rural Households in East Pakistan, 1965–66' (unpublished proformas).

[27] Rao, V. K. R. V. (ed.), *Agricultural Labour in India* (Bombay: Asia Publishing House, 1962).

NOTES ON CONTRIBUTORS

Asbjorn Bergan, economist at the Distriktenes Utbyggings-fond, Oslo; Adviser to the Pakistan Planning Commission and the Pakistan Institute of Development Economics; author of several papers on Pakistan and the economic structure of Norway.

Swadesh R. Bose, Senior Research Economist at the Pakistan Institute of Development Economics; M.A., Dacca University; Ph.D., Cambridge; author of several papers on Pakistan's agricultural development, foreign trade and employment.

Keith Griffin, Fellow and Tutor in Economics, Magdalen College, Oxford; Economic Adviser to the Algerian Government, the Pakistan Institute of Development Economics and various international agencies; graduate of Williams College; D.Phil., Oxford; author of *Underdevelopment in Spanish America*, co-author of *Planning Development* and editor of *Financing Development in Latin America*.

Nurul Islam, Director, Pakistan Institute of Development Economics; Professor of Dacca University; consultant to the Economic Development Institute of the World Bank and Economic Growth Centre, Yale; M.A., Dacca University; Ph.D., Harvard; author of *A Short-Term Model of the Pakistan Economy, Foreign Capital and Economic Development, Studies in Consumer Behaviour* and of numerous articles on foreign trade and economic development.

Hiromitsu Kaneda, Professor of Economics, University of California, Davis; graduate of Doshisha University and Amherst College; Ph.D., Stanford; adviser to the Pakistan Institute of Development Economics; author of papers on Japanese and Pakistani agriculture.

Azizur Rahman Khan, Senior Research Fellow, Nuffield College, Oxford; Research Director, Pakistan Institute of

Development Economics; Editor, *Pakistan Development Review*; M.A., Dacca University; Ph.D., Cambridge; author of papers on multi-sectoral planning models and various aspects of development economics; editor of *The Strategy and Technique of Development Planning*.

Ronald Soligo, Associate Professor, Rice University; graduate of the University of British Columbia, Ph.D., Yale; adviser to the Pakistan Institute of Development Economics; author of papers on rural–urban migration, international migration and development problems in Pakistan.

Joseph J. Stern, Lecturer, Department of Economics and Research Associate, Center for International Affairs, Harvard; graduate of Queens College; Ph.D., Harvard; Adviser, Harvard Development Advisory Group, Pakistan and Pakistan Institute of Development Economics; author of studies on interindustry economics and planning problems in Pakistan.

Gordon C. Winston, Professor of Economics, Williams College, and Senior Adviser, Pakistan Institute of Development Economics; Ph.D., Stanford; author of papers on industrial efficiency, capacity utilisation and industrial planning.

Index